Microsoft

Microsoft® ASP.NET Coding Strategies with the Microsoft ASP.NET Team

D1502414

Matthew Gibbs
Rob Howard

PUBLISHED BY
Microsoft Press
A Division of Microsoft Corporation
One Microsoft Way
Redmond, Washington 98052-6399

Library of Congress Cataloging-in-Publication Data
Gibbs, Matthew, 1971-
    Microsoft ASP.NET Coding Strategies with the Microsoft ASP.NET Team / Matthew Gibbs.
       p. cm.
    Includes index.
    ISBN 0-7356-1900-X
    1. Active server pages.   2. Web sites--Design.   3. Microsoft .NET.   I. Howard, Rob, 1973-
    II. Title.

    TK5105.8885.A26G53   2003
    005.2'76--dc21   2003056218

Printed and bound in the United States of America.

1 2 3 4 5 6 7 8 9   QWT   8 7 6 5 4 3

Distributed in Canada by H.B. Fenn and Company Ltd.

A CIP catalogue record for this book is available from the British Library.

Microsoft Press books are available through booksellers and distributors worldwide. For further information about international editions, contact your local Microsoft Corporation office or contact Microsoft Press International directly at fax (425) 936-7329. Visit our Web site at www.microsoft.com/mspress. Send comments to *mspinput@microsoft.com*.

Acquisitions Editor: Anne Hamilton   **Technical Editors:** Mike Fitzgerald, Robert Brunner
Project Editor: Barbara Moreland

Body Part No. X09-45919

Table of Contents

Acknowledgments

We would like to thank the talented people we have worked with on this book. Anne Hamilton got the book going and helped keep it moving. Barbara Moreland did a fantastic job as project editor. Technical editors Mike Fitzgerald and Robert Brunner made sure we didn't let errors get through, and Ina Chang helped us learn to write better by relentlessly improving on what we did.

I would like to thank my wife, Heather, and my two children, Josh and Kelley, for their extreme patience and understanding while I worked on this book. I missed a lot of weekend activities with them to make this book a reality. Thanks also go to Dmitry Robsman, David Ebbo, and Shanku Niyogi, with whom I have worked for the past few years. I have expanded my abilities by collaborating with them on designs and by brainstorming about problems.

Matt

Thanks to my family and friends for their patience with yet another book project.

Rob

Introduction

In this book, we'll look at the ASP.NET platform for developing Web applications. We take it for granted that you have some experience with Microsoft ASP.NET and are looking for more ideas for tackling Web development tasks and leveraging what ASP.NET has to offer. However, we'll review some of the basics about how the page framework and server controls work. We'll also examine the features of ASP.NET and discuss how they are designed. Lots of code examples will illustrate our coding strategies, and along the way we include Tips that will help you make the most of ASP.NET.

Prerequisites

This book assumes some familiarity with HTML and Web application development. Code samples are written in C# but do not typically utilize complex language features, so developers familiar with C/C++, Java, or Microsoft Visual Basic should be able to follow along without difficulty.

Structure of This Book

Most of the chapters in this book, which discuss various ASP.NET features and development topics, are freestanding—that is, you don't have to read the chapters in order. Throughout we include Tips and Notes to help you leverage ASP.NET in developing dynamic Web applications. We created these Notes based on our experiences developing ASP.NET and on our work with customers, in which we explored the challenges of creating large and small Web sites, as well as sites intended for access by internal corporate groups and by the general public.

Sample Files

The complete set of sample code can be downloaded from the book's Web site (*http://www.microsoft.com/mspress/books/6578.asp*). Click Companion Content in the More Information box on the right side of this page to bring up the Companion Content page.Following the structure of the book, the code samples are organized into a set of chapter subdirectories, making it easy to create a virtual directory and try out the code on your own machine.

Software Needed to Run the Samples

The .NET Framework SDK, which includes ASP.NET, is required to run the sample code. ASP.NET requires either Microsoft Windows 2000, Microsoft Windows XP Professional, or Microsoft Windows Server 2003. You can use Microsoft Windows XP Home Edition for development, but Microsoft Internet Information Services (IIS) is not available for that platform. An alternative is to use a development Web server. The .NET Framework SDK can be downloaded for free from *http://go.microsoft.com/fwlink/?linkid=8862*.

Creating an IIS Virtual Directory

ASP.NET handles requests issued to a Web server, which is typically IIS on the Microsoft Windows platform. If you are using Visual Studio to create Web pages, Visual Studio will automatically create a virtual directory for you. When using the .NET Framework without Visual Studio, you will need to create a virtual directory unless you are using the default Web site physical directory.

To set up an IIS virtual directory for ASP.NET, you must first have a directory on disk to be used for the application. Of course, we assume that you also have IIS and the .NET Framework installed. In this example, we'll use a sample directory created at C:\SampleApplication. To create the IIS virtual directory, perform the following steps:

1.   On Windows 2000, select Programs from the Start menu, and then select Administrative Tools and Internet Services Manager. If you are using Windows XP, select Control Panel from the Start menu. Choose Performance And Maintenance, Administrative Tools, and then Internet Information Services. Alternatively, you can type **inetmgr** at the prompt you see after selecting Run from the Start menu.

2.   Expand the local computer node followed by the Web Sites node.

3.   Right-click the Default Web Site node. Select New and then Virtual Directory from the expanded menu.

4.   On the first page of the Virtual Directory Creation Wizard, click Next. Then enter the alias for the application, which will be part of the URL path used to access the Web pages of the new application. For example, you would type **SampleApplication** and the URL to get to the application from that machine: *http://localhost/SampleApplication*. Click Next to continue.

5.   Enter the physical location where the Web application will exist. In our example, we would use C:\SampleApplication. Click Next to get to the Access Permission page.

6.   Many any necessary changes to the security for the application. See Chapter 9 for detailed information about security considerations. Click Next and then click Finish.

The IIS Virtual Directory now exists, and .ASPX pages that you place in the physical location (C:\SampleApplication) are accessible from the newly created virtual directory at *http://MachineName/SampleApplication*.

Web.config Code Samples

Many of the discussions in this book evolve around configuration settings placed in configuration files. The configuration data is inherited from application roots that already exist in the Web address. For example, consider the sample URL *http://localhost/SomeApplication/page.aspx*. Some configuration data specified in the machine.config file can be overridden in a web.config file placed in the physical directory of the Default Web Site. Again, in the SomeApplication directory, settings can be modified in a web.config file.

To avoid a lot of code samples being named web.config, throughout the book we have used more descriptive names for configuration files. When using the sample .config files, remember to rename them to web.config, or the sample .ASPX pages will not behave as expected.

Other Resources

The ASP.NET Web site (*http://www.asp.net*) provides up-to-date information on ASP.NET and hosts a variety of discussion forums relating to ASP.NET and development with the .NET Framework. The developer community works together on this site to ask and answer questions, and they take advantage of an archive of previous discussion topics. The authors of this book, along with the rest of the ASP.NET team, work directly with the community and enjoy receiving feedback, working through technical challenges, and discussing potential features for future versions of ASP.NET. The forums can be accessed directly at *http://www.asp.net/forums*.

Support

We have worked diligently to ensure accuracy in this book. Microsoft Press provides corrections through the World Wide Web at:

> *http://www.microsoft.com/mspress/support*

The address to use to connect to the Microsoft Press Knowledge Base and submit a query is:

> *http://www.microsoft.com/mspress/support/search.asp*

Submit comments, questions, or ideas regarding this book to Microsoft Press using either of the following:

Postal Mail:

Microsoft Press
Attn: Microsoft ASP.NET Coding Strategies with the Microsoft
ASP.NET Team, Editor
One Microsoft Way
Redmond, WA 98052-6399

E-Mail:

MSINPUT@MICROSOFT.COM

Please note that the preceding addresses do not offer product support for ASP.NET or the .NET Framework. For product support, please visit the Microsoft Product Standard Support Web site at:

> *http://support.microsoft.com*

1

ASP.NET Page Framework

In this chapter, we'll examine the ASP.NET page framework, but before we get into the details, let's look briefly at the big picture and history of Web development. When the user types a URL into the address bar of the browser or clicks on a link, the client Web browser issues a request to the Web server. The Web server processes the request and sends back a page of markup. The client browser receives the markup and renders the page. For most activity on the Web, the markup language is still HTML, but in Chapter 4 we look at how ASP.NET supports Compact HTML (cHTML) and XML vocabularies such as WML and XHTML.

In the early days of Web development, pages on the server were static HTML. The Common Gateway Interface (CGI) was created to provide a way to write programs that could handle client requests and be executed by the Web server. CGI provided great flexibility, enabling developers to create Web applications that could react dynamically based on user input as well as process business logic. However, it also required developers to build complicated programs to deal with all aspects of generating the markup.

The next phase of Web development on Microsoft Windows platforms involved the Internet Server Application Programmer's Interface (ISAPI), which was introduced to give developers a better means for interacting with the Web server. ISAPI applications are packaged in a DLL on the Microsoft Windows operating system and can be used simultaneously by multiple threads. This was an improvement over CGI on the Windows platform, because the process-per-request overhead was prohibitive. Still, the burden was on the developer to deal with almost all aspects of the client interaction.

Microsoft then introduced Active Server Pages (ASP), which was an ISAPI but didn't require the developer to write C or C++ code to render HTML. Instead, the developer could use Microsoft JScript or Microsoft Visual Basic

1

Script (VBScript). But it wasn't just the ability to write pages in an interpreted scripting language that set Active Server Pages apart. ASP also provided a set of intrinsic objects for managing cookies, getting server variables from the Web server, and accessing form data submitted by the user. ASP even managed user sessions automatically. Essentially, it introduced an easy way to manage user state, even though the underlying HTTP protocol was stateless. This was a great leap forward and quickly set a standard for dynamic Web development. However, when you compare this model to the rich rapid application development environment of Visual Basic, ASP seemed lacking.

The Microsoft team tackled the task of taking Web development to the next level by making the environment richer, the intrinsic features more comprehensive, and the platform faster. What came next was Microsoft ASP.NET, which is part of the new Microsoft .NET Framework. Figure 1-1 shows how the common language runtime (CLR), the first layer of the .NET Framework, is built on top of the operating system. The CLR is an execution environment that provides for garbage collection and true language interoperability. Components written for the .NET Framework in one language can easily be utilized from another language. Beyond this, components written for the CLR are free from many of the memory management chores that are the source of various programming problems. The CLR takes intermediate language binaries, and just-in-time (JIT) compiles them for the platform. You no longer need to compile code separately for different versions of Windows; the code will undergo the final machine-specific compilation on demand. Microsoft provides compilers to generate intermediate language files from C#, Visual Basic .NET, Microsoft JScript .NET and Microsoft J# .NET.

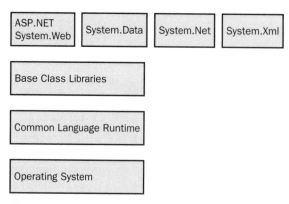

Figure 1-1   ASP.NET and the .NET Framework

In Figure 1-1 we see that on top of the CLR is a set of libraries that provide much of the base functionality needed to accomplish basic development tasks:

threading, input and output, math primitives, and string manipulation. On top of these base class libraries are other features built into the .NET Framework, including socket communications, data access, support for XML, and the *System.Web* namespaces in which most of the ASP.NET and XML Web Services features exist. The classes of the .NET Framework leverage each other to provide a sophisticated programming platform for developing both server-based and client-based applications.

ASP.NET, as part of the .NET Framework, allows us to use the language of our choice in developing dynamic Web applications and achieve better performance with this compiled code than the equivalent pages written in interpreted script languages. ASP.NET provides an event-driven programming model on top of the stateless HTTP protocol, allowing us to write richer applications with less code.

The page framework uses server controls, objects that encapsulate functionality, and user interface elements. The server controls participate in the life cycle of a Web request and are the building blocks for creating dynamic ASP.NET applications. Previously it would have been necessary to write lots of code to restore the user's view of the page, but ASP.NET can now carry the data between browser requests and restore it automatically, making the server controls a more powerful primitive for Web development. In Chapter 2 we look more closely at server controls, and in Chapter 3 we focus on server controls for working with data. After that, we look at the mobile page and mobile controls that provide adaptive rendering for targeting browsers in handheld devices and Web-enabled cell phones before looking in more depth at the infrastructure features of ASP.NET.

In addition to the run time features of the ASP.NET page framework and controls, Microsoft Visual Studio .NET provides an environment conducive to rapid application development, including support for source-level debugging of Web applications and IntelliSense statement completion.

Understanding ASP.NET Request Processing

When a request is received by the Web server, Internet Information Services (IIS) must first determine whether it is handling the request directly or the file extension is configured to be handled by an ISAPI extension DLL. Several types of files are configured for the aspnet_isapi.dll including ASP.NET pages (.aspx), XML Web Services (.asmx), and HTTP Handlers (.ashx). Figure 1-2 shows how a request for an .aspx page is processed.

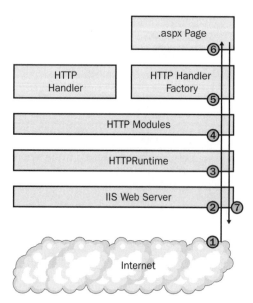

Figure 1-2   ASP.NET request processing

Let's examine the process illustrated in Figure 1-2. The request for the .aspx page is made by the client Web browser. The Web server parses the request and hands it off to the aspnet_isapi.dll for processing. The ASP.NET run time then examines the request to determine which modules need to participate in the processing pipeline and which HTTP handler or HTTP handler factory will be given the request for processing.

The modules configured to participate in this request have an opportunity to modify the headers and output at several stages during processing, both before and after the handler or handler factory has processed the request.

ASP.NET pages are configured for an HTTP handler factory, which generates and compiles pages to handle the request. The page is executed, including a set of virtual page methods and events for which the developer might have provided custom code. The Web server returns the collected output back to the Web client.

IHttpHandler Interface

In the ASP.NET processing architecture, the request is ultimately handled by an object that implements either the *IHttpHandler* interface or the *IHttpHandler-Factory* interface. ASP.NET pages are handled by an *IHttpHandlerFactory*, which in turn instantiates and executes the page. The page itself implements *IHttpHandler*. To illustrate this, we implement our own *IHttpHandler* in Code

Listing 1-1, SimpleHandler.cs. The SimpleHandler program implements the two elements of the *IHttpHandler* interface: the *IsReusable* property and the *ProcessRequest* method. By returning *true* for the *IsReusable* property, we indicate to the ASP.NET run time that a single instance of the handler can be used repeatedly. If we return *false*, a new instance must be created for every request.

> **Tip**   When implementing an *IHttpHandler*, you can get improved performance if ASP.NET is able to reuse a single instance of the handler. The object must be stateless to avoid introducing bugs related to multithreading.

The other interface member implemented in SimpleHandler.cs is the method that does the work. The *ProcessRequest* method is passed an *HttpContext* from which it can access the ASP.NET processing intrinsics such as *HttpRequest* and *HttpResponse*. In the SimpleHandler.cs sample in Code Listing 1-2, we render a simple HTML page that shows the current time on the server.

Code Listing 1-1   SimpleHandler.cs

```
using System;
using System.Web;

namespace CodingStrategies {

public class SimpleHandler : IHttpHandler {

    public bool IsReusable {
        get {
            return true;
        }
    }

    public void ProcessRequest(HttpContext context) {
        context.Response.Write("<html><head><title>SimpleHandler</title></
head><body>");
        context.Response.Write("<h2>The time is ");
        context.Response.Write(DateTime.Now.ToString());
        context.Response.Write(".</h2></body></html>");
    }
}

}
```

Code Listing 1-2 is a batch file for compiling the handler code into an assembly contained in a DLL. We specify that the type is a library and include a reference to System.Web.dll, where the handler interface and ASP.NET intrinsic classes are defined.

Code Listing 1-2   BuildSimpleHandler.bat

```
csc /target:library /reference:System.Web.dll /
out:CodingStrategies.dll SimpleHandler.cs
```

We also need to set up ASP.NET to use our handler instead of the regular *IHttpHandlerFactory*. Code Listing 1-3, HandlerWeb.config, is a web.config file that adds our handler to the configuration system. By setting the *verb* attribute to an asterisk, we indicate that all HTTP verbs are eligible. The path indicates which type of request should go to this handler. Here we specify the full page, time.axd. Requests for time.axd in this Web application will be routed to the *SimpleHandler* class. The *path* attribute also supports wildcards. We have chosen the .axd extension because it is already mapped in IIS to the ASP.NET ISAPI. You can create your own file extension for use in a handler, but you must add it to scriptmaps on the mappings tab of the Application Configuration dialog box in the Internet Information Services (IIS) Manager MMC snap-in. You can launch the snap-in from the command line by typing **start inetmgr**. Right-click the Web site or application icon and select Properties to get the Properties dialog box. When configuring a Web site, click the Configuration button on the Home Directory tab of the dialog box to reach the Application Configuration dialog box. To reach it when working with an application, click the Configuration button on the Virtual Directory tab. The *type* attribute in the web.config file specifies the assembly and class that implement the *IHttpHandler* interface.

Code Listing 1-3   HandlerWeb.config

```
<configuration>
    <system.web>
        <httpHandlers>
            <add verb="*" path="time.axd"
                 type="CodingStrategies.SimpleHandler" />
        </httpHandlers>
    </system.web>
</configuration>
```

IHttpModule Interface

When a request is handled by the ASP.NET run time, in addition to selecting a final *IHttpHandler* or *IHttpHandler* factory, a pipeline of *IHttpModules* is created based on the machine and application configuration files. The *IHttpModule* interface has just two methods, *Dispose* and *Init*. In the *Init* method, the module can add itself as a handler for events exposed by the page or by other modules. For example, ASP.NET uses modules for authentication and exposes an event that can be used by other modules or in the global.asax application code file. When the event occurs, code that has been registered as a handler for the event will be executed.

Part of the initial ASP.NET request processing is the creation of an *Http-Context* that is used throughout the rest of the pipeline to access information about the request, and to utilize the intrinsic objects like *HttpRequest*, *Http-Response*, *HttpCache*, and *Session*, just as we do in the *SimpleHandler*.

Tip   The final implementation *HttpHandler* or *HttpHandlerFactory* might never be invoked if one of the *HttpModules* ends the request. This can minimize the load on the server when requests are serviced from the cache. When a request fails authentication or authorization checks, there is also no need to execute the handler.

The architecture of the ASP.NET request processing pipeline allows us to achieve the same type of functionality in *HttpModules* as is available with more complex ISAPI filters, and we can do it with managed code, leveraging the common language runtime. Code Listing 1-4, SimpleModule.cs, shows that an *HttpModule* can participate in and even take over a request.

Code Listing 1-4   SimpleModule.cs

```
using System;
using System.Web;

namespace CodingStrategies {

class SimpleModule : IHttpModule {

    public void Init(HttpApplication application) {
        application.BeginRequest += new
```

```
            EventHandler(this.Application_BeginRequest);
    }

    public void Dispose() {
    }

    public void Application_BeginRequest(object source, EventArgs e) {
        HttpApplication application = (HttpApplication)source;
        application.Context.Response.Write("a module can end the request");
        application.Context.Response.End();
    }
}
}
```

The *HttpModule* must be registered with the ASP.NET configuration, much like the *IHttpHandler*. Code Listing 1-5, ModuleWeb.config, is a web.config file with a single entry in the *HttpModules* section. This file does not replace the *HttpModules* configured in the machine.config but adds to that set.

Code Listing 1-5   ModuleWeb.config

```
<configuration>
    <system.web>
        <httpModules>
            <add name="SimpleModule"
                 type="CodingStrategies.SimpleModule,
                       CodingStrategies" />
        </httpModules>
    </system.web>
</configuration>
```

In the *Init* method, which is called on application startup by ASP.NET, we register our *EventHandler* for the *BeginRequest* event. That *EventHandler* is then called for each request. For more details about the events that occur during each request, see the section "Understanding the ASP.NET Page Life Cycle" later in this chapter.

Tip   The order in which *HttpModules* registered for an event are called is not guaranteed. Do not count on one *HttpModule* being called before another.

The object passed to the *BeginRequest* event is an *HttpApplication* object. From this object, we access the *HttpResponse* intrinsic, which we use to write output and then end the request.

Understanding the ASP.NET Page Life Cycle

We've seen that ultimately a Web request for an .aspx page handled by ASP.NET goes to an object that implements the *IHttpHandlerFactory* interface. The pipeline created by ASP.NET to process the request includes a set of *IHttpModule* objects that can participate in certain events. The ASP.NET *IHttpHandlerFactory* object ultimately delegates execution to a *Page* class. The Page classes created by ASP.NET are the result of generating *IHttpHandler* objects from the .aspx page itself, which can be a mix of declarative server controls as well as user code.

The page execution has a set of events that can be leveraged by user code in the page itself or from within code in user controls (which will be discussed in more detail in Chapter 2). Much of the page developer's code utilizes the set of page life-cycle events. We'll be using them in examples throughout the book, beginning here. There are additional virtual page methods for which the developer can provide overrides. What is different about these events is that by providing user code with the well-known name, the event binding is performed automatically by ASP.NET, which further simplifies the mainstream scenario of developers utilizing these events.

Page_Init

The *Page_Init* method corresponds to the *Init* event and occurs very early in the life cycle. ASP.NET utilizes this event for, among other things, processing posted form data to restore controls to the state they were in on the previous request. In Code Listing 1-6, PageEvents.aspx demonstrates using this well-known method to write directly to the output.

This event occurs early enough in the page life cycle that it is too early for much of the Web application code you will be writing. Application functional code is better placed in the *Page_Load* method, after state has been restored.

Page_Load

Much of the Web application developer's code is placed in the *Page_Load* method. At this point, the control tree is created and the properties have been restored to any values previously stored in viewstate. Again, in Code Listing 1-6 is code for this method, which simply writes to the output stream, allowing us to see when the events occur.

Page_Unload

After the page has executed and all other page and control events have been raised, the *Unload* event is called. The *Page_Unload* method is ideal for closing any temporary connections or calling *Dispose* on objects that would otherwise keep valuable operating system resources held until garbage collection.

When you view the output from the PageEvents.aspx in Figure 1-3, notice that the order of events is as you would probably expect: first is the output from the *Page_Init* method, followed by that of the *Page_Load* method. Next comes the output from the controls on the page. Although we have a call to *Response.Write* in the *Page_Unload* method, it is commented out. At the point that the *Unload* event occurs, the *HttpContxt* no longer provides us with the ability to write to the output stream.

Code Listing 1-6   PageEvents.aspx

```
<script language="C#" runat="server">
protected void Page_Init(object o, EventArgs e) {
    Response.Write("Page_Init method called <br/>");
}

protected void Page_Load(object o, EventArgs e) {
    Response.Write("Page_Load method called <br/>");
}

protected void Page_Unload(object o, EventArgs e) {
    //cannot use the Response object here, the page is unloading
    //Response.Write("Page_Unload method called <br/>");
}
</script>
<form runat="server">
    <asp:label runat="server" Text="output from label server control"/><br/>
</form>
```

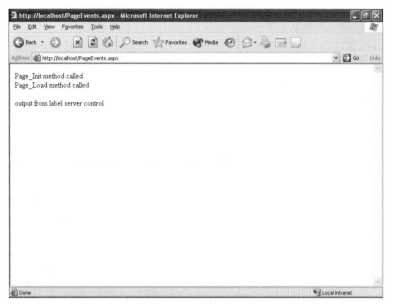

Figure 1-3   Page events output

Controlling Page Execution

The page makes a natural boundary for grouping pieces of the user interface (UI) and application functionality, but often we want to move between pages without user interaction. For example, it is common to have situations in which you want to stop execution of the current page and move the user to another page. This might be the result of a user choice that is detected in code, or it might be a way to retire an application and get users automatically moved to the improved Web site. ASP.NET has several ways of controlling page execution, each appropriate for different circumstances.

Using *Response.Redirect*

The *Response.Redirect* method is useful for getting the user to a different page. The HTTP status code returned to the browser changes from the typical 200 to 302. The 302 status code is a signal to the browser that it will receive a new location and should follow it to get to the content. Most browsers follow the redirect directive immediately, and users will hardly notice that an extra request is taking place, although there is a slight delay as the browser issues the second request. In Code Listing 1-7, RedirectToMSN.aspx demonstrates how to use one of the two method signatures of *Response.Redirect*. The URL passed as a parameter is the MSN home page.

Code Listing 1-7   RedirectToMSN.aspx

```
<script language="C#" runat="server">
protected void Page_Load(object o, EventArgs e) {
    Response.Redirect("http://www.msn.com");
}
</script>
<form runat="server">
You are being redirected to MSN.  Click this link to continue:
    <a href="www.msn.com">www.msn.com</a>
</form>
```

Although we have included content with a link to the new destination, most browsers follow the 302 redirect immediately, so the content is never actually seen by the user. The other version of *Response.Redirect* takes a second Boolean parameter to indicate whether the remainder of the page should be executed. When this second parameter is not given, the result is the same as though *false* were specified. No matter which override is chosen, the page will end with a *ThreadAbortException*, which is part of the normal ASP.NET processing for *Response.Redirect*. The exception occurs as the result of a call to *Response.End*, which terminates the rest of the page execution. Allowing the rest of the page to execute can be useful when you can detect the need to move the user to another page early but still want code that will execute in a later part of the page life cycle to complete.

> **Tip**   There is a certain amount of overhead related to throwing exceptions in the .NET Framework. Avoid throwing an excessive number of exceptions as part of the regular course of an application.

When using *Response.Redirect*, the browser must make two requests in order to display the final page to the user. Although the delay might be marginal, the server and the user both pay a price for the round trip.

When a browser receives a 302 Redirect as the result of a *GET* request, and no form variables are being posted, the browser can simply issue another *GET* request to the new location. However, when the redirect response comes from a *POST* request, the browser must decide whether to submit the form variables again to the new location. The HTTP specification states that the browser must first ask the user for permission before posting form data again. Presumably to avoid this potentially confusing question, most browsers follow the redirect without prompting the user and avoid the specification noncompliance by making a *GET* request and not submitting any form data.

Using *Server.Transfer*

Response.Redirect sends the user to a new page in the same application or to a different Web site altogether. If you want to send the user to a Web page within the same application, *Server.Transfer* might be a better choice. It functions in essentially the same way as *Response.Redirect* in that the current page is aborted, a call to *Response.End* is made along with the corresponding *ThreadAbortException* being thrown, and the new page is then executed. However, the extra round trip between client and server is eliminated. With *Response.Redirect*, you can include a query string in the new location parameter, but the form variables will not be available in the new page. *Server.Transfer* allows us to preserve the query string and data submitted by the user. The page is executed without the user having any idea that anything other than the original page completed.

Code Listing 1-8 demonstrates transferring page control to another page. In this case, we just give the user a text box and perform the transfer in the *OnClick* handler for the form's button.

```
Code Listing 1-8   TransferSource.aspx
<script runat="server" language="C#">
protected void DoTransfer(object o, EventArgs e) {
    Server.Transfer("TransferDest.aspx", true);
}
</script>
<form runat="server">
    Input Something: <asp:textbox id="theFormInput" runat="server" />
    <asp:button type="submit" runat="server" Text="Go"
        OnClick="DoTransfer"/>
</form>
```

The second parameter to the *Transfer* method indicates whether the form and query string should be available in the destination page. If not specified, the default is to preserve the data. The destination page is shown in Code Listing 1-9. TransferDest.aspx sets the value of a label to the value the user submitted to the source page. Notice that we do this when *IsPostBack* is *false*.

Although the source page was processing a postback, the destination page is not treated as a postback. The value is carried in view state for subsequent postbacks in which the *Transfer* handling logic is not involved.

Code Listing 1-9   TransferDest.aspx

```
<script language="C#" runat="server">
protected void Page_Load(object o, EventArgs e) {
    handlerLabel.Text = HttpContext.Current.Handler.ToString();
    executionPath.Text = Request.CurrentExecutionFilePath;
    if(!IsPostBack) {
        theLabel.Text=Server.HtmlEncode(Request["theFormInput"]);
    }
}
</script>
<form runat="server">
    Handler: <asp:label runat="server" id="handlerLabel" /><br />
    ExecutionPath: <asp:label runat="server" id="executionPath"/><br>
    <asp:label runat="server" id="theLabel" Text="default text" />
    <asp:button type="submit" runat="server" Text="PostBack" />
</form>
```

We also display the name of the handler from the current *HttpContext* as well as the *CurrentExecutionFilePath* from the *Request* intrinsic. When first transferred to the page, the handler name and *CurrentExecutionFilePath* do not match. This is because the handler listed is still the compiled type of the original request page, ASP.TransferSource_aspx, whereas *CurrentExecutionFilePath* represents the source page being executed, TransferDest.aspx. When the button on the destination page is clicked, the handler and the file path are again in sync.

Using *Server.Execute*

ASP.NET provides another option for controlling page execution. The *Server.Execute* API transfers control to another page, but only temporarily. When the page execution completes, control is returned to the calling page. There is no call to *Response.End* and no associated *ThreadAbortException*. Although we've pointed out the side effect of the exception, this side effect should not be your primary motivation in choosing a particular API. Rather, you should be aware of what is causing exceptions so that real problems do not go unnoticed.

Code Listing 1-10, ExecutePage.aspx, uses *Server.Execute* to gather and display the output of another executed page. The page being called, ExecutionFilePath.aspx, is shown in Code Listing 1-11. The first of the two method signatures takes just the path to the target page; the second takes a *TextWriter* that receives the output from the target page. In ExecutePage.aspx, we create a

StringWriter to collect the output and display it after we write the result of our own call to retrieve *ExecutionFilePath*.

Code Listing 1-10   ExecutePage.aspx

```
<%@Import namespace="System.IO" %>
<script runat="server" language="C#">
protected void Page_Load(object o, EventArgs e) {
    Response.Write("the current execution file path is:");
    Response.Write(Request.CurrentExecutionFilePath + "<br>");

    Response.Write("the Server.Execute file path is:");
    StringWriter sw = new StringWriter();
    Server.Execute("ExecutionFilePath.aspx", sw);
    Response.Write(sw.ToString() + "<br>");
}
</script>
```

The page output demonstrates that control returns to the calling page after the call to *Server.Execute* and the original page continues its execution.

Code Listing 1-11   ExecutionFilePath.aspx

```
<script runat="server" language="C#">
protected void Page_Load(object o, EventArgs e) {
    Response.Write(Request.CurrentExecutionFilePath);
}
</script>
```

> **Tip**   *Server.Transfer* is essentially the equivalent of *Response.End* followed by a call to *Server.Execute*.

Implementing a Wizard

In a Web application, you often need to walk the user through a series of steps—for example, to set up a new account—to gather information for the application. This type of user interface is typical in Windows applications. The user is presented with a set of pages that break down the bigger task into a series of steps; these steps collect smaller sets of input. When the user finishes the final step in the set, all the information has been gathered, and the task is completed.

In this section, we'll walk through two approaches for implementing the wizard functionality easily in ASP.NET. There are pros and cons to both, so you might need only one or a combination of approaches to accommodate your needs.

The first approach is to use a single page that leverages view state. The data being gathered is sent along in the response for each request and returned on each postback. Code Listing 1-12, SinglePageWizard.aspx, is an example of a single-page wizard. The page is constructed of several panels; each panel represents a single step in the wizard. In this example, we gather only the user's name in Step 1 and his favorite hobby in Step 2. The final panel displays the results gathered. On each request, we explicitly set the panel's visibility so that the user is viewing only a single wizard step.

Code Listing 1-12   SinglePageWizard.aspx

```
<%@Page language="c#" runat="server" %>
<script runat="server">
protected void Page_Load(object o, EventArgs e) {
    step1.Visible = false;
    step2.Visible = false;
    step3.Visible = false;
    if(!IsPostBack) {
        step1.Visible = true;
        return;
    }
}

protected void ClickStep1(object o, EventArgs e) {
    step2.Visible = true;
}

protected void ClickStep2(object o, EventArgs e) {
    theFinalName.Text = theName.Text;
    theFinalHobby.Text = theHobby.Text;
    step3.Visible = true;
}
</script>

<form runat="server">

<asp:panel id="step1" runat="server">
    Name: <asp:textbox id="theName" runat="server" />
    <asp:button type="submit" id="submitStep1" runat="server" Text="Go"
        onClick="ClickStep1"/>
</asp:panel>
```

```
<asp:panel id="step2" runat="server">
    Hobby: <asp:textbox id="theHobby" runat="server"/>
    <asp:button type="submit" id="submitStep2" runat="server" Text="Go"
        onclick="ClickStep2" />
</asp:panel>

<asp:panel id="step3" runat="server">
    Done!<br />
    Name: <asp:label id="theFinalName" runat="server" /><br/>
    Hobby: <asp:label id="theFinalHobby" runat="server" /><br/>
</asp:panel>

</form>
```

Because the wizard is a single page, the approach in Code Listing 1-12 has both advantages and disadvantages. One advantage is simplicity. A small wizard can easily be implemented on a single page; it doesn't have to take explicit action along the way to store the accumulated input in session state or a backend database. Be aware that the data is carried in a hidden field of the HTML form managed by the ASP.NET run time called *view state*. For every variable accumulated in the wizard, the size of the view state will grow. This isn't really a concern for user input of reasonable size, but as the amount of data being gathered grows, an increasing view state might become a concern. The size of data being carried along with each request can be problematic because it has an impact on performance and download time, particularly when the user has a slower connection.

In addition to the potentially large view state size, all the control values must be carried between client and server on postbacks, meaning that the control must be present in the control tree. This can be a limiting factor. Controls created dynamically that are part of the wizard will need to be created on each request—even when the controls are in an invisible panel, they need to be part of the control tree. There is a certain performance hit both in terms of memory usage and execution overhead for the controls to be instantiated and participate in the page processing. As the complexity of the wizard grows, so does the size of the page, so we'll explore another option for gathering user input.

The second approach to writing a wizard moves us beyond the single page scenario. Just as in Active Server Pages, ASP.NET provides intrinsic support for session-oriented storage. In Chapter 5, we will look more closely at the different options for configuring session state support, ranging from the fastest in-process option to back-end database storage that supports a Web farm. We'll also look at how it can be configured to scale from the fastest in-process support to Web farm configurations with persistent storage and even higher reliability. For this example, we aren't concerned about how session state is configured; we just need it to allow us to accumulate data for a single user as he progresses through the wizard, without restricting him to a single page. For simplicity, we will duplicate the single-page wizard in multiple pages. In Code Listing 1-13, MultiPageWizard_PageOne.aspx, the first page of the wizard gathers only the user name. Notice that we aren't using a *panel* server control as we did in SinglePageWizard.aspx to control visibility of the various steps. Instead, when the page is posted back, we store the data in session and use *Server.Transfer* to get to the next step.

Code Listing 1-13   MultiPageWizard_PageOne.aspx

```
<%@Page language="c#" runat="server" Debug="true" %>
<script runat="server">
protected void Page_Load(object o, EventArgs e) {
    if(IsPostBack) {
        Session["theName"] = (string)theName.Text;
        Server.Transfer("MultiPageWizard_PageTwo.aspx", false);
    }
}
</script>

<form runat="server">
    Name: <asp:textbox id="theName" runat="server" />
    <asp:button type="submit" id="submitStep1" runat="server" Text="Go"/>
</form>
```

After the user enters his name and clicks the button to submit the form, the *IsPostBack* property is *true*. The value of the text box is stored in session, and the user is transferred to MultiPageWizard_PageTwo.aspx, as shown in Code Listing 1-14.

Code Listing 1-14   MultiPageWizard_PageTwo.aspx

```
<%@Page language="c#" runat="server" %>
<script runat="server">
protected void Page_Load(object o, EventArgs e) {
    if(IsPostBack) {
    Session["theHobby"] = theHobby.Text;
    Server.Transfer("MultiPageWizard_PageFinal.aspx");
    }
}
</script>
```

```
<form runat="server">
    Hobby: <asp:textbox id="theHobby" runat="server"/>
    <asp:button type="submit" id="submitStep2" runat="server" Text="Go"/>
</form>
```

MultiPageWizard_PageTwo.aspx is essentially the same as MultiPage-Wizard_PageOne.aspx. Again, we take the hobby information submitted by the user and add it to the values being accumulated in the *HttpSession* object.

> **Tip**   Add validators to the wizard pages that verify the set of expected values is in session. If all the required values aren't present, redirect the user to the step where the first missing piece is to be submitted.

In Code Listing 1-15, MultiPageWizard_PageFinal.aspx, we pull the accumulated values out of session and, for the sake of the example, display them. In a real-world wizard, you would no doubt have more values to collect and would be performing some action with a back-end database.

Code Listing 1-15   MultiPageWizard_PageFinal.aspx

```
<%@Page language="c#" runat="server" %>
<script runat="server">
protected void Page_Load(object o, EventArgs e) {
    theFinalName.Text = (string)Session["theName"];
    theFinalHobby.Text = (string)Session["theHobby"];
}

</script>

<form runat="server">
Done!<br />
    Name: <asp:label id="theFinalName" runat="server" /><br/>
    Hobby: <asp:label id="theFinalHobby" runat="server" /><br/>
</form>
```

Of course, as with the single-page wizard, there are pros and cons to the multi-page version. The data submitted by the wizard is stored in session state, which utilizes more server resources, but it avoids the need to send potentially significant quantities of data back and forth between the browser and the server. The default time-out for individual sessions is 20 minutes, so a user who gets distracted in the middle of his session can find that the data he already submitted is no longer available.

> **Tip**   Add validators at each step of the wizard to enforce the entering of correct input by the user. For more information on validators, see "Controls for Validating User Input" in Chapter 2. Let the user proceed only after the values accumulated to that point are satisfactory and errors are corrected, because gathering missing information becomes more complicated after the user reaches the end of the wizard.

Working With Dynamic Controls

One big advantage of ASP.NET pages is the ability to get powerful application functionality without writing a lot of code. By simply including the tag for the server control on the page, the control is automatically instantiated by the ASP.NET run time, the view state is managed, and the control's events are fired. Of course, sometimes you won't know that a control or set of controls will be needed until the page is running. We can declare the controls and set the *Visible* property to *false* when the controls aren't needed, but there is performance overhead associated with a control as long as it exists. Alternatively, a control can be created dynamically and added to the control tree.

When working with dynamically created controls, you must add them back to the control tree early enough in the page life cycle to effectively participate in postback. Use the *Init* method on the page to create these controls. The controls will then be able to manage events just as though they were placed on the page declaratively.

Another challenge when working with controls dynamically is remembering information about the dynamic controls. Of course, the view state of the controls themselves will function in the same way as static controls, but you might need information about which controls need to be created during postback. The dynamic controls must be created for the postback processing to handle the view state information they stored in the previous request. Code Listing 1-16, DynamicTextbox.aspx, demonstrates creating a *Textbox* control during the initial request. We record the fact that the control was created in the page view state. During the postback, we examine that stored information, which lets us know that we need to recreate that type of control so that it is part of the control tree and can handle the view state information that it saved previously.

Code Listing 1-16   DynamicTextbox.aspx

```csharp
<%@Page language="C#" debug="true" %>
<script runat="server" language="C#">
protected void Page_Init(object o, EventArgs e) {
    if(!IsPostBack) {
        CreateTextBox();
    }
    else {
        if(shouldCreateTextBox == true) {
            CreateTextBox();
        }
    }
}

protected override void LoadViewState(object savedState) {
    if(savedState != null) {
        object[] state = (object[])savedState;
        base.LoadViewState(state[0]);
        shouldCreateTextBox = (bool)state[1];
    }
}

protected override object SaveViewState() {
    object[] state = new object[2];
    state[0] = base.SaveViewState();
    state[1] = shouldCreateTextBox;
    return state;
}

private void CreateTextBox() {
    TextBox t = new TextBox();
    theForm.Controls.Add(t);
    shouldCreateTextBox = true;
}

private static bool shouldCreateTextBox = false;
</script>
<form runat="server" id="theForm">
    <asp:button runat="server" type="Submit" Text="Go" />
</form>
```

The page view state is automatically sent to the client for us and posted back to the server on the subsequent request. (We'll look at this in more detail in Chapter 2 when we discuss how server controls work.) In this example, we are overriding the methods to add and retrieve our own piece of state information and then delegating to the base class implementations to take care of the rest of the state. There is no <asp:textbox> in the page itself, yet the textbox is present in the rendered output; if you enter data in it and perform a postback, it tracks the posted data between requests. The textbox works normally because the code in the page creates it and adds it to the Controls collection of the form, based on the value stored in the page view state.

Summary

In this chapter, we looked at the ASP.NET Web development platform. We saw how to leverage the infrastructure provided by the ASP.NET page framework to help us write sophisticated and dynamic Web applications. We examined how the request pipeline is constructed and how we can create our own *IHttp-Handlers* to process requests and *IHttpModules* to participate in the request pipeline. You also learned how to use events that are exposed on the page so that you can easily add your application logic directly to the page, where we also are using the power of the ASP.NET declarative syntax to build pages with server controls.

You saw how easy it is to leverage the built-in controls of ASP.NET to provide wizard-type functionality that can gather data from the user, control page execution in code, and add controls to pages dynamically. The page framework is the foundation on which we can rapidly develop rich Web applications that take advantage of the powerful libraries of the .NET Framework.

2

Server Controls

In Chapter 1, we talked about the ASP.NET page framework and briefly discussed ASP.NET server controls. In this chapter, we'll look more closely at the server controls. Although we assume you have some familiarity with ASP.NET, we will begin this chapter by introducing a few server control basics and then look at some ways you can leverage that knowledge to accomplish the tasks associated with developing dynamic Web applications.

The server control object encapsulates a discrete piece of application functionality and is also typically responsible for producing the associated markup. The support for specifying a server control on a page is a blending of the familiar declarative tag structure of HTML markup and the ability to manipulate the object behavior at runtime in code.

Like the HTML page, an ASPX page is composed of a tree structure of elements. With a static HTML page, the markup is read by the browser and rendered to the user. The content of an ASPX page is first parsed into a tree of server controls that participate in the life cycle of the page, providing the opportunity to dynamically produce the markup sent to the browser. In fact, an HTML page can be turned into a server page by simply changing the file extension to .ASPX. A page like this would consist entirely of literal controls that render exactly as they appear in the source file, but this example illustrates why the server control architecture should feel natural to a Web developer.

Code Listing 2-1, HtmlHelloWorld.htm, is a simple HTML file that demonstrates the simplicity of the server controls concept.

Code Listing 2-1   HtmlHelloWorld.htm

```html
<html>
    <form>
        <input type="text" value="Hello" />
        <input type="submit" value="Go"/>
    </form>
</html>
```

If we rename the code in Code Listing 2-1 to HtmlHelloWorld.aspx, the markup sent to the client would be exactly the same, but the page would be parsed and compiled into a page class on the server. When requested, a tree of controls is built. In this case, the control tree consists of just the page object and a single literal control child that is the HTML content specified in the page. However, the control tree opens the door to manipulating the output dynamically. Later in this chapter, we'll explore the life cycle of the server-side events for the controls.

There are two major types of server controls: HTML controls and Web controls. HTML controls provide a quick way to leverage existing knowledge of HTML while allowing you to easily add and manipulate dynamic features. Web controls typically have a bigger set of properties and methods that provide a higher degree of functionality encapsulation and expose richer programming features.

HTML Controls

The HTML controls are a set of HTML elements that expose server events and can participate directly in the control's life cycle. The HTML server controls are primarily designed for moving existing HTML content to ASP.NET and for leveraging existing knowledge of HTML markup. These controls enable you to take advantage of the rapid application development features of ASP.NET without rewriting applications and losing the Web development efforts.

In Code Listing 2-2, HtmlControlsHelloWorld.aspx, we converted the code from HtmlHelloWorld.htm into HTML server controls.

Code Listing 2-2   HtmlControlsHelloWorld.aspx

```html
<html>
    <form runat="server">
        <input type="text" runat="server" value="Hello" />
        <input type="submit" runat="server" value="Go" />
    </form>
</html>
```

At first glance, the markup looks almost identical to the markup in Code Listing 2-1, except that we added the *'runat="server"* attribute assignment to the *form* and *input* elements. The control tree has been changed more significantly. Figure 2-1 shows the control tree built from this page. The literal controls between HtmlForm, HtmlInputText, and HtmlInputSubmit are the carriage returns from the source file. Generally speaking, ASP.NET turns all elements that are not marked with *'runat="server"* into literal controls and renders them to the client directly.

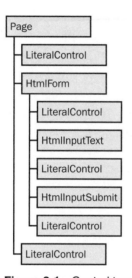

Figure 2-1   Control tree for HtmlControlsHelloWorld.aspx

You can see that the HTML server controls look like their familiar HTML counterparts, which facilitates the development of dynamic applications. The server controls expose events for which we can provide code. This event-driven programming model has been key to meeting the demands of rapid application development. Code Listing 2-3 adds to our previous example an event handler that is invoked when the user clicks the Submit button. In this example, we simply change the value of the text box from *Hello* to *GoodBye* when the form is submitted.

> **Tip**   A certain amount of overhead is associated with all server controls. To preserve application performance when leveraging existing HTML content, do not turn HTML elements into HTML server controls unless you are taking advantage of server events.

Code Listing 2-3   HelloGoodbye.aspx

```
<script runat="server" language="C#" >
protected void MySubmitHandler(object o, EventArgs e) {
    inputText.Value = "GoodBye";
}
</script>
<html>
    <form runat="server">
        <input id="inputText" type="text" runat="server"
            value="Hello" />
        <input type="submit" runat="server" value="Go"
            onServerClick="MySubmitHandler"/>
    </form>
</html>
```

ASP.NET does not include HTML server control equivalents for all HTML elements. The purpose of the provided set of server controls is to enable the server-side code interactions you would benefit most from. The following are HTML elements for which there are corresponding HTML server controls:

<a>	*<input type=button>*
<button>	*<input type=submit>*
<form>	*<input type=reset>*
<img>	*<input type=checkbox>*
<select>	*<input type=file>*
<table>	*<input type=hidden>*
<td>	*<input type=image>*
<th>	*<input type=radio>*
<tr>	*<input type=text>*
<textarea>	*<input type=password>*

It is no coincidence that half of the HTML elements with HTML server control equivalents correspond to the *input* element. The *input* element expects data from the user, and the application typically must act on the user-supplied data.

Web Controls

All server control classes inherit either directly or indirectly from the *System.Web.UI.Control* base class. The HTML controls inherit indirectly through the *System.Web.UI.HtmlControls.HtmlControl* class. The other type of ASP.NET server controls, the Web controls, inherit from the *Control* base class through a different common base class: *System.Web.UI.WebControls.WebControl*. The Web controls are a richer set of controls than the HTML server controls. Because both types of controls are server controls, they have the same fundamental capabilities:

- They expose events unique to the control, for which the developer can provide handlers.

- They automatically manage ViewState so that user input is maintained between requests.

- They participate in the page and control life cycle, allowing them to be manipulated dynamically in code.

Web controls offer even more than their familiar HTML element counterparts. For example, validation controls simplify the process of checking user input. Other Web controls display lists of data as well as bind to record sets from a database. In addition to user interaction controls such as the Button and Textbox controls are more sophisticated controls such as Calendar and AdRotator.

Code Listing 2-4 demonstrates how a Web control can produce advanced rendering and provide events for interacting with the user. In this example, the Label and Calendar Web controls are placed inside an HTML form server control. You'll also notice an event handler for the calendar's *SelectionChanged* event. In the event handler, we simply change the text of the label to display the newly selected date.

Code Listing 2-4   Calendar.aspx

```
<%@Page language="C#" %>
<script runat="server">
protected void Calendar_Changed(object o, EventArgs e) {
    theLabel.Text = "You selected " +
        theCalendar.SelectedDate.ToShortDateString();
}
</script>
<form runat="server">
    <asp:label id="theLabel" runat="server"
        text="select a date" />
    <asp:calendar id="theCalendar" runat="server"
        OnSelectionChanged="Calendar_Changed" />
</form>
```

Figure 2-2 shows the page before and after a date has been selected. The calendar user interface (UI) as well as the logic for navigating between months is produced by the Web control. These updates are accomplished transparently during automatic postbacks to the server that occur when the user makes a selection. Notice that we didn't include a button in the form for submitting the calendar. The calendar days and month navigation UI render as links that submit the form.

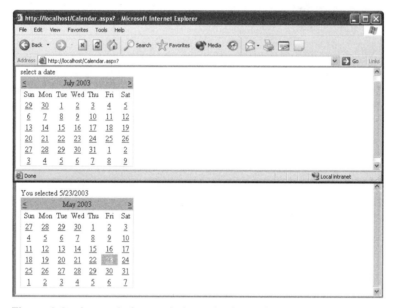

Figure 2-2   A page before and after selecting a date

ASP.NET Web Control Hierarchy

We've mentioned the different types of ASP.NET Web controls and pointed out that they inherit from a common base class. Figure 2-3 shows the inheritance hierarchy. Notice again that the Web controls are more focused on functional elements for Web development than the HTML server controls and familiar client-side elements.

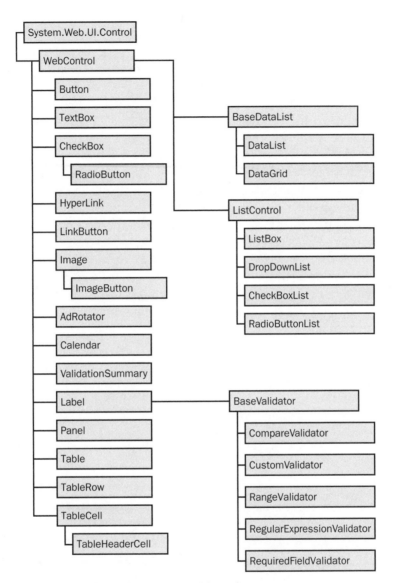

Figure 2-3   ASP.NET Web control hierarchy

Three controls in Figure 2-3—*BaseValidator, BaseDataList,* and the *List-Control*—are abstract classes used to encapsulate functionality for the derived types. As such, they can't be instantiated directly. The functionality for each of these controls is apparent from their names, so we won't go into details in this chapter. We do, however, discuss the list controls and validator controls in more detail, and Chapter 3 is devoted to the data controls.

Leveraging User Controls

As you can see, the ASP.NET Web controls provide a set of fundamental building blocks for building dynamic Web applications. You can also use them to build more complex functionality for the entire site. ASP.NET provides a simple means for encapsulating groups of controls in the user control model. User controls are constructed just like ASPX pages, with event handlers and a control tree, but they utilize the .ASCX file extension and aren't requested directly by the user. Instead, they are included in the ASPX page like a server control and are used as larger building blocks comprised of server controls for application development. They provide a simple way to encapsulate a piece of functionality created with other controls such that they can be re-used. User controls can expose properties, methods, and events just like a server control but can be created declaratively instead of requiring you to compile a separate control inheriting from *Control* or *WebControl*.

Code Listing 2-5 is a user control that we can use in other pages as a footer to display the time. Although the code is simple, including the code and set of controls on many pages without encapsulating it all as a user control might be tedious—particularly if you had to change the footer—because you'd have to edit each page, cutting and pasting changes in numerous files. It would be an error-prone and unpleasant task at best. The user control allows you to centralize code and control declarations for re-use.

Code Listing 2-5   CurrentTime.ascx
```csharp
<script runat="server" language="c#">
protected void Page_Load(object o, EventArgs e) {
    timeLabel.Text = DateTime.Now.ToString();
}
</script>
<center>
    <b>
    <asp:label runat="server" id="timeLabel" style="color:red" />
    </b><br/>
    <i>Time brought to you by ASP.NET Coding Strategies</i>
</center>
```

By encapsulating the functionality in an ASCX file, we can utilize it in multiple ASPX pages. Changes to the user control are reflected in all pages that contain it. Code Listing 2-6 shows how to incorporate this user control in a page.

Code Listing 2-6   IncludeCurrentTime.aspx

```
<%@Register TagPrefix="CodingStrategies" TagName="Time"
    Src="CurrentTime.ascx" %>
<form runat="server">
    page content goes here <br />
    followed by the user control <br />
    <CodingStrategies:Time runat="server" />
</form>
```

> **Tip**   Remember that updating a user control will cause the compiled pages that reference the user control to become invalidated. When the pages are next requested, they will have to be recompiled.

Not only does the ASCX file offer us the advantage of encapsulating pieces of the application into reusable pieces—it also allows us to cache user controls separately. Chapter 6 has more details about utilizing the cache, but it's important to note here that user controls support the *OutputCache* directive. In particular, read-only views of data in multiple pages of an application can benefit from being placed in a user control that is temporarily cached independently from the containing page because doing so reduces trips to the database.

The encapsulation in user controls goes beyond just including content from somewhere else in the page. We can provide public properties, fields, and methods on the user control that can be used from the page that utilizes the user control. In addition, we can hide members of the user control from the containing page by setting the member-access modifiers. However, remember that the controls themselves are in the control tree, and the page code is free to manipulate them at will. The user control in Code Listing 2-7 provides a public property setter that updates the color it is displaying.

Code Listing 2-7   FavoriteColor.ascx

```
<%@Import namespace="System.Drawing" %>
<script runat="server" language="C#">
protected Color favoriteColor = Color.Black;
protected void Page_Load(Object o, EventArgs e) {
    theLabel.Text = favoriteColor.Name;
}
public Color Color {
    set {
        favoriteColor = value;
        theLabel.Text = favoriteColor.Name;
```

```
        theLabel.ForeColor = favoriteColor;
    }
}
</script>
<h2><asp:label id="theLabel" runat="server"/></h2>
```

Code Listing 2-8 shows the page that uses the user control. In it, the user is given a text box to enter a favorite color. The name provided by the user is then turned into a color structure and set on the FavoriteColor user control.

Code Listing 2-8   SetFavoriteColor.aspx

```
<%@Import Namespace="System.Drawing" %>
<%@Register TagPrefix="CodingStrategies" TagName="Color"
    Src="FavoriteColor.ascx" %>
<script language="C#" runat="server">
protected void SetColor(object o, EventArgs e) {
    Color color = Color.FromName(theTextbox.Text);
    colorControl.Color = color;
}
</script>
<form runat="server">
    Name your favorite color
    <asp:textbox runat="server" id="theTextbox"
        OnTextChanged="SetColor" Value="Black"/><br />
    Your favorite color is:
    <CodingStrategies:Color runat="server"
        id="colorControl" /><br />
    <asp:button type="submit" runat="server" Text="Go" />
</form>
```

> **Note**   The members of a user control in the output cache can't be accessed from pages that contain the control. The output of the cached control will be included in the page, but the user control object itself will not be available. Attempting to access it will result in an error message.

Extending Web Controls

In addition to using the HTML server controls and the Web controls, you can create your own controls. You can also choose from among an impressive market of third-party controls that provide features not included in ASP.NET.

You can choose to inherit directly from *Control* or indirectly via the *WebControl* class. We won't begin to cover the topic of writing your own controls in this book, but we can recommend another title, *Developing Microsoft ASP.NET Server Controls and Components* by Nikhil Kothari and Vandana Datye (Microsoft Press, 2002) to help you. The book covers in great detail the control architecture and how to take advantage of it, and it includes information on providing design-time behavior to enhance the developer's work when using the control from Microsoft Visual Studio or another developer tool.

Displaying a Message Box

Debugging ASP.NET applications is covered in Chapter 10, but we'll examine one related topic here. Developers frequently look for quick ways to simply output a message. A typical way of doing this in Web development is to use the browser to display a message box, which the user dismisses to continue interacting with the page. Developers often get accustomed to the ease provided by the user controls, and find in the documentation a *MessageBox* object. However, when you create one of these controls in code (as you would on the client) and try to display it, nothing shows up. The .NET Framework has a *MessageBox* object, but when you call its *Show* method in an ASPX page, the system tries to show the object on the server, not on the client.

Code Listing 2-9 demonstrates including a client-side message box. We have a server-side method named *CreateClientSideMessageBox* that takes a single string parameter. It writes out the JavaScript code in the output to invoke the browser's *alert* method by using the string message passed in to the server-side method. This *alert* method causes a client-side message box to be displayed, instead of showing a message box on the server. Notice that we separate the last line of the script block. The */s* is an escape sequence that can cause a compilation failure, so we concatenate the strings to avoid the issue.

Code Listing 2-9   Alert.aspx

```
<script language="C#" runat="server">
protected void Page_Load(object o, EventArgs e) {
    if(IsPostBack) {
        CreateClientSideMessageBox("IsPostBack is true");
    }
    else {
        CreateClientSideMessageBox("IsPostBack is false");
    }
}

protected void CreateClientSideMessageBox(string message) {
    Response.Write("<script language=\"javascript\">");
    Response.Write("alert(\"" + message + "\");");
    Response.Write("</" + "script>");
}
</script>

<form runat="server">
    this page displays a client side message box<br/>
    <asp:button runat="server" Text="go" />
</form>
```

> **Note**   If you have to import the *System.Windows.Forms* namespace
> into your page or Microsoft Visual Studio .NET Web application project,
> chances are your code is using server-side resources that have no visi-
> ble desktop on which to be displayed. Thus, they must be disposed of to
> avoid introducing resource issues under heavy load. Verify that you are
> not mistakenly trying to display UI elements on the server.

Controls for Lists

In Web applications, users commonly interact with a list of items. Four ASP.NET
list controls inherit from the abstract *ListControl* base class. They differ in the
user interface presented to the user and in the constraints that they offer. The
list controls contain a collection of *ListItem* objects that can be data-bound (discussed in more detail in Chapter 3) or set directly as the inner text of the list
controls. You can also create the list items dynamically and add them to the control's *Items* collection. When the value property of an item is not set explicitly, that
control's value will default to the *Text* property of the control. Let's compare the
different types of list controls and the way the data is presented to the user.

CheckBoxList

The list items in a CheckBoxList are presented as check boxes. Multiple items from the list can be selected at the same time. In Code Listing 2-10, the Check-BoxList is populated declaratively. The control tracks which items are selected, allowing us to provide an event handler that is fired when the selected items are changed and posted back to the server; that is, the code reacts only when the user takes action that changes the selected items in the list. In the handler for the *SelectedIndexChanged* event, we iterate over all items in the list and output all that are selected. The code does not clear previous collections, leaving it to the user to add and remove items at will. The ViewState management keeps track of the selected items between requests and automatically restores them to their selected state during the next rendering.

Code Listing 2-10   CheckBoxList.aspx

```
<script language="C#" runat="server">
protected void CheckBoxListSelectionChanged(
    object o, EventArgs e) {
    bool valueSet = false;
    foreach(ListItem item in languageCheckBoxList.Items) {
        if (item.Selected) {
            if(valueSet) {
                favoriteLanguage.Text += ", " + item.Text;
            }
            else {
                favoriteLanguage.Text = item.Text;
                valueSet = true;
            }
        }
    }
}
</script>
<form runat="server">
    <asp:CheckBoxList id="languageCheckBoxList" runat="server"
        OnSelectedIndexChanged="CheckBoxListSelectionChanged" >
        <asp:ListItem runat="server">C#</asp:ListItem>
        <asp:ListItem runat="server">VB.NET</asp:ListItem>
        <asp:ListItem runat="server">JScript.NET</asp:ListItem>
    </asp:CheckBoxList><br/>
    Favorite Language:
    <b><asp:label runat="server" id="favoriteLanguage"
        style="color:blue" Text="Not Set" /></b><br />
    <asp:button runat="server" Text="Submit"/>
</form>
```

Notice in Code Listing 2-10 that we iterate over the collection of items in the *OnSelectedIndexChanged* event handler to ascertain the complete set of selected values.

> **Tip**   If the user interface supports multiple simultaneous selections, accessing *SelectedItem*, *SelectedIndex*, and *SelectedValue* will return the first item the control finds when it iterates over the items. To get the complete set of selected items, loop through all items from the list.

ListBox

The ListBox control, like CheckBoxList, also supports multiple simultaneous selections on the part of the user, but these can be restricted to a single selection by setting the *SelectionMode* property to the *Single* value of the *ListSelectionMode* enumeration. In Code Listing 2-11, the set of languages in Code Listing 2-10 is in our list again, but this time we add the list items to the ListBox dynamically in the *Page_Load* event. Notice that we need to add the items only in the initial request. The set of items is restored automatically from ViewState during postbacks.

Code Listing 2-11   ListBox.aspx

```csharp
<script language="C#" runat="server">
protected void Page_Load(object o, EventArgs e) {
    if(!IsPostBack) {
        ListItem item;
        item = new ListItem("C#");
        languageListBox.Items.Add(item);
        item = new ListItem("VB.NET");
        languageListBox.Items.Add(item);
        item = new ListItem("JScript.NET");
        languageListBox.Items.Add(item);
        languageListBox.Rows = 3;
    }
}

protected void ListBoxSelectionChanged(object o, EventArgs e) {
    bool valueSet = false;
    foreach(ListItem item in languageListBox.Items) {
        if (item.Selected) {
            if(valueSet) {
                favoriteLanguage.Text += ", " + item.Text;
            }
```

```
            else {
                favoriteLanguage.Text = item.Text;
                valueSet = true;
            }
        }
    }
}
</script>
<form runat="server">
    <asp:ListBox id="languageListBox" runat="server"
        SelectionMode="multiple"
        OnSelectedIndexChanged="ListBoxSelectionChanged" /><br />
    Favorite Language: <b>
    <asp:label runat="server" id="favoriteLanguage"
        style="color:blue" Text="Not Set" /></b><br />
    <asp:button runat="server" Text="Submit"/>
</form>
```

We set the *Rows* property to the number of items from the list. Of course, this wouldn't be a suitable approach when the list contains a lot of items because the *Rows* property corresponds to the number of items from the list that are displayed without scrolling. Vertical scroll bars are provided automatically when the number of items in the list exceeds the row count.

> **Tip**   Items added to a list control are carried between client and server in ViewState. If the set of items is a significant size, consider disabling ViewState. That way the control will not bloat the payload by unnecessarily carrying the ViewState in a round trip between client and server. In this case, be aware that the selected items are no longer available, so you must provide code to ascertain when the selected items were changed.

DropDownList

The DropDownList provides a compact approach for selecting a single item from a list. In the other lists, you start with a default of no selection, but the DropDownList differs in that an item from the list is always selected. In Code Listing 2-12, we use the previous example of selecting a favorite language but instead use the DropDownList, explicitly initializing the label of the selected language with the selected item. Even though we didn't set the *Selected* property of any item in the list, the first item added takes on this value.

Also important to note in Code Listing 2-12 is that the text of a *ListItem* is set to the content of the *Value* attribute only when a value is not specified in the body of the *ListItem*. In DropDownList.aspx, we set unique values and display those instead. Doing this is particularly useful when working with database back ends in which the friendly text displayed to the user might be only a convenience and the important field is available as the *ListItem* value.

Tip   To create a drop-down list that does not appear to have an initially selected value, add an item to the top of the list that is selected by default and corresponds to no user selection.

Code Listing 2-12   DropDownList.aspx

```csharp
<script language="C#" runat="server">
protected void Page_Load(object o, EventArgs e) {
    if(!IsPostBack) {
        ListItem item;
        item = new ListItem("C#", "1");
        languageDropDownList.Items.Add(item);
        item = new ListItem("VB.NET", "2");
        languageDropDownList.Items.Add(item);
        item = new ListItem("JScript.NET", "3");
        languageDropDownList.Items.Add(item);

        favoriteLanguage.Text
            = languageDropDownList.SelectedItem.Value;
    }
}

protected void DropDownListSelectionChanged(object o, EventArgs e) {
    favoriteLanguage.Text
        = languageDropDownList.SelectedItem.Value;
}
</script>
<form runat="server">
    <asp:DropDownList id="languageDropDownList" runat="server"
        OnSelectedIndexChanged="DropDownListSelectionChanged" >
    </asp:DropDownList><br/>
    Favorite Language: <b>
    <asp:label runat="server" id="favoriteLanguage"
        style="color:blue" /></b><br />
    <asp:button runat="server" Text="Submit"/>
</form>
```

RadioButtonList

The RadioButtonList control, like the DropDownList control, provides an interface for the user to select a single item from a list. With this rendering, the user is presented with a set of radio buttons from which to make a single selection. When an item is selected, the previously selected item is cleared. The *SelectedIndexChanged* event is not fired until the form is posted back to the server. The user is thus free to change the value on the page without invoking the server-side handler until some other action on the page causes a postback.

Code Listing 2-13 is another example of selecting a favorite language. Notice that we do not try to access the *SelectedItem* property of the RadioButtonList control until the *SelectedIndexChanged* event handler. Until the user makes a selection, or *SelectedIndex* is set explicitly in code, the *SelectedItem* property is null.

Code Listing 2-13   RadioButtonList.aspx

```
<script language="C#" runat="server">
protected void Page_Load(object o, EventArgs e) {
    if(!IsPostBack) {
        ListItem item;
        item = new ListItem("C#", "1");
        languageRadioButtonList.Items.Add(item);
        item = new ListItem("VB.NET", "2");
        languageRadioButtonList.Items.Add(item);
        item = new ListItem("JScript.NET", "3");
        languageRadioButtonList.Items.Add(item);
    }
}


protected void DropDownListSelectionChanged(object o,
    EventArgs e) {
    favoriteLanguage.Text
        = languageRadioButtonList.SelectedItem.Value;
}
</script>
<form runat="server">
    <asp:RadioButtonList id="languageRadioButtonList"
        runat="server"
        OnSelectedIndexChanged="DropDownListSelectionChanged" >
    </asp:RadioButtonList><br/>
    Favorite Language: <b>
    <asp:label runat="server" id="favoriteLanguage"
        style="color:blue" /></b><br />
    <asp:button runat="server" Text="Submit"/>
</form>
```

Figure 2-4 shows the default appearance of the four ASP.NET list controls. Each is filled with the sample set of .NET Framework languages used in the previous examples in this chapter.

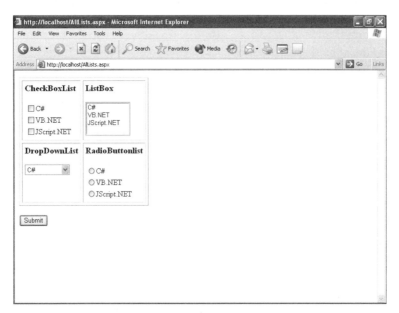

Figure 2-4   Rendering of the ASP.NET list controls

Controls for Validating User Input

A large percentage of the code in a typical application is devoted to validating the input received from the user. ASP.NET dedicates five server controls to making this step more manageable: RequiredFieldValidator, CompareValidator, RangeValidator, RegularExpressionValidator, and CustomValidator. These validation controls all inherit from the abstract *BaseValidator* class, which is derived from the *Label* class. An additional control can be used in conjunction with the validators, ValidationSummary, to present the set of errors in a cohesive and consistent manner.

Each of these validation controls has a *ControlToValidate* property used to set the ID of the target control. When the form is posted, the *Validate* method is called automatically; when validation fails, the *ErrorMessage* text is displayed. For some browsers, the validation controls are able to take advantage of client-side script to perform the validation check and display an error message without completing the postback.

> **Tip**   If necessary, you can disable client-side validation by using the *Page* directive's *ClientTarget* attribute. Setting this directive to *downlevel* causes ASP.NET to treat the browser as though it does not support JScript.

The *Display* property is used to indicate whether space should be reserved in the rendering for the error message. It can be set to one of the two *ValidatorDisplay* enumeration values: *Static* or *Dynamic*. The *Static* setting, where space is allocated but not immediately filled, works only when the client supports client-side scripting and the *Page* directive's *ClientTarget* attribute has not been set to *downlevel*.

RequiredFieldValidator

The RequiredFieldValidator control enforces data entry on the part of the user. No constraints are placed on the value of the data provided, but some type of data must be entered. Code Listing 2-14 demonstrates using the RequiredField-Validator control to ensure that data has been entered for an e-mail address.

Code Listing 2-14   EmailRequired.aspx

```
<form runat="server">
    Please enter your email address
    <asp:RequiredFieldValidator runat="server" id="required1"
        ControlToValidate="emailTextbox"
        ErrorMessage="email required" Display="Static" />
    <asp:Textbox runat="server" id="emailTextbox"/>
    <asp:button type="submit" runat="server" Text="Submit" />
</form>
```

> **Note**   When used with sophisticated clients, client-side validation can reduce server load and improve the customer experience by providing immediate feedback about a problem without issuing a request to the server.

CompareValidator

The CompareValidator control can check against static or dynamic values. In addition, it can compare the value with the value of another control. To compare with a value, use the *ValueToCompare* property. Switch to the *ControlTo-Compare* property to use the value of another control from the page. The use of these properties is mutually exclusive. Code Listing 2-15 demonstrates using the CompareValidator control to check that the provided string, when converted to an integer, is greater than or equal to 18.

Code Listing 2-15   CompareValidator.aspx

```
<form runat="server">
    Enter your age:
    <asp:CompareValidator runat="server" Type="integer"
        ValueToCompare="18" ControlToValidate="ageTextBox"
        ErrorMessage="Must be 18 to vote."
        Operator="GreaterThanEqual"/>
    <asp:TextBox runat = "server" id="ageTextBox" />
    <asp:Button type="submit" runat="server" Text="Submit" />
</form>
```

The *operator* property can be set to any of the values from the *Validation-CompareOperator* enumeration: *Equal*, *NotEqual*, *GreaterThan*, *Greater-ThanEqual*, *LessThan*, *LessThanEqual*, and *DataTypeCheck*. The *DataTypeCheck* operator is an interesting operator that can be applied in unique ways. Normally, the value of the control being validated is converted to the type specified by the *Type* property, and an exception is thrown if the conversion fails. The *DataTypeCheck* operator provides a means of explicitly checking that the type entered can be converted, but it does not cause an exception to be thrown for illegal conversions. The *ValueToCompare* and *ControlToCompare* properties are not used, even when specified, when the validator's *operator* property is set to *DataTypeCheck*. (Note that if the *operator* property is not specified, the default is to check for value equality.)

RangeValidator

The RangeValidator control has properties for specifying minimum and maximum values. The value being confirmed must fall between those values inclusive of the range limits. In Code Listing 2-16 we add a programmatic check against the validator. Once the data is found to be valid against the coded constraints, the instructions are changed to provide more appropriate information.

Code Listing 2-16   RangeValidator.aspx

```
<script runat="server" language="C#" >
protected void Page_Load(object o, EventArgs e) {
    if(IsPostBack && rangeValidator.IsValid ){
        message.Text = "Thanks, see you in September.";
    }
    else {
        message.Text = "Please start vacations on 2003/08/01";
    }
}
</script>
<form runat="server">
    Enter your desired vacation start date:
    <asp:Textbox runat="server" id="theDate" />
    <asp:RangeValidator runat="server" id="rangeValidator"
        ControlToValidate="theDate"
        ErrorMessage="vacations must start on August 1st"
        Type="Date" MinimumValue="2003/08/01"
        MaximumValue="2003/08/01"/><br />
    <b><asp:label runat="server" id="message" /></b><br />
    <asp:button type="submit" runat="server" Text="Submit" />
</form>
```

RegularExpressionValidator

The ability to use regular expressions in validators opens up great possibilities for powerful input checking without writing lots of code. The RegularExpressionValidator control accepts a string in the *ValidationExpression* property that is applied to the input contained in the control specified by the *ControlToValidate* property. A new regular expression is created using *ValidationExpression*, and the value is tested for conformity. If you've written code to verify that an e-mail address does indeed appear to be an e-mail address without using regular expressions, you'll appreciate the sample address validation in Code Listing 2-17. Notice that an empty string will pass the regular expression in the sample. Use a RegularExpressionValidator in conjunction with a RequiredFieldValidator to ensure input. In many circumstances, the combination of several validators is simpler than producing a single regular expression that accounts for all the desired validity checks.

Code Listing 2-17   RegularExpressionValidator.aspx

```
<form runat="server">
    Enter your email address, which will be sold to third parties:
    <asp:textbox id="emailAddress" runat="server" /><br />
    <asp:RegularExpressionValidator runat="server"
        ValidationExpression
            ="\w+([-+.]\w+)*@\w+([-.]\w+)*\.\w+([-.]\w+)*"
        ControlToValidate="emailAddress"
        ErrorMessage="At least make it look like a real address."/>
    <br />

    <asp:button type="submit" runat="server" Text="Submit" />
</form>
```

CustomValidator

The CustomValidator control differs from the other validators in that it lets you provide custom client-side and server-side validation code. The *ClientValidationFunction* property can be set to a script block string that will be passed through to the browser for execution when the form is being submitted. If the custom code sets the argument object's *IsValid* property to *false*, the form will not be submitted.

The value of the control specified in the *ControlToValidate* property is passed to the custom validation code as the *Value* property of the *ServerValidateEventArgs* parameter. In Code Listing 2-18, we provide an event handler for the *OnServerValidate* event that demonstrates accessing the value and setting the *IsValid* property of the same object to indicate whether the user's input has passed scrutiny. In this example, the user can't succeed because we always set *IsValid* to *false* and customize the *ErrorMessage* to encourage the user to modify her input no matter what she enters.

Code Listing 2-18   CustomValidator.aspx

```
<script runat="server" language="C#">
protected void ServerAddMoreValidation(object o,
    ServerValidateEventArgs e) {
    try {
        //whatever they enter, it is insufficient by one
        int theInput = Int32.Parse(e.Value);
        if (theInput < 0) {
            theValidator.ErrorMessage
                = "please enter a positive value";
        }
        else {
            theValidator.ErrorMessage = "please enter at least "
                + (theInput + 1).ToString();
```

```
            }
        }
        catch {
        }
        e.IsValid = false;
    }
</script>
<form runat="server">
    Enter the quantity:
    <asp:textbox runat="server" id="quantity" />
    <asp:CustomValidator runat="server" id="theValidator"
        ControlToValidate="quantity"
        OnServerValidate="ServerAddMoreValidation"
        ErrorMessage="Try Again"/><br />
    <asp:label runat="server" id="theFeedback"/><br />
    <asp:button type="submit" runat="server" Text="Submit" />
</form>
```

Be aware that the client script provided for the CustomValidator control should act only as the first line of defense in the validation work. A malicious user can get around the script code and post bogus data directly to the server.

> **Tip**   Always verify the data received by the server, even when client-side validation code has been provided. You can't safely assume anything—the client might not have run the code, and the user might have constructed a malicious request by hand with values that would not pass the examination of the client-side code.

ValidationSummary

As you've learned, when verifying user input, the validation controls can save you lines and lines of custom code. In many cases, you will add several validators to the page for a field requiring a single input: a RequiredField validator control to enforce the submission of data as well as a RangeValidator or CustomValidator control to more closely scrutinize the data. The proliferation of error messages on a page can be somewhat daunting for the user, particularly if the *Display* property is dynamic, which causes the HTML elements to potentially shift slightly based on the presence of error messages. The ValidationSummary control coalesces the page's error messages into a central location. The control's *HeaderText* is displayed at the top of the error message list, which is generated from the controls failing validation.

Uploading a File

A less common but important functionality to offer is a way for the user to upload a file to the server. Often, this task is the foundation upon which Web applications are built. If the user is not acting on server data from a back-end database, he might be working on having the server act on files uploaded by the server. The ASP.NET control for enabling this functionality is from the set of HTML controls. The HtmlInputFile control requires that we modify the *form* element so that the browser will be able to submit the file.

The first step is to consider the impact on the server of allowing users to upload files. This is the kind of functionality that is quickly discovered by inquisitive anonymous users and can sometimes lead to a barrage of large files or file upload requests that don't seem to make progress. Consider restricting access to the Web root in which file upload occurs only for authenticated users. Chapter 8 discusses in detail the various types of authentication supported by ASP.NET. By denying anonymous users access to the site, you can eliminate big problems. Users seem to behave better when their actions can be traced back to them, and with the logging capabilities of IIS, you can easily ascertain the source of inappropriate uploads.

The second step is to configure the application for the maximum supported file size for upload. Consider the amount of storage that is allocated for housing the uploaded files. The *httpRuntime* element contains a *maxRequest-Length* attribute that corresponds to the number of kilobytes a user can upload or post before receiving an error. The default is 4096 KB. Code Listing 2-19 is a web.config file that limits the request length to 2 MB. If the size of the uploaded files is assured to be significantly smaller, consider reducing this from the default 4 MB. If the limit will increase, seriously consider the impact on performance if you were to buffer the upload files and write them to disk.

Code Listing 2-19   RequestLengthWeb.config
```
<configuration>
    <system.web>
        <httpRuntime maxRequestLength="2048" />
    </system.web>
</configuration>
```

> **Tip**   Use the *SaveAs* method of the *PostedFile* member of the Html-InputFile control to specify where the file should be placed on disk. Target a directory that exists on a separate partition, where filling the partition will have minimum impact on the operations of the server.

The third and final step in preparing to handle the uploading of files is to configure a location with permissions in which the ASP.NET worker process can write files. (In Chapter 8, you'll look at security mechanisms and user impersonation and also examine directory write privileges and identity.) Isolate the save location from other applications and operating system files to guard against overwriting an existing file.

Code Listing 2-20 demonstrates setting the *form* element's *enctype* attribute to the correct type and includes adding the HTML server control to enable file uploads, via the *runat* attribute. The code that saves the file from memory to disk simply gets the current time in milliseconds, but note that this doesn't scale. As unlikely as it might seem, you can't safely assume that two users couldn't cause this code to execute simultaneously.

Code Listing 2-20   UploadFile.aspx

```
<script language="C#" runat="server">
protected void PhotoSubmit(object o, EventArgs e) {
    if(thePhoto.PostedFile != null) {
        try {
            // does NOT handle multiple users uploading at
            // exactly the same time
            string filepath
                = "C:\\temp\\" + DateTime.Now.Ticks.ToString();
            thePhoto.PostedFile.SaveAs(filepath);
            status.Text = "File saved as " + filepath;


        }
        catch {
            status.Text = "An Error occurred processing the file.";
            status.Text += " Please try again.";
        }
    }
}
</script>
<form runat="server" enctype="multipart/form-data">
    Please select an image to submit:
    <input id="thePhoto" type="file" runat="server"><br />
    <input type="button" runat="server" value="Proceed"
        OnServerClick="PhotoSubmit" />
    <asp:label runat="server" id="status" />
</form>
```

> **Tip**   If you need to generate random numbers in your application, create a *Random* object and store it in application scope. The object is seeded when it is created and can then be used throughout the application to get differing values easily.

Using ViewState with Sensitive Data

By now, you're aware that ASP.NET maintains state between requests in the stateless HTTP protocol. How does this work? The process is actually straightforward once you get a feel for what is happening behind the scenes. To recall the previous state, each control can contribute some ViewState that it needs to have access to when the postback occurs. This ViewState from the page controls is put together into a hidden form field and sent to the client. When the page is posted back to the server, the ViewState is broken up and given back to the controls that asked for it to be saved. When you look at the source of a page in the browser, you'll see that the ViewState data is contained in a hidden form field that is not as easily readable as you might have expected. This is for two reasons. First, the data is base64-encoded for transmission to and from the client. By simply base64-decoding it, you can easily see the real values. Second, the ViewState data is hashed with a server key in what is referred to as the ViewState MAC. This guards against users modifying the ViewState and posting data back to the servers that differs from what was sent.

Encoding and hashing the ViewState is not equivalent to encrypting the data. Data encryption is computationally expensive and is therefore not the default for ViewState. ASP.NET does provide support for automatically encrypting and decrypting the ViewState. Always make sure that the ViewState MAC is enabled when you are using ViewState. When working with confidential data, be sure that the ViewState MAC is enabled, and set the *machineKey* validation attribute to 3DES. ASP.NET then automatically encrypts and decrypts the page ViewState, protecting it from prying eyes and from client-side tampering. Of course, using Secure Sockets Layer (SSL) on the page gives an even greater degree of protection against any information being discovered by someone watching data go by.

Code Listing 2-21 is a sample web.config file that sets the *enableView-StateMAC* key to *true*, which is the default despite the comment in machine.config that says otherwise. It also sets the option to enable encryption by setting the validation algorithm to Triple DES. Note that setting the *validation* attribute to 3DES causes encryption. The validation against ViewState tampering is actually controlled by the *enableViewStateMac* attribute.

Code Listing 2-21 EncryptionWeb.config

```
<configuration>
    <system.web>
        <pages enableViewStateMac="true" />
        <machineKey validation="3DES" />
    </system.web>
</configuration>
```

> **Tip** When deploying in a Web farm without server affinity (meaning that for each request, a client session can be handled by a different server), the validation key must be set explicitly and synchronized between the machines. If the default AutoGenerate setting is used, postbacks handled by a machine other than the one in which the View-State was generated will not be processed correctly, and the user will get an error.

Summary

In this chapter, we examined the ASP.NET server controls—the two main types of controls included as part of ASP.NET, the HTML server controls, and the Web controls. The HTML server controls let you rapidly move to server-side development because you can take advantage of your knowledge of HTML elements. The Web controls provide a richer abstraction but also allow event-driven programming.

We looked at the User control model for encapsulating pieces of a Web application and discussed the opportunities for third parties to create and sell additional Web application programming elements that plug directly into Visual Studio .NET.

We examined the ASP.NET Web controls associated with lists and user selection as well as the validation controls, which greatly reduce the amount of code necessary to ensure that user input conforms to the required level of quality.

We finished this chapter by demonstrating how to use ASP.NET to manage file uploads and how to enable validation and encryption to include sensitive data in our controls, protect it from prying eyes, and guard against tampering. In the next chapter, we will look at the data-binding mechanism of ASP.NET and how to work with back-end databases to provide users with sophisticated data access.

Controls

Data is at the heart of all applications. Granted, there are exceptions to this statement, but more often than not, Web applications are used for viewing, searching, and updating data. In this chapter, we'll look at the features of ASP.NET that focus on binding user interface elements to data. Because binding to records from a sample database would unnecessarily complicate our sample code and detract from the focus on data controls, we create small datasets where appropriate directly in the page and bind to them. In practice, of course, your data would be retrieved from calls to middle-tier business objects or by accessing a back-end database directly.

Connecting data to server controls is referred to as *data-binding*. In Code Listing 3-1, we data-bind to a field declared on the page. In the *Page_Load* method, we set the *theTime* variable to the current time and then call the *Data-Bind* method on the page. Note the <%# syntax (it is not censored text) prior to the variable name. This code sequence is an indicator to ASP.NET that what follows is code that the ASP.NET page parser will inject into the page. That code—called a *data-binding expression*—is then called when the *DataBind* operation is performed on the page.

Code Listing 3-1   DataBindField.aspx

```csharp
<script language="C#" runat="server">
DateTime theTime;
protected void Page_Load(object o, EventArgs e) {
    theTime = DateTime.Now;
    Page.DataBind();
}
</script>
The time is: <%# theTime %><br/>
```

Figure 3-1 shows part of the code that ASP.NET generates for Code Listing 3-1. (Remember that this code is automatically generated and is not guaranteed to be consistent between versions of ASP.NET.) When DataBindField.aspx is executed, the *BuildControlTree* method is called. This method calls another automatically generated method (which has a mangled name) to build the data-bound string, which is accomplished using an instance of the *DataBoundLiteralControl* class. This method attaches an event handler to the newly created *DataBoundLiteralControl* for the *DataBinding* event. The *Page_Load* method calls the *DataBind* method, which then invokes this event handler code. The event handler calls the *SetDataBoundString* method on the original DataBoundLiteralControl to get the value of the field being used. The *Text* property of DataBoundLiteralControl is finally set to the field's value, which is displayed when the control is rendered.

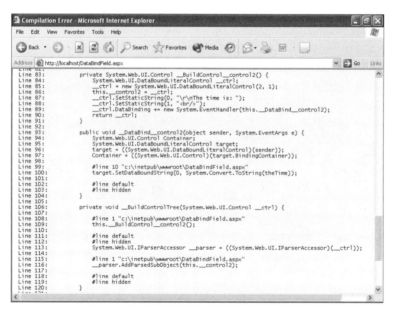

Figure 3-1   Code generated for data-binding a page field

To display a simple value, the automatically generated code for the simple ASPX page shown in Code Listing 3-1 must seem like overkill. After all, we're already writing code to set the value for the field, and it's trivial to add another line to set the *Text* property of a control directly.

We can begin to see more power in the databinding construct in Code Listing 3-2. In this example, the expression is expanded to include values from two server controls on the page. Because we are assuming that the controls are integers, we really should validate the datatype, as discussed in Chapter 2.

```
Code Listing 3-2   DataBindControlValue.aspx
<script runat="server" language="C#">
protected void Page_Load(object o, EventArgs e) {
    if(IsPostBack) {
        Page.DataBind();
    }
}
</script>
<form runat="server">
    Add two numbers:
    <asp:TextBox runat="server" id="operand1" /> +
    <asp:TextBox runat="server" id="operand2" /><br />
    <asp:Button type="submit" runat="server" Text="Submit" /><br />
    The DataBound result =
    <%# Int32.Parse(operand1.Text) + Int32.Parse(operand2.Text) %>
</form>
```

Code Listing 3-2 shows that data-binding offers a shortcut for simple coding expressions or method invocations. You don't have to declare a server control explicitly, provide code elsewhere to collect the values from the sources, and then assign the result. Instead, the data-binding support allows us to easily declare the expression inline. Notice that the *Page_Load* method in the example performs the *DataBind* operation only when the page is a postback. Because we provide no default values for the textbox controls, we wait until the user has had a chance to post their inputs. Often, the scenario is reversed and the data-bind operation is performed only when the request is *not* a postback. When a control can carry the data it is bound to between requests in ViewState, you can avoid performing expensive calculations or database operations again.

> **Tip**   Use data-binding to declaratively control the display of values combined from the value of other controls.

Code Listing 3-3 demonstrates how data-binding also supports invoking methods automatically. In this example, input is gathered from the user. The use of validators assures us that some value has been provided and that it is a positive number and sufficiently small to calculate its factorial quickly. The data-binding expression is code to invoke the *CalculateFactorial* method. The *CalculateFactorial* method expects an integer type and returns a double, so the data-binding expression takes care of the type conversions to and from the string.

Code Listing 3-3   DataBindMethod.aspx

```
<script runat="server" language="C#">
protected void Page_Load(object o, EventArgs e) {
    if(IsPostBack) {
        Page.DataBind();
    }
}
protected double CalculateFactorial(int input) {
    double result = 1;
    for(;input > 0; input--) {
        result *= input;
    }
    return result;
}
</script>
<form runat="server">
    Databind the result of a method call.
    <asp:Textbox runat="server" id="theInput" /><br/>
    <asp:RequiredFieldValidator runat="server"
        ControlToValidate="theInput"
        ErrorMessage="input is required" />
    <asp:RangeValidator runat="server"
        ControlToValidate="theInput"
        ErrorMessage="input must be >= 0 and < 20"
        Type="integer" MinimumValue="0" MaximumValue="20" /><br/>
    <asp:Button runat="server" type="submit"
        Text="Calculate Factorial" /><br/>
    The result is: <b>
    <%# CalculateFactorial(Int32.Parse(theInput.Text)).ToString() %>
    </b>
</form>
```

In Chapter 2, we said that the items of the list controls could be set declaratively, dynamically, or by using data-binding. When you data-bind the list controls, the data source you specify must support at least one of a set of interfaces. If the data source does not implement *IEnumerable* or *IlistSource*, an exception will be thrown. In Code Listing 3-4, we convert the DropDownList sample from Chapter 2 to bind to an *ArrayList*.

> **Note**   Avoid unnecessary data-binding. If the control has ViewState enabled, it needs to be data-bound only for initialization and then again when the underlying data source changes. However, if you disable ViewState for the control or for the page, you must call *DataBind* on every page load to re-populate the items.

Code Listing 3-4   DataBindDropDownList.aspx

```csharp
<script language="C#" runat="server">
protected void Page_Load(object o, EventArgs e) {
    if(!IsPostBack) {
        ArrayList arrayList = new ArrayList();
        arrayList.Add("C#");
        arrayList.Add("VB.NET");
        arrayList.Add("JScript.Net");

        languageDropDownList.DataSource = arrayList;
        languageDropDownList.DataBind();

        favoriteLanguage.Text
            = languageDropDownList.SelectedItem.Value;
    }
}

protected void DropDownListSelectionChanged(object o, EventArgs e) {
    favoriteLanguage.Text = languageDropDownList.SelectedItem.Text;
}
</script>
<form runat="server">
    <asp:DropDownList id="languageDropDownList" runat="server"
        OnSelectedIndexChanged="DropDownListSelectionChanged" >
    </asp:DropDownList><br/>
    Favorite Language:
    <b><asp:Label runat="server" id="favoriteLanguage"
        style="color:blue" /></b><br />
    <asp:Button runat="server" Text="Submit"/>
</form>
```

Tip   Add dynamic items after data-binding. When adding items to a DropDownList control from both a data source and code in the page, be aware of the order in which they are added. The data-binding operation clears all the items that exist in the control and replaces them with the set from the data source. After *DataBind* is called, you can safely add items to the data-bound list. A good example of where this tip can prove valuable is when you want to add a default value of "Make a Selection" at the top of a drop-down list.

The Repeater, DataList, and DataGrid Controls

ASP.NET has three primary controls for easily displaying sets of data: Repeater, DataList, and DataGrid. In this section, we'll explain the major differences in their feature sets, examine how to use them, and discuss their limitations so that you pick the correct control for your development task.

Repeater

The Repeater control has no implicit markup to render. Instead, you are required to specify templates that indicate to the containing control which markup—typically HTML—to render for each item in the data source. Markup is specified declaratively; you don't need to know how many items will exist when the data-binding occurs. Because the Repeater control does not offer a default rendering, it is probably the most flexible of the three controls. However, selecting, editing, and deleting items is more difficult with Repeater. Repeater does not offer a rich set of style properties to set because the appearance is controlled entirely by what is in the templates. Code Listing 3-5 shows a Repeater control in action, including using the full set of templates: Header-Template, FooterTemplate, ItemTemplate, AlternatingItemTemplate, and SeparatorTemplate.

Code Listing 3-5   Repeater.aspx

```csharp
<script language="C#" runat="server">
public class State {
    string _name;
    string _timezone;
    public State(string name, string timezone) {
        _name = name;
        _timezone = timezone;
    }
    public string Name {
        get { return _name; }
    }
    public string TimeZone {
        get { return _timezone; }
    }
}
protected void Page_Load(object o, EventArgs e) {
    if(!IsPostBack) {
        ArrayList states = new ArrayList();
        states.Add(new State("Washington", "Pacific"));
        states.Add(new State("Utah", "Mountain"));
        states.Add(new State("Wisconsin", "Central"));
```

```
        states.Add(new State("New York", "Eastern"));

        repeaterVertical.DataSource = states;
        repeaterHorizontal.DataSource = states;

        repeaterVertical.DataBind();
        repeaterHorizontal.DataBind();
    }
}
</script>
<form runat="server">
    <asp:Repeater runat="server" id="repeaterVertical">
        <HeaderTemplate>
            <table><tr><th>State</th><th>TimeZone</th></tr>
        </HeaderTemplate>
        <ItemTemplate>
            <tr bgcolor="blue">
                <td><%#((State)(Container.DataItem)).Name) %></td>
                <td><%#DataBinder.Eval(Container,
                    "DataItem.TimeZone") %></td>
            </tr>
        </ItemTemplate>
        <SeparatorTemplate>
            <tr bgcolor="white"><td><hr></td></tr>
        </SeparatorTemplate>
        <AlternatingItemTemplate>
            <tr bgcolor="red">
                <td><%#((State)(Container.DataItem)).Name %></td>
                <td><%#DataBinder.Eval(Container,
                    "DataItem.TimeZone") %></td>
            </tr>
        </AlternatingItemTemplate>
        <FooterTemplate></table></FooterTemplate>
    </asp:Repeater>

    <hr/>

    <asp:Repeater runat="server" id="repeaterHorizontal">
        <HeaderTemplate>
            <table><tr><th>State<br/>TimeZone</th>
        </HeaderTemplate>
        <ItemTemplate>
            <td bgcolor="blue">
                <%#DataBinder.Eval(Container.DataItem,
                    "Name") %><br />
                <%#DataBinder.Eval(Container.DataItem,
                    "TimeZone") %>
            </td>
```

```
        </ItemTemplate>
        <AlternatingItemTemplate>
            <td bgcolor="red">
                <%#DataBinder.Eval(Container.DataItem,
                    "Name") %><br />
                <%#DataBinder.Eval(Container.DataItem,
                    "TimeZone") %>
            </td>
        </AlternatingItemTemplate>
        <FooterTemplate></tr></table></FooterTemplate>
    </asp:Repeater>
</form>
```

The output from Code Listing 3-5 is shown in Figure 3-2. The script block in Repeater.aspx first contains a simple class that holds a state name and its time zone. In the *Page_Load* method, a small set of these objects is created and added to an *ArrayList*, which is then set as the data source property of the two Repeater controls on the page. The first Repeater control displays the items from the list horizontally in a table, whereas the second Repeater control displays them vertically. Notice that the header and footer templates are used to render the beginning and ending tags of the table. The ItemTemplate and AlternatingItemTemplate are then used in turn for the items from the data source.

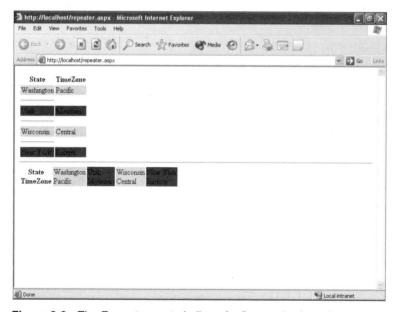

Figure 3-2 The Repeater control allows for flow and column layout

Another aspect to note about Code Listing 3-5 is the different syntax used in the data-binding expressions. In the first data-binding instance, the *Repeater-Item* object returned from *Container.DataItem* is explicitly cast to the *State* object type stored in the data source. The *Name* property accessor of the *State* object is then accessed directly. In the second data-binding instance, the *Data-Binder.Eval* method is used to automatically perform reflection on the *Container* to retrieve the *TimeZone* property of the *State* object, which is stored in the *DataItem* property. In the second Repeater control, an alternate form of the *DataBinder.Eval* method is used in which the first parameter is resolved directly to the item, and the property is then resolved through reflection. These two syntax statements can be used interchangeably.

DataList

The DataList control provides rendering behavior in addition to supporting a set of templates for controlling the control's appearance. Unlike the Repeater control, which supports only flow layout rendering, the DataList control supports both table and flow layout. In table layout, the templates are rendered as part of a *Table* element. In flow layout, the templates are rendered inside span tags. With either type of layout, the DataList allows you to control whether the items are repeated in a horizontal or vertical orientation as well as how many columns of items appear across the page. Code Listing 3-6 has an example of the DataList control. In addition to the templates supported by the Repeater control, DataList supports EditItemTemplate and SelectedItemTemplate for editing and selection, respectively.

Code Listing 3-6   DataList.aspx

```csharp
<script language="C#" runat="server">
public class State {
    string _name;
    string _timezone;
    public State(string name, string timezone) {
        _name = name;
        _timezone = timezone;
    }
    public string Name {
        get { return _name; }
    }
    public string TimeZone {
        get { return _timezone; }
    }
}
protected void Page_Load(object o, EventArgs e) {
```

```
    if(!IsPostBack) {
        ArrayList states = new ArrayList();
        states.Add(new State("Washington", "Pacific"));
        states.Add(new State("Utah", "Mountain"));
        states.Add(new State("Wisconsin", "Central"));
        states.Add(new State("New York", "Eastern"));

        datalist.DataSource = states;
        datalist.DataBind();
        datalist.SelectedIndex = 0;
    }
}
</script>
<form runat="server">
    <asp:DataList runat="server" id="datalist" BackColor="tan"
        RepeatDirection="Vertical" BorderWidth="1"
        BorderColor="Black" Repeatcolumns="2"
        CellSpacing="3" CellPadding="4" >
        <SelectedItemStyle BackColor="beige" >
        </SelectedItemStyle>
        <ItemTemplate>
            <%# DataBinder.Eval(Container.DataItem, "Name") %> is in
            <%# DataBinder.Eval(Container, "DataItem.Timezone") %>
        </ItemTemplate>
    </asp:DataList>
</form>
```

DataGrid

The DataGrid control is the most commonly used of the three controls. It renders the items as a table with each item contained inside a single row, so it does not support a choice of column or flow layout. Unlike the Repeater and DataList controls, the DataGrid control supports paging of content as well as sorting. Although the DataGrid control is generally easier to use, it doesn't offer you a high degree of templating control with the exception of offering support for templating entire columns. Code Listing 3-7 shows a basic DataGrid control bound to data created directly on the page. Additional code samples follow that demonstrate how to accomplish specific tasks with the DataGrid control.

Code Listing 3-7   DataGrid.aspx

```
<%@Import namespace="System.Data" %>
<script language="C#" runat="server">
protected void Page_Load(object o, EventArgs e) {
    datagrid.DataSource = GetData();
    DataBind();
}


DataTable GetData() {
    DataTable data = new DataTable();
    data.Columns.Add(new DataColumn("TheID", typeof(Int32)));
    data.Columns.Add(new DataColumn("Name", typeof(string)));
    data.Columns.Add(new DataColumn("TimeZone", typeof(string)));

    DataRow dr;
    dr = data.NewRow();
    dr[0] = 1; dr[1] = "Washington"; dr[2] = "Pacific";
    data.Rows.Add(dr);
    dr = data.NewRow();
    dr[0] = 2; dr[1] = "Utah"; dr[2] = "Mountain";
    data.Rows.Add(dr);
    dr = data.NewRow();
    dr[0] = 3; dr[1] = "Wisconsin"; dr[2] = "Central";
    data.Rows.Add(dr);
    dr = data.NewRow();
    dr[0] = 4; dr[1] = "New York"; dr[2] = "Eastern";
    data.Rows.Add(dr);
    dr = data.NewRow();
    dr[0] = 5; dr[1] = "Florida"; dr[2] = "Eastern";
    data.Rows.Add(dr);

    return data;
}
</script>
<form runat="server">
    <asp:DataGrid runat="server" id="datagrid" />
</form>
```

Figure 3-3 shows the basic rendering that this approach produces. In the "Adding Styles To the DataGrid" section later in this chapter, Code Listing 3-9 adds styles and templated header text to demonstrate the flexibility and sophisticated user interface available in the DataGrid control.

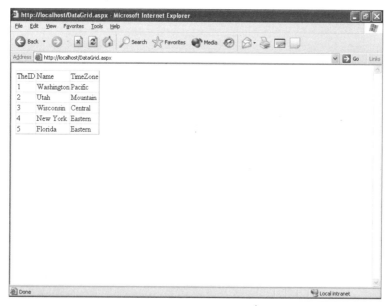

Figure 3-3   Basic DataGrid rendering

In DataGrid.aspx, the data source is a *DataTable* object created directly on the page; however, this data-binding approach is not the most common. When a Web application needs to provide support for manipulating and modifying data, a *DataSet* object is populated from a back-end database. The local view of the data can thus be manipulated over time through a series of requests and committed back to the database later. On the other hand, when a Web application needs only to display and not update data, using *SqlDataReader* is a better choice, since *SqlDataReader* provides a read-only view of the data and has less overhead than the *DataSet*. However, be aware that when using *SqlDataReader*, the DataGrid will not perform sorting and paging directly. If sorting and pagination are required, use a *DataSet* or a *DataView*.

> **Tip**   For frequently accessed but rarely changed data, use the application cache or partial page caching (discussed in Chapter 6) to cut down on trips to the database.

Managing ViewState Size

When ViewState is enabled, as it is by default, the data from the data source makes a round trip between the client and server on each request. When the data is significantly large, this round trip can have a negative impact on the user experience. Look at the size of the ViewState for the DataGrid control by using tracing (discussed in Chapter 10) to understand exactly what kind of impact the ViewState is having on page size.

If ViewState size is problematic for an application, a couple of solutions are available. First, you can completely disable ViewState in configuration or on the page or for an individual control. Without ViewState, the DataGrid control can no longer automatically store information about the paging state, the item being edited, or the current sort expression. You would need to maintain this data separately.

Second, you can simply reduce ViewState by following these steps:

1. Set *AutoGenerateColumns* to *false* and explicitly declare only those columns that are necessary.

2. Set the styles in the code explicitly instead of establishing them declaratively.

3. Do not use the *DataKeyField* member.

Specifying Columns Explicitly

In DataGrid.aspx, we take advantage of the DataGrid control's ability to automatically render the structure of the data source in the user interface. The column headers are the names of the columns, and the column order replicates that of the *DataColumn* objects in the *DataTable*. There is a performance cost associated with the reflection required to produce this automatic rendering.

Another drawback with the auto-generated columns is that in production databases, column names are rarely names that would mean much to the user, and the query might include columns that are intended for use by the application but should not be used by or shown to the user. The DataGrid control allows us to override this behavior by setting the *AutoGenerateColumns* property to *false* and providing a collection of *BoundColumn* definitions within a *Columns* element declaratively in the page. Only the specified fields from the bound data are displayed instead. Code Listing 3-8 is a modified version of the previous DataGrid example in which *AutoGenerateColumns* is set to *false* and we provide explicit header names for the columns. In the coming examples, we will continue to modify this listing of states and their time zones to illustrate ways of using and controlling the DataGrid.

Code Listing 3-8   DataGridColumns.aspx

```csharp
<%@Import namespace="System.Data" %>
<script language="C#" runat="server">
protected void Page_Load(object o, EventArgs e) {
    datagrid.DataSource = GetData();
    DataBind();
}

DataTable GetData() {
    DataTable data = new DataTable();
    data.Columns.Add(new DataColumn("TheID", typeof(Int32)));
    data.Columns.Add(new DataColumn("Name", typeof(string)));
    data.Columns.Add(new DataColumn("TimeZone", typeof(string)));

    DataRow dr;
    dr = data.NewRow();
    dr[0] = 1; dr[1] = "Washington"; dr[2] = "Pacific";
    data.Rows.Add(dr);
    dr = data.NewRow();
    dr[0] = 2; dr[1] = "Utah"; dr[2] = "Mountain";
    data.Rows.Add(dr);
    dr = data.NewRow();
    dr[0] = 3; dr[1] = "Wisconsin"; dr[2] = "Central";
    data.Rows.Add(dr);
    dr = data.NewRow();
    dr[0] = 4; dr[1] = "New York"; dr[2] = "Eastern";
    data.Rows.Add(dr);
    dr = data.NewRow();
    dr[0] = 5; dr[1] = "Florida"; dr[2] = "Eastern";
    data.Rows.Add(dr);

    return data;
}
</script>
<form runat="server">
    <asp:DataGrid runat="server" id="datagrid"
        AutoGenerateColumns="false">
        <Columns>
            <asp:BoundColumn HeaderText="ID" DataField="TheID" />
            <asp:BoundColumn HeaderText="Name" DataField="Name" />
            <asp:BoundColumn HeaderText="Time Zone"
                DataField="TimeZone" />
        </Columns>
    </asp:DataGrid>
</form>
```

Combining Data-Bound and Static Items

When a control is data-bound, the items collection is cleared. Any statically declared items, items from an earlier data-binding, or items restored from ViewState are lost—not always an ideal situation. Sometimes the goal is to combine items from a back-end database with statically known data or with user-provided data. The *DataGridItemCollection* does not permit inserts or additions, so you combine sets of data before the data is bound to the control. Select the data from the database and then add the user-defined data. The *DataBind* operation will bind the augmented set of data to the control, reflecting the changes appropriately.

DataBinder.Eval

We discussed earlier that the *DataBinder.Eval* method is used to declare which members of the *DataItem* to use in the output. The *Eval* method uses reflection to get the second parameter from the first. This approach typically has *Container.DataItem* as the first parameter, which yields a *DataRowView*. The second parameter is the name of the data field within the *DataRowView*. There is a performance cost associated with reflection, so you might want to think twice about the volume of required operations. The *DataSet* is a primary data source for the DataGrid control, however, and its performance in rendering is remarkable given the sheer volume of operations required to produce the output.

Adding Styles to the DataGrid

The DataGrid control supports a sophisticated set of styles just as the other Web controls do. Font, color, and border styles can be set directly on a control. In addition, the DataGrid provides support for a set of template styles. These template styles are applied to pieces of the output, not to the whole control.

In Code Listing 3-9, we add styles to the short list of states in the DataGrid. We also set the *ShowFooter* property to *true* to render both header and footer rows for the data. We can modify the appearance of the DataGrid's table layout by specifying *ItemStyle* and *AlternatingItemStyle*.

Code Listing 3-9   DataGridStyles.aspx

```csharp
<%@Import namespace="System.Data" %>
<script language="C#" runat="server">
protected void Page_Load(object o, EventArgs e) {
    datagrid.Columns[0].ItemStyle.ForeColor
        = System.Drawing.Color.Red;
    datagrid.DataSource = GetData();
    DataBind();
}

DataTable GetData() {
    DataTable data = new DataTable();
    data.Columns.Add(new DataColumn("TheID", typeof(Int32)));
    data.Columns.Add(new DataColumn("Name", typeof(string)));
    data.Columns.Add(new DataColumn("TimeZone", typeof(string)));

    DataRow dr;
    dr = data.NewRow();
    dr[0] = 1; dr[1] = "Washington"; dr[2] = "Pacific";
    data.Rows.Add(dr);
    dr = data.NewRow();
    dr[0] = 2; dr[1] = "Utah"; dr[2] = "Mountain";
    data.Rows.Add(dr);
    dr = data.NewRow();
    dr[0] = 3; dr[1] = "Wisconsin"; dr[2] = "Central";
    data.Rows.Add(dr);
    dr = data.NewRow();
    dr[0] = 4; dr[1] = "New York"; dr[2] = "Eastern";
    data.Rows.Add(dr);
    dr = data.NewRow();
    dr[0] = 5; dr[1] = "Florida"; dr[2] = "Eastern";
    data.Rows.Add(dr);

    return data;
}
</script>
<form runat="server">
    <asp:DataGrid runat="server" id="datagrid"
        AutoGenerateColumns="false"
        font-name="tahoma" font-size="12 pt" font-bold="true"
        ShowFooter="true" BackColor="#667788" ForeColor="#FFFFFF" >
        <HeaderStyle BackColor="tan" BorderColor="#000000"
            ForeColor="#334455" HorizontalAlign="center"
            font-size="14 pt" />
        <FooterStyle BackColor="tan" BorderColor="#000000"
            ForeColor="#334455" HorizontalAlign="center"
            font-size="14 pt" />
```

```
            <ItemStyle BackColor="#667788" ForeColor="#ffffff" />
            <AlternatingItemStyle BackColor="#ffffff"
                ForeColor="#334455" />
            <Columns>
                <asp:BoundColumn HeaderText="ID" FooterText="ID"
                    DataField="TheID" />
                <asp:BoundColumn HeaderText="Name" FooterText="Name"
                    DataField="Name" />
                <asp:BoundColumn HeaderText="Time Zone"
                    FooterText="Time Zone" DataField="TimeZone" />
            </Columns>
        </asp:DataGrid>
    </form>
```

Sorting the DataGrid

One of the primary features of the DataGrid is the ability to automatically sort its contents. When the *AllowSorting* property is set to *true*, the DataGrid generates LinkButton controls in the column headers of the columns that have a value for the *SortExpression* property. Auto-generated columns will automatically set the *SortExpression* property to the name of the field to which the column is bound. The *OnSortCommand* event is fired when the user clicks one of these LinkButton controls. This functionality can be used when customizing the user interface, such as using a Button control or ImageButton consistently throughout the site to create a standard appearance. The sorting functionality can be invoked when the user selects an element that has been created in place of the LinkButton controls.

Code Listing 3-10 has two DataGrid controls, both using the same set of data. The first DataGrid control leverages the built-in support for paging. The *AllowSorting* property is set to *true*, and the *SortDataGrid* event handler is invoked when a column is selected. We are using a *DataView* to take advantage of the ability to set the column name as the sort expression. This event handler creates the data with the new sort expression and rebinds the DataGrid. The second DataGrid on the page does more work to customize the output. In addition to its own data-sorting event handler, a new event handler is provided that is called whenever a new item is created. In the *ItemCreated* event handler, we only act if the item being created is the header. When the header is being created, we retrieve the individual cells from the DataGrid and add a new *Button* to the Controls collection. The second DataGrid still has the sorting functionality, but we created Button controls instead of the default LinkButton controls.

When Does the DataGrid Control Need to Be Data-Bound?

The answer to this question is a common source of confusion. If the *Data-Bind* method is not called, stale data might be rendered, or perhaps no data at all is rendered. Calling *DataBind* too often will decrease performance and might cause updates to fail because the modified inputs are lost. *DataBind* needs to be called when the page first loads and the *IsPostBack* property is *false*. If ViewState is disabled, *DataBind* must be called on every page load, even when *IsPostBack* is *true*. When a property is changed that will cause the output to change, such as when the user starts editing or cancels editing, or when a sort operation is taking place, the *DataBind* method must be called. Normally, you call this method in the event handler after the updated DataGrid properties are set. A *Select* command is an exception to this rule. When the user selects a row, *SelectedItemIndex* changes and, if appropriate, the *SelectedItemIndexChanged* event is called, but a repeated data-binding operation is not necessary because the data is not changing.

Code Listing 3-10   DataGridSorting.aspx

```csharp
<%@Import namespace="System.Data" %>
<script language="C#" runat="server">
protected void Page_Load(object o, EventArgs e) {
    if(!IsPostBack) {
        datagrid.DataSource = GetData("");
        datagrid2.DataSource = GetData("");
        DataBind();
    }
}


protected void SortDataGrid(object o,
    DataGridSortCommandEventArgs e) {
    datagrid.DataSource = GetData(e.SortExpression);
    datagrid.DataBind();
}

protected void SortDataGrid2(object o,
    DataGridSortCommandEventArgs e) {
    datagrid2.DataSource = GetData(e.SortExpression);
    datagrid2.DataBind();
}
```

```
DataView GetData(string sortString) {
    DataTable data = new DataTable();
    data.Columns.Add(new DataColumn("TheID", typeof(Int32)));
    data.Columns.Add(new DataColumn("Name", typeof(string)));
    data.Columns.Add(new DataColumn("TimeZone", typeof(string)));

    DataRow dr;
    dr = data.NewRow();
    dr[0] = 1; dr[1] = "Washington"; dr[2] = "Pacific";
    data.Rows.Add(dr);
    dr = data.NewRow();
    dr[0] = 2; dr[1] = "Utah"; dr[2] = "Mountain";
    data.Rows.Add(dr);
    dr = data.NewRow();
    dr[0] = 3; dr[1] = "Wisconsin"; dr[2] = "Central";
    data.Rows.Add(dr);
    dr = data.NewRow();
    dr[0] = 4; dr[1] = "New York"; dr[2] = "Eastern";
    data.Rows.Add(dr);
    dr = data.NewRow();
    dr[0] = 5; dr[1] = "Florida"; dr[2] = "Eastern";
    data.Rows.Add(dr);

    DataView view = new DataView(data);
    view.Sort = sortString;
    return view;
}

void DataGrid_ItemCreated(object o, DataGridItemEventArgs e) {
    if(e.Item.ItemType == ListItemType.Header) {
        Button b = new Button();
        b.Text = "ID";
        b.CommandName = "Sort";
        b.CommandArgument="TheID";
        TableCell tc = e.Item.Cells[0];
        tc.Controls.Add(b);

        b = new Button();
        b.Text = "Name";
        b.CommandName = "Sort";
        b.CommandArgument = "Name";
        tc = e.Item.Cells[1];
        tc.Controls.Add(b);

        b = new Button();
        b.Text = "Time Zone";
        b.CommandName = "Sort";
        b.CommandArgument = "TimeZone";
```

```
            tc = e.Item.Cells[2];
            tc.Controls.Add(b);
        }
    }
</script>
<form runat="server">
    <asp:DataGrid runat="server" id="datagrid" AllowSorting="true"
        OnSortCommand="SortDataGrid" ShowHeader="true" />
    <asp:DataGrid runat="server" id="datagrid2"
        AutoGenerateColumns="false" OnSortCommand="SortDataGrid2"
        AllowSorting="true" OnItemCreated="DataGrid_ItemCreated">
        <Columns>
            <asp:BoundColumn DataField="TheID" />
            <asp:BoundColumn HeaderText="Name" DataField="Name" />
            <asp:BoundColumn HeaderText="Time Zone"
                DataField="TimeZone" />
        </Columns>
    </asp:DataGrid>
</form>
```

Paging the DataGrid

The DataGrid control provides for automatic as well as custom pagination of contents, which gives users many options for viewing data. Users commonly want to page through smaller pieces of a larger data set. Sometimes the desired piece of information is only a subset of the total data, or maybe the data must be viewed with a collection to allow for comparison with the neighboring data.

Automatic pagination is simple. You set the *AllowPaging* property to *true* and provide a *PageIndexChanged EventHandler* that sets the *CurrentPageIndex* to the *NewPageIndex* and calls *DataBind* on the DataGrid.

Custom pagination requires that both the *AllowPaging* property and the *AllowCustomPaging* property be set to *true*. The *PageIndexChanged EventHandler* can then bind the control to a subset of the total data the user is perusing. The code must then set the *VirtualItemCount* property of the Data-Grid to indicate what the total count is. When allowing custom pagination, the DataGrid can no longer derive the total item count from the bound items, so you must explicitly provide this information.

Code Listing 3-11 demonstrates both automatic and custom paging of the DataGrid. The calls to the *GetData* method for the automatically paginated control always calculate the full set of squares, although only 10 of them are being displayed at once, whereas the custom-paginated DataGrid requires that only 10 samples be calculated for any given page view.

Note   Custom paging of the DataGrid can be particularly beneficial when the entire set of data being used is quite large or when retrieving it is expensive. Custom paging can also be used when the data source is a *DataReader* but you still require paging support on the DataGrid. In this scenario, you are responsible for managing the paging in the code, but you might achieve a better result with custom controls than you would by using a *DataSet* with automatic paging.

Code Listing 3-11   DataGridPaging.aspx

```csharp
<%@Import namespace="System.Data" %>
<script language="C#" runat="server">
protected void Page_Load(object o, EventArgs e) {
    if(!IsPostBack) {
        datagrid.DataSource = GetData(0, 100);
        datagrid2.DataSource = GetData(0, 10);
        datagrid2.VirtualItemCount = 100;
        DataBind();
    }
}

DataTable GetData(int startIndex, int count) {
    DataTable data = new DataTable();
    data.Columns.Add(new DataColumn("TheNumber", typeof(Int32)));
    data.Columns.Add(new DataColumn("Squared", typeof(Int32)));

    DataRow dr;
    for(int i = 0; i < count;i++) {
        dr = data.NewRow();
        int theNumber = i+startIndex;
        dr[0] = theNumber;
        dr[1] = theNumber * theNumber;
        data.Rows.Add(dr);
    }
    return data;
}

void ChangePage(object o, DataGridPageChangedEventArgs e) {
    datagrid.CurrentPageIndex = e.NewPageIndex;
    datagrid.DataSource = GetData(0, 100);
    datagrid.DataBind();
}
```

```
void CustomChangePage(object o, DataGridPageChangedEventArgs e) {
    datagrid2.CurrentPageIndex = e.NewPageIndex;
    datagrid2.DataSource = GetData(e.NewPageIndex*10, 10);
    datagrid2.DataBind();
    datagrid2.VirtualItemCount = 100;
}

</script>
<form runat="server">
    <asp:DataGrid runat="server" id="datagrid"
        AllowPaging="true" OnPageIndexChanged="ChangePage"/>
    <asp:DataGrid runat="server" id="datagrid2"
        AllowPaging="true" AllowCustomPaging="true"
        OnPageIndexChanged="CustomChangePage"/>
</form>
```

Selecting Rows in the DataGrid

Now that you can bind data and understand how to page and sort data in the DataGrid, let's look at how to enable the user to select individual items from within the DataGrid.

The DataGrid automatically recognizes when the user clicks an item by using a command name that is part of a known set. When the *Select* command is invoked, the DataGrid automatically updates the appearance of the individual item by using *SelectedItemStyle*. In Code Listing 3-12, *SelectedItemStyle* uses several of the styles available. The full set of available styles belongs to the *TableItemStyle* class and includes *BackColor*, *ForeColor*, *BorderColor*, and *CssClass*.

When the selected index is changed, not only does the appearance of the selected item within the DataGrid changed automatically, but an event is also fired. This allows a developer to provide an appropriate event handler that can be used to update a separate user interface element on the page based on the item selected in the DataGrid.

Tip   Use two DataGrid controls on a page to allow for a master view and a details view. Synchronize the *SelectedItemIndexChanged* event in the master DataGrid to update the contents of the details view DataGrid.

Code Listing 3-12   DataGridSelect.aspx

```
<%@Import namespace="System.Data" %>
<script language="C#" runat="server">
DataTable data;
protected void Page_Load(object o, EventArgs e) {
    GetData();
    datagrid1.DataSource = data;
    if(!IsPostBack) {
        datagrid1.DataBind();
    }
}


DataTable GetData() {
    data = Session["data"] as DataTable;
    if(data != null) {
        return data;
    }
    data = new DataTable();
    DataColumn primaryColumn
        = new DataColumn("carid", typeof(Int32));
    data.Columns.Add(primaryColumn);
    data.Columns.Add(new DataColumn("year", typeof(Int32)));
    data.Columns.Add(new DataColumn("make", typeof(string)));
    data.Columns.Add(new DataColumn("model", typeof(string)));
    DataRow dr;
    dr = data.NewRow();
    dr[0] = 1; dr[1] = 1998; dr[2] = "Isuzu"; dr[3] = "Trooper";
    data.Rows.Add(dr);
    dr = data.NewRow();
    dr[0] = 2; dr[1] = 2000; dr[2] = "Honda"; dr[3] = "Civic";
    data.Rows.Add(dr);
    DataColumn[] primaryColumns = new DataColumn[1];
    primaryColumns[0] = primaryColumn;
    data.PrimaryKey = primaryColumns;
    Session["data"] = data;
    return data;
}

</script>

<form runat="server">
    <asp:DataGrid runat="server" DataKeyField="carid" id="datagrid1"
        AutoGenerateColumns="false">
        <selectedItemStyle BackColor="tan" Font-Bold="true" />
        <Columns>
            <asp:ButtonColumn CommandName="Select" Text="Select" />
            <asp:BoundColumn DataField="carid" ReadOnly="true"
```

```
              HeaderText="id" />
        <asp:BoundColumn DataField="year" HeaderText="year" />
        <asp:BoundColumn DataField="make" HeaderText="make" />
        <asp:BoundColumn DataField="model" HeaderText="model" />
      </Columns>
   </asp:DataGrid><br/>
</form>
```

Editing Data in the DataGrid

We looked at how to use the DataGrid to display data. The next step is to allow the user to update the data. The DataGrid has built-in events that make the updating task relatively simple. The DataGrid has a property named *EditItemIndex* that is usually set to -*1*, indicating that no row is currently being edited. We use this property to control the appearance of the DataGrid and work with the three events related to editing data: *EditCommand*, *CancelCommand*, and *UpdateCommand*.

Typically, you enable editing by setting the *EditItemIndex* in the *EditCommand* event handler, and abandon the changes by setting the *EditItemIndex* back to -*1* in the *CancelCommand* event handler. The update is performed when the user submits changes within the *UpdateCommand* event handler.

The first step is to provide an *EditCommandColumn* and provide text for the LinkButtons control that will be automatically rendered. When *EditItemIndex* is -*1*, the value of the *EditText* attribute is displayed in the *EditCommandColumn*; otherwise, the values of the *UpdateText* and *CancelText* attributes are displayed for the selected row. When the user clicks a LinkButton, the *EditCommand* event handler for the control is invoked. In Code Listing 3-13, notice that the DataGrid is bound at the end of the event handlers so that the updated view is rendered for the user.

The *CancelCommand* event handler simply sets the *EditItemIndex* back to -*1*, implicitly abandoning any modified data, and calls *DataBind*.

The majority of the work is usually done in the *UpdateCommand* event handler. In Code Listing 3-13, in which we bind to data in the page and temporarily store the data in Session state, we find the row in the *DataTable* and update it with the text from the updated *DataGridItem*. Notice that we index into the *TableRow* contained by the *DataGridItem* to retrieve the TextBox that was used to allow the user to update the item. Don't forget to update the data source—in this example, that means updating the Session data. In many situations, the DataGrid is bound against data that is disconnected from the back-end database and manipulated locally, as shown in this example. Although the data might continue to look correct to the user, the developer must explicitly commit any local changes back to the real data source.

Code Listing 3-13 DataGridEdit.aspx

```
<%@Import namespace="System.Data" %>
<script language="C#" runat="server">
DataTable data;
protected void Page_Load(object o, EventArgs e) {
    GetData();
    datagrid1.DataSource = data;
    if(!IsPostBack) {
        datagrid1.DataBind();
    }
}


DataTable GetData() {
    data = Session["data"] as DataTable;
    if(data != null) {
        return data;
    }
    data = new DataTable();

    DataColumn primaryColumn
        = new DataColumn("carid", typeof(Int32));
    data.Columns.Add(primaryColumn);
    data.Columns.Add(new DataColumn("year", typeof(Int32)));
    data.Columns.Add(new DataColumn("make", typeof(string)));
    data.Columns.Add(new DataColumn("model", typeof(string)));
    DataRow dr;
    dr = data.NewRow();
    dr[0] = 1; dr[1] = 1998; dr[2] = "Isuzu"; dr[3] = "Trooper";
    data.Rows.Add(dr);
    dr = data.NewRow();
    dr[0] = 2; dr[1] = 2000; dr[2] = "Honda"; dr[3] = "Civic";
    data.Rows.Add(dr);

    DataColumn[] primaryColumns = new DataColumn[1];
    primaryColumns[0] = primaryColumn;
    data.PrimaryKey = primaryColumns;

    Session["data"] = data;
    return data;
}

protected void OnEdit(object o, DataGridCommandEventArgs e) {
    datagrid1.EditItemIndex = e.Item.ItemIndex;
    datagrid1.DataBind();
}
```

```
protected void OnCancel(object o, DataGridCommandEventArgs e) {
    datagrid1.EditItemIndex = -1;
    datagrid1.DataBind();
}

protected void OnUpdate(object o, DataGridCommandEventArgs e) {

    int year;
    try {
        year = Int32.Parse((
            (TextBox)e.Item.Cells[2].Controls[0]).Text);
    }
    catch(System.FormatException fe) {
        Response.Write(
            "Invalid year specified. Update not completed");
        return;
    }
    string make = ((TextBox)e.Item.Cells[3].Controls[0]).Text;
    string model = ((TextBox)e.Item.Cells[4].Controls[0]).Text;
    DataRow row = data.Rows.Find(e.Item.Cells[1].Text);
    if(row != null) {
        row["year"] = year.ToString();
        row["make"] = make;
        row["model"] = model;

    }
    data.AcceptChanges();
    datagrid1.EditItemIndex = -1;
    datagrid1.DataBind();
    Session["data"] = data;
}
</script>

<form runat="server">
    <asp:DataGrid runat="server" DataKeyField="carid" id="datagrid1"
        AutoGenerateColumns="false" OnEditCommand="OnEdit"
        OnCancelCommand="OnCancel" OnUpdateCommand="OnUpdate" >
        <Columns>
            <asp:EditCommandColumn EditText="Edit"
                CancelText="Cancel" UpdateText="Update" />
            <asp:boundcolumn DataField="carid" ReadOnly="true"
                HeaderText="id" />
            <asp:BoundColumn DataField="year" HeaderText="year" />
            <asp:BoundColumn DataField="make" HeaderText="make" />
            <asp:BoundColumn DataField="model" HeaderText="model" />
        </Columns>
    </asp:DataGrid><br/>
</form>
```

Deleting Data in the DataGrid

Deleting data from the DataGrid is not as complex as updating it. Because no item is being edited directly and there is only an indication that the row should be deleted, entering and exiting an editing mode is unnecessary. Code Listing 3-14 is a modified version of Code Listing 3-13 that allows only the deletion of items. Notice that the way a LinkButton is displayed for deleting is the inclusion of a *ButtonColumn* with the *CommandName* attribute for the buttons set to *Delete*. This indicates to the DataGrid to fire the event handler specified in its *OnDeleteCommand* attribute.

Code Listing 3-14   DataGridDelete.aspx

```
<%@Import namespace="System.Data" %>
<script language="C#" runat="server">
DataTable data;
protected void Page_Load(object o, EventArgs e) {
    GetData();
    datagrid1.DataSource = data;
    if(!IsPostBack) {
        datagrid1.DataBind();
    }
}

void DeleteRow(object o, DataGridCommandEventArgs e) {
    DataRow row = data.Rows.Find(e.Item.Cells[1].Text);
    if(row != null) {
        data.Rows.Remove(row);
    }
    data.AcceptChanges();
    datagrid1.DataBind();
    Session["data"] = data;
}

DataTable GetData() {
    data = Session["data"] as DataTable;
    if(data != null) {
        return data;
    }
    data = new DataTable();
    DataColumn primaryColumn
        = new DataColumn("carid", typeof(Int32));
    data.Columns.Add(primaryColumn);
    data.Columns.Add(new DataColumn("year", typeof(Int32)));
    data.Columns.Add(new DataColumn("make", typeof(string)));
    data.Columns.Add(new DataColumn("model", typeof(string)));
    DataRow dr;
    dr = data.NewRow();
```

```
    dr[0] = 1; dr[1] = 1998; dr[2] = "Isuzu"; dr[3] = "Trooper";
    data.Rows.Add(dr);
    dr = data.NewRow();
    dr[0] = 2; dr[1] = 2000; dr[2] = "Honda"; dr[3] = "Civic";
    data.Rows.Add(dr);
    DataColumn[] primaryColumns = new DataColumn[1];
    primaryColumns[0] = primaryColumn;
    data.PrimaryKey = primaryColumns;
    Session["data"] = data;
    return data;
}

</script>

<form runat="server">
    <asp:DataGrid runat="server" DataKeyField="carid" id="datagrid1"
        AutoGenerateColumns="false" OnDeleteCommand="DeleteRow">
        <Columns>
            <asp:ButtonColumn CommandName="Delete" Text="Delete" />
            <asp:BoundColumn DataField="carid" ReadOnly="true"
                HeaderText="id" />
            <asp:BoundColumn DataField="year" HeaderText="year" />
            <asp:BoundColumn DataField="make" HeaderText="make" />
            <asp:BoundColumn DataField="model" HeaderText="model" />
        </Columns>
    </asp:DataGrid><br/>
</form>
```

Filtering Data with the DataGrid

As we mentioned earlier, when users view data in a DataGrid, they often want to filter the data to look at only a subset of the entire selection. You can allow them to view only a portion of the data without returning to the database with a revised query. The *DataView* object supports a *RowFilter* property for limiting the data, which is employed when the view is used for data-binding or enumeration.

> **Note**   Consider providing for data filtering and sorting without return trips to the database for throughput. Be aware, however, that storing data in Session has an impact on the amount of memory used on the server. Also, using ViewState to enable the data to make a round trip has an impact on the size of the page and the post data that will be submitted in subsequent requests.

In Code Listing 3-15, we return to the data example of displaying states and their time zones. A DropDownList has been added with a corresponding handler that updates the *RowFilter* of the *DataView*. Notice that when the *Row-Filter* is set to the empty string, no filtering is performed.

Code Listing 3-15   DataGridFilter.aspx

```
<%@Import namespace="System.Data" %>
<script language="C#" runat="server">
DataTable data;
DataView view;
protected void Page_Load(object o, EventArgs e) {
    GetData();
    datagrid1.DataSource = view;
    if(!IsPostBack) {
        datagrid1.DataBind();
    }
}

void GetData() {
    view = Session["view"] as DataView;
    if(view != null) {
        return;
    }
    data = new DataTable();
    data.Columns.Add(new DataColumn("TheID", typeof(Int32)));
    data.Columns.Add(new DataColumn("Name", typeof(string)));
    data.Columns.Add(new DataColumn("TimeZone", typeof(string)));

    DataRow dr;
    dr = data.NewRow();
    dr[0] = 1; dr[1] = "Washington"; dr[2] = "Pacific";
    data.Rows.Add(dr);
    dr = data.NewRow();
    dr[0] = 2; dr[1] = "Utah"; dr[2] = "Mountain";
    data.Rows.Add(dr);
    dr = data.NewRow();
    dr[0] = 3; dr[1] = "Wisconsin"; dr[2] = "Central";
    data.Rows.Add(dr);
    dr = data.NewRow();
    dr[0] = 4; dr[1] = "New York"; dr[2] = "Eastern";
    data.Rows.Add(dr);
    dr = data.NewRow();
    dr[0] = 5; dr[1] = "Florida"; dr[2] = "Eastern";
    data.Rows.Add(dr);

    Session["data"] = data;
```

```
    view = new DataView(data);
    return;
}

void FilterData(object o, EventArgs e) {
    string selectedZone = TimeZoneFilter.SelectedItem.Value;
    if(selectedZone == "Pacific") {
        view.RowFilter = "TimeZone = 'Pacific'";
    }
    else if(selectedZone == "Mountain") {
        view.RowFilter = "TimeZone = 'Mountain'";
    }
    else if (selectedZone == "Central" ) {
        view.RowFilter = "TimeZone = 'Central'";
    }
    else if (selectedZone == "Eastern") {
        view.RowFilter = "Timezone = 'Eastern'";
    }
    datagrid1.DataBind();
}

</script>

<form runat="server">
    <asp:DataGrid runat="server"  id="datagrid1"
        AutoGenerateColumns="false">
        <Columns>
            <asp:ButtonColumn CommandName="Select" Text="Select" />
            <asp:BoundColumn DataField="TheID" ReadOnly="true"
                HeaderText="id" />
            <asp:BoundColumn DataField="Name" HeaderText="year" />
            <asp:BoundColumn DataField="TimeZone"
                HeaderText="make" />

        </Columns>
    </asp:DataGrid><br/>
    <b>Filter by time zone:</b>
    <asp:DropDownList runat="server"
        OnSelectedIndexChanged="FilterData"
        AutoPostBack="true" id="TimeZoneFilter">
        <asp:ListItem>None</asp:ListItem>
        <asp:ListItem>Pacific</asp:ListItem>
        <asp:ListItem>Mountain</asp:ListItem>
        <asp:ListItem>Central</asp:ListItem>
        <asp:ListItem>Eastern</asp:ListItem>
    </asp:DropDownList>
</form>
```

Advanced DataGrid

In the previous sections, we examined how to accomplish some common tasks using the DataGrid's built-in support. In this section, we'll look at some tasks that are a little more esoteric and require a bit more code, taking advantage of the DataGrid control's flexibility.

Adding Data

As you've seen, the DataGrid has built-in support for updating data, offers a simple way to work with selected data, and makes deleting data easy. But when you deal with dynamic Web applications, you need to allow the user to add new data. To accomplish this, you add a Button control outside of the DataGrid, and in the associated *Click* event handler you add a new row to the data source of the DataGrid. At the same time, you set the *EditItemIndex* to the new item and call *DataBind*. The user is presented with the familiar DataGrid editing interface to add values for the new row. Notice in Code Listing 3-16 that we modified Code Listing 3-13 to include the ability to add a new row. The *CancelCommand* event handler has been modified to remove a row from the *DataSet* that has not been updated. When the user clicks the Add button, the *CancelCommand* event handler is invoked explicitly. This prevents you from adding a new empty row when the previous row is not completed. Actually, the incomplete row is removed and then a new row with the same defaults is added again, but to the user the result is the same—the incomplete data is not persisted.

Code Listing 3-16   DataGridAdd.aspx

```
<%@Import namespace="System.Data" %>
<script language="C#" runat="server">
DataTable data;
protected void Page_Load(object o, EventArgs e) {
    GetData();
    datagrid1.DataSource = data;
    if(!IsPostBack) {
        datagrid1.DataBind();
    }
}

DataTable GetData() {
    data = Session["data"] as DataTable;
    if(data != null) {
        return data;
    }
```

```
    data = new DataTable();

    DataColumn primaryColumn
        = new DataColumn("carid", typeof(Int32));
    data.Columns.Add(primaryColumn);
    data.Columns.Add(new DataColumn("year", typeof(Int32)));
    data.Columns.Add(new DataColumn("make", typeof(string)));
    data.Columns.Add(new DataColumn("model", typeof(string)));
    DataRow dr;
    dr = data.NewRow();
    dr[0] = 1; dr[1] = 1998; dr[2] = "Isuzu"; dr[3] = "Trooper";
    data.Rows.Add(dr);
    dr = data.NewRow();
    dr[0] = 2; dr[1] = 2000; dr[2] = "Honda"; dr[3] = "Civic";
    data.Rows.Add(dr);

    DataColumn[] primaryColumns = new DataColumn[1];
    primaryColumns[0] = primaryColumn;
    data.PrimaryKey = primaryColumns;

    Session["data"] = data;
    return data;
}

protected void StartAdd(object o, EventArgs e) {
    OnCancel(null, null);
    DataRow dr = data.NewRow();
    dr["carid"] = data.Rows.Count + 1;
    dr["year"] = 2000;
    dr["make"] = "";
    dr["model"] = "";
    data.Rows.InsertAt(dr, 0);
    datagrid1.EditItemIndex = data.Rows.Count - 1;
    datagrid1.DataBind();
}

protected void OnEdit(object o, DataGridCommandEventArgs e) {
    datagrid1.EditItemIndex = e.Item.ItemIndex;
    datagrid1.DataBind();
}

protected void OnCancel(object o, DataGridCommandEventArgs e) {
    DataRow dr = data.Rows.Find(data.Rows.Count);
    if((int)dr["year"] < 1930 || (int)dr["year"] > 2004
        || dr["make"] == "" || dr["model"] == "") {
        Response.Write("removing row");
        data.Rows.Remove(dr);
    }
```

```
        datagrid1.EditItemIndex = -1;
        datagrid1.DataBind();
}


protected void OnUpdate(object o, DataGridCommandEventArgs e) {
    int year;
    try {
        year = Int32.Parse((
            (TextBox)e.Item.Cells[2].Controls[0]).Text);
    }
    catch(System.FormatException fe) {
        Response.Write(
            "Invalid year specified. Update not completed");
        return;
    }
    string make = ((TextBox)e.Item.Cells[3].Controls[0]).Text;
    string model = ((TextBox)e.Item.Cells[4].Controls[0]).Text;
    DataRow row = data.Rows.Find(e.Item.Cells[1].Text);
    if(row != null) {
        row["year"] = year.ToString();
        row["make"] = make;
        row["model"] = model;

    }
    data.AcceptChanges();
    datagrid1.EditItemIndex = -1;
    datagrid1.DataBind();
    Session["data"] = data;
}
</script>
<form runat="server">
    <asp:DataGrid runat="server" DataKeyField="carid" id="datagrid1"
        AutoGenerateColumns="false" OnEditCommand="OnEdit"
        OnCancelCommand="OnCancel" OnUpdateCommand="OnUpdate" >
        <Columns>
            <asp:EditCommandColumn EditText="Edit"
                CancelText="Cancel" UpdateText="Update" />
            <asp:boundcolumn DataField="carid" ReadOnly="true"
                HeaderText="id" />
            <asp:BoundColumn DataField="year" HeaderText="year" />
            <asp:BoundColumn DataField="make" HeaderText="make" />
            <asp:BoundColumn DataField="model" HeaderText="model" />
        </Columns>
    </asp:DataGrid><br/>
    <asp:button runat="server" type="submit"
        OnClick="StartAdd" Text="Add"/>
</form>
```

Summarizing Data

In the previous code examples, we included header text for the columns in the column declarations. The DataGrid also supports the inclusion of a footer row, and this is enabled by setting the *ShowFooter* property to *true*. The DataGrid creates the space for the footer information automatically, but it does not fill the data in. The summary information can be calculated on the fly as each item is added and then set explicitly when the footer item is added. The footer item is added after all the items and alternating items. Code Listing 3-17 illustrates how to summarize data by adding an *ItemCreated* event handler and then accumulate the value from the items as they are added. Notice that when the *FooterItem* is added, the contents of the *TableCell* are set explicitly with the markup and the total.

Code Listing 3-17 DataGridSummary.aspx

```csharp
<%@Import namespace="System.Data" %>
<script language="C#" runat="server">
protected void Page_Load(object o, EventArgs e) {
    if(!IsPostBack) {
        datagrid.DataSource = GetData();
        DataBind();
    }
}

DataView GetData() {
    DataTable data = new DataTable();
    data.Columns.Add(new DataColumn("aNumber", typeof(Int32)));
    DataRow dr;
    dr = data.NewRow(); dr[0] = "70"; data.Rows.Add(dr);
    dr = data.NewRow(); dr[0] = "58"; data.Rows.Add(dr);
    dr = data.NewRow(); dr[0] = "62"; data.Rows.Add(dr);
    dr = data.NewRow(); dr[0] = "54"; data.Rows.Add(dr);
    dr = data.NewRow(); dr[0] = "57"; data.Rows.Add(dr);
    dr = data.NewRow(); dr[0] = "50"; data.Rows.Add(dr);
    dr = data.NewRow(); dr[0] = "52"; data.Rows.Add(dr);
    dr = data.NewRow(); dr[0] = "49"; data.Rows.Add(dr);
    dr = data.NewRow(); dr[0] = "46"; data.Rows.Add(dr);
    DataView view = new DataView(data);
    return view;
}

int total;
void DataGrid_ItemCreated(object o, DataGridItemEventArgs e) {
    if((e.Item.ItemType == ListItemType.Item) ||
        (e.Item.ItemType == ListItemType.AlternatingItem)) {
```

```
            total += (int)(DataBinder.Eval(e.Item.DataItem, "aNumber"));
            return;
        }
        if(e.Item.ItemType == ListItemType.Footer) {
            e.Item.Cells[0].Text = "<b><i>" + total + "</i></b>";
        }
    }
</script>
<form runat="server">
    <asp:DataGrid runat="server" id="datagrid"
        AutoGenerateColumns="false"
        OnItemCreated="DataGrid_ItemCreated" ShowFooter="true">
        <Columns>
            <asp:BoundColumn DataField="aNumber"
                HeaderText="Number"/>
        </Columns>
    </asp:DataGrid>
</form>
```

> **Tip**   Reflecting on the individual items has an impact on performance. For large sets of data with numerous columns to summarize, leveraging the database directly for calculated values might be more efficient.

Summary

In this chapter, we examined some ways to work with data in ASP.NET. We compared the Repeater, DataList, and DataGrid controls, and because the Data-Grid in particular offers powerful support for templating, controlling styles, and editing, we walked through some of the more useful ways to take advantage of it. We also examined what is necessary for adding and deleting rows from the underlying data and how to filter and sort data. Finally, we looked at summarizing data dynamically.

Many Web sites are primarily driven by the need to access and modify back-end data. It pays to become proficient at enabling the user to manipulate data effectively, but be sure you understand the performance implications associated with working with large sets of data.

4

Developing for Mobile Browsers

A growing number of handheld and mobile devices come with built-in browsers. The disparity between the features of these browsers is far greater than it is among more full-featured desktop PC browsers. The most fundamental difference is that the various mobile browsers demand different kinds of markup. An HTML page that renders fine on a desktop browser won't work at all on many mobile browsers, and the markup language used by one mobile browser might not work on another. In this chapter, we'll look at writing Web applications for mobile browsers using Microsoft ASP.NET Mobile Controls and the *MobilePage* class. You'll also examine how to leverage ASP.NET so that you can minimize what you need to learn about mobile browsers and deploy a mobile-enabled application successfully.

> **Tip** You might encounter references to the Microsoft Mobile Internet Toolkit on the Web, in magazine articles, and in newsgroups. When version 1.0 of ASP.NET was released, mobile support was not included. Instead, support was available as part of a separate download called the Microsoft Mobile Internet Toolkit. This mobile support is now included as part of ASP.NET.

Introducing Mobile Pages and Mobile Controls

Traditional Web development has us thinking in terms of the HTML tags we need to use. You probably have ideas about how your desired user interface (UI) can be realized using specific HTML markup, but in the world of mobile devices, this mindset won't get you very far. Some browsers support the Wireless Markup Language (WML), which is part of the Wireless Application Protocol, also referred to as WAP. Other browsers support a subset of HTML specifically designed for mobile devices, called Compact HTML (cHTML). Compact HTML is particularly popular where wireless bandwidth infrastructure supports faster access to more data, such as in Japan. Some more sophisticated handheld devices have browsers that support HTML 3.2 but do not include client-side script support, whereas others have script support as well as some features of HTML 4.

The server controls architecture in ASP.NET moves us away from thinking directly in terms of HTML. It lets us more easily focus on the application logic and high-level user interface (UI) design because the controls render the HTML we need. ASP.NET mobile controls move the emphasis even further from being markup-specific, and guide the developer to think in terms of application functionality. The controls in the *System.Web.UI.MobileControls* namespace extend the *system.Web.UI.MoblieControls.MobileControl* class and add a new construct for rendering the different markup required by handheld devices and embedded browsers. Figure 4-1 shows how *MobileControls* and *MobilePage* extend the base *Page* and *Control* classes.

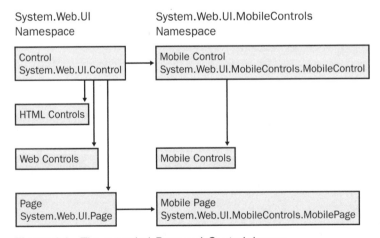

Figure 4-1   The extended *Page* and *Control* classes

The mobile controls do not actually handle the rendering of markup. Each *MobileControl* class has an associated set of *adapters* that renders the different kinds of markup. (The section titled "Selecting Page and Control Adapters," later in this chapter, gives more detail about how an adapter is associated with a control during the page life cycle.) The control is responsible for the primary functionality, whereas the adapters manage the markup. The mobile control delegates the rendering as well as other page framework events to the adapter so that the adapter can effectively manage any unique requirements of the requesting device. This adaptive quality of *MobilePage* means that you can support a variety of browsers without necessarily learning the associated markup language. For example, to get calendar functionality in your application, you can place a *Calendar MobileControl* on a *MobilePage*. The mobile page gets the correct adapter for the requesting device. WML, cHTML, and HTML calendar adapters perform the rendering when the page is executed. Each calendar adapter produces markup targeting a specific language. Figure 4-2 shows how the adapters fit into the page life cycle.

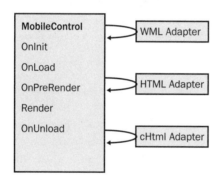

Figure 4-2   The role of the adapter in the life of a mobile page

Other approaches to the problem of multiple markup languages have had limited success, in part because applications are still written with HTML. One such approach is to simply translate the HTML into the markup supported by the requesting device, but this presents the problem of what to do when the translation isn't straightforward. A way to deal with this complication is to discard pieces of the original content—a solution that's far from ideal.

ASP.NET mobile controls don't attempt to translate one type of markup into another. Instead, the controls are themselves an abstraction for the functionality. You program against those controls and their object model, and the adapters emit the markup necessary for the requesting device.

Selecting Page and Control Adapters

We said earlier that each control has an associated set of adapters responsible for rendering different kinds of markup. Let's look a little more closely at what this means.

When a *MobilePage* executes, it examines the headers in the HTTP request to determine the capabilities of the requesting browser. In the *browserCaps* section of the configuration file, a set of regular expressions is applied to headers, starting with the *User-Agent* string. When a matching expression is found, the default browser capabilities are overridden by the values specified by that match. Often a matching regular expression will cause a set of nested regular expressions to execute to further define specific browser capabilities, which allows you to detect and handle variations between device models and browser versions. When the regular expression does not match, the associated capability settings and nested matches will not be applied for that browser type.

After this preliminary information about the browser is gathered, the page can select an adapter to handle page framework behavior specific to the page being executed. Perhaps it's more accurate to express this in reverse by saying that a page adapter selects itself. The page adapters expose a method configured as the *DeviceQualifies* predicate in machine.config or web.config files. The *DeviceQualifies* code is tasked with ascertaining whether it can render for the capabilities of the requesting device. The *DeviceQualifies* methods are executed in the order they appear in the configuration until one returns *true*, essentially selecting itself to manage the current request. The page adapter is responsible for managing view state, postback data, and postback handlers; for providing the appropriate *TextWriter* for handling page output; and for selecting adapters for the controls contained in the page. The page adapter participates in the page life cycle events and delegates to the adapters as well.

In the machine.config file, you'll notice that adapters are grouped into adapter families, with a page adapter as the parent that contains a set of compatible control adapters. These control adapters are used to render the output and process events for the associated control.

The concept of the control tree is essentially duplicated in the adapter hierarchy. The page control contains a set of child controls, and each mobile control has an associated adapter. The adapters can create child controls to produce the user interface appropriate for the functionality of the associated server control on a specific device. Page events such as *OnInit*, *OnLoad*, *OnPreRender*, and *OnUnload* can be handled by the adapter or left for the control to manage.

Designing for Mobile Browsers

At first, developers are inclined to create a single site for both desktop and mobile browsers. And by a "single site," we don't just mean that the pages are all deployed in a single Web application root of Microsoft Internet Information Services (IIS). Developers want to have their site functionality simply ported to mobile browsers. However, many pieces of functionality don't translate well to the mobile Web environment. For example, data entry can be tedious for the user, especially for longer forms. The first step in developing your site for mobile devices is to determine what subset of the application functionality should be exposed to the user. The most successful mobile pages are those that provide information with minimum user input.

> **Tip** Mobile pages should limit the amount of input required by the user. Strive for maximum relevant information with the fewest key clicks. Entering data can be tedious on a small form factor, and networks for mobile devices are still relatively slow compared to wired devices, so performing postbacks and following links can be somewhat time consuming.

On their desktop browsers, users are accustomed to accessing rich cascading menus and having dynamic interactions with a large quantity of available selections. Mobile device users, however, are often connected to the Internet through relatively slow wireless connections on machines without powerful processors. Every postback and action requiring a round trip to the server can be painfully slow, so navigation should be simple and allow the user to get to the end page easily—not more than three clicks from the home page is a good rule of thumb. This mobile UI strategy is likely to be a significant shift from the desktop UI you currently present in your applications.

Many developers neglect the problems posed by slower connections when designing their pages. You should create pages that reduce the number of round trips to the server, but you don't have to limit page content to the size of the screen. Most devices provide vertical scrolling keys to make page reading easier for the user.

Also be aware that many mobile browsers have strict limits on the amount of content that can be returned in a page, so you need to be reasonable when addressing a single page request and judicious about the amount of content to be displayed. If you exceed that content limit, the user will get an error message. Too little content frustrates the user with too many waiting periods, and too much content turns the page into a browser error.

Taking Advantage of Emulators

When developing an application, you need to act like the user so that you can see what he sees. That means you must test the application for errors and verify functionality on the devices the user is likely to employ. In the past, you might have had to test a couple of types of desktop browsers, and possibly even several versions of those browsers. When you develop an application that targets mobile browsers, however, this testing becomes a significantly bigger challenge. There are numerous form factors to consider, with various methods of connectivity, and browsers are often "burned" into the firmware of the devices. An additional complication is the considerable cost of buying so many devices and the associated connectivity service plans. Fortunately, many browser producers and device manufacturers provide software *emulators* that make the process of testing a Web application more manageable.

Before scouring the Web for every emulator you can find, you should first narrow the scope of your search by defining your target devices, if you can. In many scenarios you can eliminate classes of devices and thus avoid customizing your application and testing for those devices. For example, consider a mobile application that is built to enable a group of employees better remote access to corporate information. A company might have employees use the PocketPC running Pocket IE, or it might have everyone use a specific type of Personal Digital Assistant (PDA). In a case like this, you wouldn't need to be concerned about tailoring your application for the cell-phone user. Alternatively, a company might standardize on SIM cards for authentication and predominantly use cell-phone-based browsers. Of course, if your application is targeting the general public, you miss out on the opportunity to focus your efforts so narrowly.

> **Tip**   Use a desktop browser as a debugging aid when developing applications for mobile browsers because debug and tracing information is not included in the output from the *MobilePage*.

Start with a Browser

Before you focus your efforts on testing with mobile device emulators, use a desktop browser. The desktop browsers are generally more stable than some of the new emulators. They also will be recognized and the HTML adapters will render appropriate markup. You can then move on to testing and refining the application using emulators with the assurance that the core functionality is in place and behaving as expected.

Using a desktop browser also provides for easy application debugging. Tracing functionality is not available for mobile pages when rendered to small form factors. Although debug information from error messages will be displayed in the output adapted for mobile devices, it will be truncated based on the characteristics of the device. There is no reason to forego the more feature-rich desktop browsers when developing a mobile-enabled application. However, user interface decisions that seem fine when viewed on the relatively large desktop monitor might seem less appropriate when scaling to the smaller real estate of the mobile device.

When using emulators to develop a mobile application, you'll want to get broad coverage for the adapters that you have available. If you've installed adapters customized for a particular browser, consider how your development can exercise those adapters as well. Generally, with the adapters that shipped with the Microsoft .NET Framework and the device updates that have been released as of the writing of this book, you'll want to be concerned with HTML, cHTML, XHTML, and WML. The cHTML family of adapters inherits from the HTML device group, so it might be sufficient to work with the Pocket PC emulator included as part of the PocketPC 2002 Software Development Kit. You can download the Pocket PC emulator from Microsoft at *http://msdn.microsoft.com/downloads*. The cHTML renderings do not take advantage of client-side script support, so you might want to turn off script support in the settings for the browser. Another way to achieve scriptless renderings during development is to override the capability by including a global match in the web.config file for the application. The web.config file in Code Listing 4-1 will cause your desktop browser to be treated as a scriptless device and receive cHTML from a mobile page.

Code Listing 4-1   Scriptless Browser Configuration Web.config

```
<configuration>
    <system.web>
        <browserCaps>
            javascript="false"
        <browserCaps/>
    </system.web>
</configuration>
```

The most recent emulators from Openwave, Ericsson, and Nokia all include support for WML and XHTML renderings. You might find that the messages from the different emulators reporting page errors are somewhat cryptic. In fact, the error reporting abilities vary significantly among the emulators. You might find it faster to start working directly with the XHTML or WML that is causing the problem. A quick search of the Web turns up a number of XHTML and WML validators in which you can paste the page output and get relatively detailed error reporting. Often, the source of the problem is the markup you've included directly. Since XHTML and WML both require strict XML compliance, you can easily overlook something that renders fine in the HTML browsers, which are traditionally more forgiving when you deviate from the standard. In addition to requiring well-formed markup, WML and XHTML browsers enforce schema validation. The tags used, and even their order or placement and nesting, must comply with the schema supported by the browser. Another approach that can help is to save to a file the page output from the emulator in which you are seeing an error. Then you can load the markup directly from the file into the different emulators and frequently isolate a problem more easily.

Using Cookieless Sessions

When you create a mobile Web project in Microsoft Visual Studio .NET, a web.config file is created as part of the project. In this configuration file, several default settings are established for the application. One of these enables cookieless sessions. (Another configuration setting defines a set of device filters, which we'll talk about more in the "Using Device Specific Filters" section later in this chapter.)

Cookies are passed between client and server as part of the request headers. Some mobile devices don't have the logic for managing cookies, and others allow the user to turn cookie use off. Normally, server sessions will not work correctly without cookies and desktop developers can treat session support as optional. In fact, to reduce use of server resources, some applications will explicitly disable server session state. Server sessions are particularly important in mobile pages because mobile pages use session state to assist in managing the view state. On regular desktop pages, the view state is passed between the client and server on each request, allowing for state to be simulated in an otherwise stateless protocol. Mobile pages minimize the amount of data that must be passed on each request and use up part of the limited browser memory by storing some view state in session. Without cookies, a new session is created on each request because the session identifier is not sent, and view state will not work correctly. In cookieless sessions, the session identifier is carried as part of the URL so that a server session exists for the user without the use of client-side cookies. When a request is first received without a session identifier as part of the request path /samplePath/somePage.aspx, the browser is redirected to the same page with a modified URL carrying a session identifier. /(sessionIdentifier)/samplePath/somePage.aspx. For the duration of the session, the session identifier is implied by relative requests, or added to fully qualified paths to keep the user connected to the current session.

To turn on cookieless sessions, include a *cookieless="true"* direction in the *sessionState* section of your web.config file. The web.config file in Listing 4-2 is simplified to include that direction.

Code Listing 4-2 Cookieless Web.config

```
<configuration>
    <system.web>
        <sessionState cookieless="true" />
    </system.web>
</configuration>
```

Tip Use cookieless sessions to ensure that your application works correctly on devices that do not support cookies.

Some browsers without built-in support for cookies still appear to work correctly when receiving and returning cookies. Prior to WAP 2, WAP browsers could not initiate HTTP requests directly to the Web server. Instead, they connected to a WAP Gateway, which acted as a proxy for them. The *gateway* translates the WAP request from the browser into an HTTP request. Figure 4-3 shows this process.

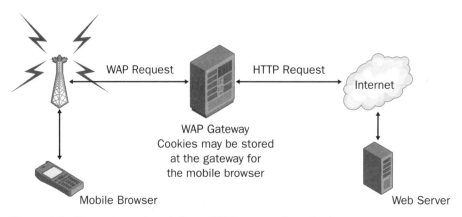

Figure 4-3   The gateway translating a WAP request from the browser

Some gateways offer additional functionality by tracking the cookies on behalf of the device. The browser never actually sees the cookie, but to the server, the browser appears to support cookies. Because this is a function of the gateway and not the browser, don't be surprised when you examine the browser capabilities and find that support for cookies is set to false, even though the tracking appears to work some of the time. Don't assume you know the capabilities of the general device and ignore the possible impact of the gateway.

Directing Users to Mobile Content

One issue that comes up often is how to get users to the mobile pages once they exist. A couple of "gotchas" can complicate this apparently simple task: users having to choose between the mobile and desktop versions of content, and users being shown the wrong content for their browser type.

Theoretically, we should just be able to look at the type of browser issuing the request and redirect the user to the correct page. However, this immediately causes a problem for many users if the page they are directed to has a redirect as well. Many mobile browsers view several back-to-back redirect status codes as an error condition. Presumably they do this to avoid infinite loops, but the error also occurs in valid scenarios. If you're using cookieless sessions, a redirect will get the session identifier in the URL. If you're using forms authentication, the user will encounter a redirect to the login page when first accessing a protected page. If you put a couple of these scenarios together, the user will get an error message from her mobile browser when trying to access the site.

Fortunately, one approach handles this redirect problem with relatively little effort on your part: designate a mobile page as the default page. You can then use *Response.Redirect* to get desktop browsers to a non-mobile page. Alternatively, you can use *Server.Transfer* to get the appropriate page for the non-mobile device. The *MobileCapabilities* object has a property with the intuitive name *IsMobileDevice* that makes it easy to tell when a request is coming from a browser recognized as suitable for adapted content. The *Page_Load* method shown in the following code snippet demonstrates how a user of a non-mobile device is directed to the content designed for her particular device.

```
<script runat="server" language="C#">
protected void Page_Load(object o, EventArgs e) {
    MobileCapabilities capabilities =
        (MobileCapabilities)Request.Browser;
    if(capabilities.IsMobileDevice == true) {
        Server.Transfer("mobileDefault.aspx");
    }
}
</script>
```

Using the *MobileCapabilities* Object

In the preceding code, notice that the *HttpBrowserCapabilities* object returned by the *Browser* property of the *Request* object is cast as a *MobileCapabilities* object. In version 1.1 of the .NET Framework, the object type associated with browser capabilities returned by the *Request.Browser* property is actually a *MobileCapabilities* object. The *MobileCapabilities* object inherits from the *HttpBrowserCapabilities* class and extends the class with support for properties that apply primarily to mobile browsers. You can see this in the *browserCaps* section of the machine.config file (shown in the following code), in which the result type specified is of type *System.Web.Mobile.MobileCapabilities*.

```
<browserCaps>
    <result type="System.Web.Mobile.MobileCapabilities,
        System.Web.Mobile, Version=1.0.5000.0, Culture=neutral,
        PublicKeyToken=b03f5f7f11d50a3a" />
</browserCaps>
```

Working with Device Updates

ASP.NET device updates provide support for additional browsers. The new support can come as new configuration data or in the form of new mobile control adapters. New configuration data consists of browser capabilities that accurately describe the browser features and map the browser to the correct adapters. The browser capabilities are also utilized by the adapters to accommodate any idiosyncrasies and to produce the best markup possible for the device. New adapters also rely on configuration data, and when the existing adapters can't render markup for the new browser, a new adapter that renders the required markup must be developed.

The *browserCaps* configuration section is often customized when adding support for a new browser, as we'll discuss in the next section. Device updates add new *browserCaps* information by adding a new file containing additional browser data. Any modifications you make directly to machine.config are left intact. The new file is referenced in the *browserCaps* section with a *file* element.

```
<browserCaps>
    <result type="System.Web.Mobile.MobileCapabilities" />
    <file src="deviceUpdate1.config" />
</browserCaps>
```

The machine.config *browserCaps* section is matched first, followed in turn by each file referenced with a *file* element. So, an expression match in a *browserCaps file* reference can override the capability setting of a match for one of the regular expressions found in machine.config. For example, support for XHTML was added in ASP.NET Device Update 2. A browser that supports both WML and XHTML might be configured in the machine.config file to use WML, but the deviceUpdate1.config file can override the preferred rendering type to XHTML-MP (a mobile profile version of XTHML) so that it can use the XHTML rendering.

Tip Device updates installed on ASP.NET 1 using the Mobile Internet Toolkit replace the *browserCaps* section in machine.config with new content. Customizations for the *browserCaps* section will be lost when installing Device Updates 1.

Adding Support for a New Browser

You can add support for a new browser in two primary ways. The first approach is to modify the configuration so that the browser is recognized with the correct capabilities and the adapters can render the proper markup, and it is successful when the markup produced by the existing adapters works with the new browser. If the browser requires markup changes that can't be configured, you need to write custom adapters and then modify the configuration so that it can utilize them. In the section "Writing a Custom Adapter," which appears later in this chapter, we'll go through the steps for writing and configuring new adapters.

The *browserCaps* section is made up of sets of *use* and *filter* elements. The *use* element indicates which request header to use in the *filter* elements that follow it. The *filter* element contains one or more *case* elements that match elements from the header being used and set the browser capabilities. For example, in the *browserCaps* section in the following code, the first *use* element specifies that we are using the *User-Agent* header. It is followed by a long list of defaults. These defaults are then overridden to more specialized values by the various matching *case* elements.

```
<browserCaps>
    <result type="System.Web.Mobile.MobileCapabilities" />
    <use var="HTTP_USER_AGENT" />
        activexcontrols=false

        …

        platform="Unknown"
        preferredRenderingType="html32"

        …

        isMobileDevice="false"
    <filter>
        <case match="Windows 95|Win95">
            platform=Win95
        </case>
        <case match="Windows 98|Win98">
            platform=Win98
        </case>
        <case match="Windows NT 5.1|Windows XP">
            platform=WinXP
        </case>
        <case match="Windows NT 5.0|Windows 2000">
            platform=Win2000
        </case>
    </filter>
</browserCaps>
```

Notice in this snippet from machine.config that after the *use* element indicates that the *User-Agent* is being examined, the default capabilities invoked are for a fairly generic HTML device that specifies the most common set of capabilities. This configuration should achieve the broadest coverage for browsers that aren't recognized specifically in the code.

Tip When a browser isn't recognized in the *browserCaps* configuration section, the default behavior is to treat it as an HTML 3.2 device without support for client-side scripting.

The *case* elements within a *filter* element act like a switch-case construct. Once a match is found, evaluating the rest of the *case* elements within that filter is unnecessary. For example, if the platform is found to be Microsoft Windows 95, the default unknown platform is overridden, and the remaining platform checks are skipped.

Let's walk through what it takes to add device information by creating configuration for an imaginary sample device. We'll do it the same way we would to add support for a real browser. This device is from a company just entering the mobile browser market. We'll call the company NewPlayer. Their new browser is the WmlColor2000. First we need to create a filter entry to match the *User-Agent* string of the device. If the device were a new model from a manufacturer recognized by the configuration, we would nest the specialization within an existing match. In our example, we create a new top-level filter element to match the *User-Agent* string: *"NewPlayer Color 2000."* We then specify the preferred rendering type and set the MIME type to be WML. These two capabilities are used in selecting the adapter and in returning the correct header values in the HTTP response.

```
<filter>
    <case match="NewPlayer Color 2000.*">
        browser="NewPlayer WmlColor2000"
        preferredRenderingType="wml11"
        preferredRenderingMime="text/vnd.wap.wml"
    </case>
</filter>
```

Ascertaining which properties will be set for a particular browser by the other filter elements can be difficult. Two simple pages can help to illustrate. The first (shown in Listing 4-3) displays just the HTTP headers sent by the device. This page gives you an idea of which headers you have available to identify the device and to set the characteristics correctly in the configuration.

Now that you have the headers available for the device, you can iterate through the capabilities being set for the browser. When you first configure a device, some of these settings will be incorrect, but by having the capability list, you can more easily identify the properties that will need to be set explicitly. This list also comes in handy when you need to find the filters that are incorrectly matching headers and setting properties for the browser. In the case of incorrect matching, you can add a specialization to the existing filter to correct the setting. Listing 4-4 writes out all the configured capabilities of the *MobileCapabilities* object for the requesting device.

Code Listing 4-3   DisplayingHeaders.aspx

```
<%@ Page Inherits="System.Web.UI.MobileControls.MobilePage" %>
<script runat="server" language="c#">
protected void Page_Load(Object sender, EventArgs e) {
    NameValueCollection nvc = Request.Headers;
    string[] keys = nvc.AllKeys;
    for(int i = 0; i < keys.Length; i++) {
        string[] values = nvc.GetValues(keys[i]);
        System.Web.UI.MobileControls.Label lbl = new
            System.Web.UI.MobileControls.Label();
        lbl.Text = keys[i] + ":" ;
            for(int j = 0; j < values.Length; j++) {
                lbl.Text += " " + values[j];
            }
        form1.Controls.Add(lbl);
    }
}
</script>
<mobile:Form id="form1" runat="server" Paginate="true" >
</mobile:Form>
```

Code Listing 4-4   ShowCapabilities.aspx

```
<%@ Page Inherits="System.Web.UI.MobileControls.MobilePage"
    Language="cs" %>
<%@ Import Namespace="System.Reflection" %>
<%@ Import Namespace="System.Web.Mobile" %>
<script runat="server" language="c#">
protected void Page_Load(Object sender, EventArgs e) {
    MobileCapabilities capabilities =
        (MobileCapabilities)Request.Browser;
    Type t = typeof(MobileCapabilities);
    PropertyInfo[] propertyInfos = t.GetProperties();
    foreach(PropertyInfo pi in propertyInfos) {
        System.Web.UI.MobileControls.Label lbl = new
            System.Web.UI.MobileControls.Label();
        lbl.Text = pi.Name + " = " + capabilities[pi.Name];
        form1.Controls.Add(lbl);
    }
}
</script>
<mobile:Form id="form1" runat="server" Paginate="true" >
</mobile:Form>
```

Understanding the large quantity of *filter* and *case* elements within the *browserCaps* section is a somewhat daunting task at first, but as you configure more and more devices, you quickly become acquainted with the *browserCaps* section's capabilities. The various groups of *filter* elements isolate particular settings such as those for the platform, or handle multiple device models from a single manufacturer. You will become proficient at manipulating browser configurations as you become more familiar with individual browser capabilities.

Writing a Custom Adapter

One significant difference in behavior between the mobile controls and the Web controls is their treatment of custom attributes. By default, custom attributes are not allowed on mobile controls. In this section, we'll talk about the reasons behind this limitation and its impact on your work. We'll also walk through the writing and configuration of your own custom adapter.

If you specify an attribute on the server control that isn't recognized by the control, a *System.Exception* is thrown during the *Load* event, stating "Cannot set custom attributes on mobile controls in this page." Web controls, however, do allow custom attributes, and do not throw an exception when loaded. Custom attributes are simply passed through to the browser as an attribute of the primary HTML tag rendered for a control. It is important to recognize the difference when using custom attributes with Web controls because you're probably used to setting extra *style* attributes, or you might be using the *FOR* attribute to leverage client-side script. With the mobile controls, this will not work without extra effort on your part because unrecognized attributes are prohibited by default.

Because the validated WML and XHTML markup used by mobile browsers mandates strict compliance to their schemas, simply passing through unknown attributes is not safe. And given the differences between client-side scripting and supported attributes, there isn't a reasonable way to translate many tags. The primary HTML tag rendered for a particular Web control typically doesn't vary based on the browser issuing the request; HTML processors in browsers simply ignore the attributes they do not know. However, with adapted output, the tag used to represent a server element can vary from markup language to markup language.

For example, consider *accessKey* attributes, which are customized shortcut keys for selecting links. Users can find them particularly useful for making selections because they don't need a mouse. Listing 4-5 shows how to use the *accessKey* in your code. It is a simple page with links to *http://www.microsoft.com /mspress* and *http://www.asp.net*. The *accessKey* attribute is specified so that when the user selects the specified shortcut key, the link is accessed. However, notice that when you try requesting the page, the *accessKey* attribute causes a run-time error.

Code Listing 4-5   accessKey.aspx

```
<%@ Page Inherits="System.Web.UI.MobileControls.MobilePage" %>
<mobile:form runat="server">
    <mobile:link runat="server"
        NavigateUrl="http://www.microsoft.com/mspress"
        AccessKey="m"
        Text="(m) MSpress" />
<mobile:link runat="server"
        NavigateUrl="http://www.asp.net"
        AccessKey="p"
        Text="(p) ASP.NET" />
</mobile:form>
```

Using Custom Attributes

To take advantage of custom attributes, you must modify the configuration so that errors aren't thrown when you use the attributes with mobile Controls. In addition, you must make use of the new server control attributes in custom adapter code, because without them, the default adapters will simply ignore the unknown attribute.

Listing 4-6 is a web.config file that overrides the machine.config default and prevents the run-time errors that usually occur when unrecognized attributes are encountered. When you set *allowCustomAttributes* to *true* on the *mobileControls* element, you no longer encounter the errors.

Code Listing 4-6   Allowing Custom Attributes Web.config

```
<configuration>
    <system.web>
        <mobileControls
            allowCustomAttributes="true" />
    </system.web>
</configuration>
```

> **Tip**   The *AllowCustomAttributes* configuration setting does not cause custom attributes to be passed through to the client. It only allows them to be specified in the server page without causing an error on the server. This setting applies only to the mobile controls where unrecognized attributes on the server controls are treated as an error by default.

Request *AccessKey.aspx* (shown in Listing 4-5) again and notice that including custom attributes no longer creates an error condition. However, pressing ALT+M or ALT+P doesn't move the focus as expected. To get the desired effect, you can create an adapter that will use the *accessKey* setting. In this example, we'll provide a new adapter for generating HTML. We create a new class that inherits from the *HtmlLinkAdapter* and overrides the *AddAttributes* method. The *AddAttributes* method is called during the *Render* method to handle any supported attributes. We will simply write the *accessKey* attribute if it is present. In Listing 4-7, we create a new link adapter that inherits from the *HtmlLinkAdapter*. It overrides the *AddAttributes* method to include support for the access key.

Code Listing 4-7   MyHtmlLinkAdapter.cs

```
using System;
using System.Web.UI;
using System.Web.UI.MobileControls.Adapters;

public class MyHtmlLinkAdapter : HtmlLinkAdapter {
  protected override void
    AddAttributes(HtmlMobileTextWriter writer) {
    string attributeValue =
      ((IAttributeAccessor)Control).GetAttribute("accessKey");
      if(attributeValue != null && attributeValue != String.Empty){
        writer.WriteAttribute("accessKey", attributeValue);
      }
    }
}
```

There is no built-in project type for Adapters in Visual Studio .NET, so you can create an empty workspace and compile the file after adding references to *System.Web.Mobile.dll* and *System.Web.dll*. From the command prompt, compile with this:

```
csc /r:system.dll,system.web.mobile.dll
    /t:library MyHtmlLinkAdapter.cs
```

The resulting dynamic-link library (DLL) will be called *MyHtmlLink-Adapter.dll* and should be placed in the *bin* directory of your test virtual root. Now request *AccessKey.aspx* and notice that there are no errors, the ALT+P key combination moves the focus to the ASP.NET link, and ALT+M shifts focus back to the MSPress link. Granted, this example doesn't get us anything spectacular—it just restores the use of one custom attribute that would have been passed through in a non-adapted page anyway. But it does illustrate how we can enable and use custom attributes in our own adapters while preserving the relative safety of not passing any arbitrary attributes through to a variety of browsers.

Working with Pagination

The idea behind server-based pagination is to automatically break up a block of content from a control or group of controls in a page into smaller pieces of rendering accessed with multiple page requests. Breaking up blocks of content can be important to enabling your application for mobile browsers because wireless connections typically have less bandwidth than bandwidth available in a wired connection and limits in client memory can be difficult to manage. It can be important in creating a user interface that is consistent and easy to navigate in a variety of devices. Without pagination, some mobile browsers tasked with rendering a large amount of content will display an error message to the user that simply states "Deck Overflow." This explanation doesn't present the user with options or even a potential workaround for the problem. (We should emphasize that pagination itself does not fix the problem of deck overflow—it simply circumvents it.)

The pagination algorithm targets page boundaries by limiting the number of lines of content that are included in the rendered output for display on the device. The memory limits of the device are, of course, not aware of any user-interface elements. The byte count can be exceeded by a single image that is too large, or the content can be within the memory limits even though the user must scroll through many pages of output.

You can enable pagination on a *form* element by setting the *Pagination* attribute to *true*, or you can specify that a control in the form be considered for pagination by setting the form's *ControlToPaginate* property equal to the ID of the control. Allowing pagination does not force the content to be split up across pages; it simply signals to the *MobilePage* class that the form should perform the pagination calculations and break up the output of the control, if warranted.

Using Device-Specific Filters

The mobile controls simplify the process of developing applications for disparate devices. They also eliminate the need to write several different kinds of markup to support the mobile user. However, often we do have the luxury of knowing that a large group of users has standardized on a single device or a class of similar devices. When trying to get the most out of adaptive renderings, it is nice to be able to exercise more fine-grained control over the output. The mobile controls support several different ways to customize based on the capabilities of a device by leveraging filters based on the capabilities of the requesting device. A *filter* is a named test used to modify control properties and affect rendering. Code Listing 4-8 is a sample web.config file that declares several filters for testing what type of markup is being used.

Code Listing 4-8   FiltersWeb.config

```
<configuration>
    <system.web>
        <deviceFilters>
            <filter
                name="prefersXHTML"
                compare="PreferredRenderingType"
                argument="xhtml-mp" />
            <filter
                name="prefersWML11"
                compare="PreferredRenderingType"
                argument="wml11" />
        </deviceFilters>
    </system.web>
</configuration>
```

When these filters are used, the *PreferredRenderingMime* property of the *Browser* object is compared against the argument. The filter is *true* when there is a match. The filters provide a declarative way to reuse these capability tests in the mobile page. We include a *deviceSpecific* element inside a control and can override the control values based on the filters. The first filter that is true is applied and the remaining ones are not tested. Code Listing 4-9 demonstrates using these device filters to change the text of a label.

Code Listing 4-9   LabelFilter.aspx

```
<%@ Page Inherits="System.Web.UI.MobileControls.MobilePage" Language="C#" %>
<script runat="server" language="C#">
public bool prefersHTML(System.Web.Mobile.MobileCapabilities
    capabilities,string argument) {

    if(capabilities["preferredRenderingType"] == "html32") {
        return true;
    }
    return false;
}
</script>
<mobile:form runat="server">
<mobile:label runat="server" Text="The Default Text">
    <deviceSpecific>
        <choice filter="prefersXHTML" Text="XHTML Text" />
        <choice filter="prefersHTML" Text="Text for HTML browser" />
        <choice filter="prefersWML11" Text="WML" />
    </deviceSpecific>
</mobile:label>
</mobile:form>
```

Notice that we use a filter not included in Code Listing 4-8. If a filter is not found in the configuration, the mobile page looks for a method on the page to be used as a delegate in performing the filter check. When the page is requested, the *preferredRenderingType* is checked. If a filter is evaluated to *true*, the value of *Text* for the label is set to the new value and filter evaluation ends. If no match is found, the current value is kept.

> **Tip**   Be careful when defining and using filters. There is a tendency to want to believe that one capability implies another. Even though the capabilities of new devices continue to advance rapidly, it is best to explicitly check for support when customizing.

In addition to being able to modify the properties and styles of controls using device filters, you can exert control over the markup itself. By using filters along with templates, you can easily customize the look of the page. The *Panel* control supports a template named *contentTemplate* that can be controlled with filters. The *Form* control supports several templates for customizing the rendering, including a *scriptTemplate* for passing through arbitrary script content to the browser as well as header and footer templates. Code Listing 4-10 demonstrates using a filter to use tables when they are supported.

Code Listing 4-10   HeaderFilter.aspx

```
<%@ Page Inherits="System.Web.UI.MobileControls.MobilePage" Language="C#" %>
<script runat="server" language="C#">
public bool supportsTables(System.Web.Mobile.MobileCapabilities capabilities,
  string argument) {

    if(Convert.ToBoolean(capabilities["tables"])) {
        return true;
    }
    return false;
}
</script>
<mobile:form runat="server">
<deviceSpecific>

<choice filter="supportsTables">
<headerTemplate>
<table><tr><td><b>ASP.NET Coding Strategies</b></td></tr>
<tr><td>
```

```
</headerTemplate>

<footerTemplate>
</td></tr></table>
</footerTemplate>
</choice>

<choice>
<headerTemplate>
<mobile:label runat="server" Text="ASP.NET" />
</headerTemplate>
</choice>
</deviceSpecific>
</mobile:form>
```

Notice in Code Listing 4-10 that we have included a *choice* element without a filter. When no filter is specified and none of the previous *choice* elements have been selected, that element automatically will be used.

Summary

In this chapter, we looked closely at how to use the mobile features of ASP.NET to target the rapidly growing segment of mobile users. For many applications, mobile-enabled content is quickly becoming of primary importance to getting key information to employees, business partners, and customers. The mobile controls rely on identifying the capabilities of the requesting device and browser. This information about capabilities is then leveraged by control adapters that produce the appropriate markup for a device. Device updates keep the supported browsers current with the marketplace, and the extensibility of the adaptive rendering architecture allows us to extend mobile applications even further.

5

Managing Client State

One of the unique opportunities for members of the ASP.NET team is reviewing the architecture design for customers, which is beneficial not only for the customer but also for us. The customer gets validation and critical feedback about their design, and we get first-hand knowledge of usage scenarios that influence decisions for the technologies we build.

A common best practice that we advocate is to factor application and client state management into the solution early in the design. State management requires developers to plan for a Web server farm and to understand and adhere to specific design patterns. For example, out-of-process session state requires that the data stored be serializable by the binary serializer. In total, there are seven different techniques for managing state in ASP.NET, which are described in Table 5-1. In this chapter, we're going to examine managing state that is stored for clients. In Chapter 6, we'll examine application and request state.

Table 5-1 Techniques for Managing State in ASP.NET

Type of State	Applies to	Description
Session	Client	State stored within the application's memory or outside of the application's memory (out of process) and available only to the user who created the data.
ViewState	Client	State stored within embedded *<input type="hidden">* HTML elements for pages that post back to themselves.
Cookie	Client	State stored in an HTTP cookie on the client's machine. Accessible until the cookie is expired or removed.

Table 5-1 Techniques for Managing State in ASP.NET

Type of State	Applies to	Description
static variables	Application	Static member variables are declared in global.asax or from an *HttpModule* and are available anywhere within the application.
Application	Application	State stored within application's memory and available anywhere within the application.
Cache	Application	State stored within application's memory and available anywhere within the application. Cache additionally supports dependencies and other features to expire items from memory.
HttpContext	Request	State stored within *HttpContext* is accessible only for the duration of the request.

In this chapter, we're going to examine managing state that is stored for clients. In Chapter 6, we'll examine application and request state.

Working with and understanding how client state is used in the application is critical to putting a good design into practice. The most common type of client state is session state. Before we look at how session state is used in ASP.NET, let's step back and review the history of session state, which will provide some context for understanding how it is used.

History of Session State

Microsoft Active Server Pages (ASP) first introduced the server-side programming model of session state. The *Session* object model has properties that are accessible within ASP and are used to store and manage user state data that needs to be persisted between browser requests. The programming model is a simple dictionary-style API in which all access is controlled through a known key. State data, such as the URL of the last page visited or the last 10 search requests, can be persisted using a key and retrieved using a key. For example, the following Visual Basic code works in both ASP and ASP.NET:

```
' Set a session value for last page visited
Session("LastPageVisited") = "http://www.asp.net/default.aspx"

' Get a session value for last page visited
lastPageVisited = Session("LastPageVisited")
```

Limitations with ASP Session State

Despite the advantages of ASP, ASP session state has three significant limitations: server affinity in Web farms, apartment model threading, and the HTTP cookie requirement. It was primarily for these three reasons that many developers avoided ASP session state.

Server Affinity in Web Farms

Prior to ASP.NET, server farms that supported session state required smart network hardware to ensure that a client was always redirected to the Web server initiating the first request. In ASP, the session data is stored within the Microsoft Internet Information Services (IIS) process that created it.

ASP runs as an ISAPI extension in the memory space of the IIS Web server. Data stored in memory by ASP is bound to that Web server process and can't be shared between servers. This limitation requires the client always to use the same Web server to guarantee consistency of its session state data. For example, if a user set data in session on server A and used server B on the next request, the session created on A would not be available data.

This connection of the client to a particular server is known as *IP affinity*, and it is a requirement for using session state. (There are other internal redirection solutions, but IP affinity is the most prevalent.) This solution usually requires complex networking hardware to load-balance the traffic. It relies on the client reusing the same IP address on multiple requests and the router maintaining a table of client IPs to server IPs. Routers then intelligently reroute requests based on the mapping of client IPs to server IPs, guaranteeing that the client goes back to the server it started with.

However, even with this IP affinity solution in place, many applications still failed to properly account for large Internet Service Providers (ISPs) such as AOL, MSN, and EarthLink. These three ISPs were the most well known for using reverse proxies for their clients, which meant that on each request the client could come from a different IP address.

Apartment Model Threading

Another limitation of ASP session state is that apartment model–threaded components are the de facto COM threading model. COM servers stored in session state cause multiple simultaneous requests to the same session value to be serialized. This problem is also common with ASP application state.

HTTP Cookies Requirement

ASP session state is also bound to an HTTP cookie. (You'll learn more about cookies later in this chapter.) When a new session starts, ASP assigns an HTTP cookie to the client; the cookie contains a unique key that the client and server share. This key, known as *SessionID*, is a unique value that the server generates and uses to associate session data with the client that posts the key. The IP address can't be used for this since the IP address can potentially change on each request.

Using an HTTP cookie works very well until a client decides not to accept cookies. In many cases this restriction breaks application functionality; since the client can't maintain a *SessionID*, the application can't rely on session state.

ASP.NET Session State

Session state still exists in ASP.NET, partly for backward compatibility, but also as a viable implementation that developers should no longer shy away from. ASP.NET session is free-threaded, but in some cases it can be accessed serially. Session state in ASP.NET still utilizes an HTTP cookie for managing the *SessionID*, however, ASP.NET also supports storing the *SessionID* in the URL if using cookies is not desirable. ASP.NET session state also supports two out-of-process modes to simplify deployment in Web server farms: out-of-process state server (*StateServer*), and out-of-process SQL Server (*SQLServer*).

In-Process Session State

ASP.NET defaults to what is known as in-process (*InProc*) session state. When in this mode, values stored within session state do not require serialization support and are stored within the memory space of the ASP.NET worker process. This behavior is identical to the way ASP stores its session data and has all the same shortcomings and limitations in a Web farm scenario. However, instead of the data being stored in the IIS process, the data is stored in managed memory within the ASP.NET worker process. (When ASP.NET is running on Microsoft Windows 2000, it defaults to the ASP.NET worker process aspnet_wp.exe. However, when ASP.NET is running on Microsoft Windows Server 2003, it will use the new IIS process model w3wp.exe.)

When stored in-process, session state data is lost whenever the process is recycled. In Microsoft Windows Server 2003 running IIS 6, the worker process automatically recycles every 29 hours, which is the default setting and is configurable. However, this does mean that every 29 hours the session data will be lost, whether it is 2:00 AM or 3:00 PM.

InProc is by far the fastest way to use session state. It doesn't support Web farm scenarios (unless you enforce client affinity). However, it also doesn't have the serialization and deserialization overhead associated with out-of-process modes. It's safe to assume that out-of-process session state is 15–30 percent slower (depending upon variables such as network speed and the size of the object or objects being serialized).

> **Important**   Use in-process session state (the default) if you have
> only a single server. In IIS 6, either use out-of-process or disable pro-
> cess recycling behavior to avoid data loss.

Code Listing 5-1 shows the configuration settings from machine.config
that specify the default settings for session state. Values that apply to *InProc*
appear in bold.

Code Listing 5-1   In-Process Session State Configuration

```
<configuration>
    <system.web>
        <sessionState mode="InProc"
                      stateConnectionString="tcpip=127.0.0.1:42424"
                      stateNetworkTimeout="10"
                      sqlConnectionString="..."
                      cookieless="false"
                      timeout="20" />
    </system.web>
</configuration>
```

The timeout value specifies the time, in minutes, after which a session is
considered timed out and its values can be removed. Session state uses a sliding
expiration: the timeout is reset each time the item is requested. A session could
theoretically be kept alive indefinitely if a request was made just once before
the value in the timeout is reached. We'll discuss the cookieless option later in
the chapter.

The name of the HTTP cookie used to store the *SessionID* in ASP.NET is
different from the cookie used to store the *SessionID* in ASP. There is no sharing
of session data between ASP and ASP.NET. (See Chapter 11 for more details
about migrating session state between ASP and ASP.NET.)

InProc session state allows any data type to be stored, and it participates
in the global session events *Session_OnStart*, which is raised when a new session is created; and *Session_OnEnd*, which is raised when a session is abandoned. These events can be programmed in either global.asax or within an
HTTP module.

> **Important**   Don't use the *Session_End* event; it can be called only for sessions created in the *InProc* mode. The event is not raised for sessions created in one of the out-of-process modes when sessions are abandoned.

Although the *InProc* session is the fastest, in some cases, you might want to trade performance for reliability or ease of management. For example, the out-of-process option is a good choice when you want to support multiple Web servers, or when you want to guarantee that session data can survive the Web server process.

Out-of-Process Session State

ASP.NET session state supports two out-of-process options, state server (*State-Server*) and SQL Server (*SQLServer*). Each has its own configuration settings and idiosyncrasies to contend with, such as managing stored types. The ASP.NET State Service is recommended for medium-size Web applications. For enterprise-size or highly-transactional Web applications, SQL Server is recommended.

> **Important**   It's important that the programming model is transparent. For example, we don't have to change how we access or use session state when we change the storage mode.

We recommend *SQLServer* for out-of-process session state because it is just as fast as *StateServer* and SQL Server is excellent at managing data. Furthermore, ASP.NET can communicate with SQL Server natively (meaning internally, using the *System.Data.SqlClient* libraries), and SQL Server can be configured to support data failover scenarios. In cases in which *SQLServer* is not available, *StateServer* works well, but it unfortunately does not support data replication or failover scenarios.

Managing Types for Out-of-Process Modes

If you're using an out-of-process mode, one of your major costs is the serialization and deserialization of items stored. Using an optimized internal method,

ASP.NET performs the serialization and deserialization of certain "basic" types, including numeric types of all sizes, such as *Int*, *Byte*, and *Decimal*, as well as several non-numeric types, such as *String*, *DateTime*, *TimeSpan*, *Guid*, *IntPtr*, and *UintPtr*.

If you have a session variable that is not one of the basic types, ASP.NET will serialize and deserialize it using the *BinaryFormatter*, which is relatively slower than the internal method. If you've created a custom class, and you want to store it in session state, you must mark it with the *[Serializable]* meta-data attribute or implement the *ISerializable* interface. (*[Serializable]* is the C# meta-data attribute. *<Serializable()>* is the Microsoft Visual Basic .NET metadata attribute.) The *SerializableAttribute* class is defined in the mscorlib.dll assembly within the *System* namespace. The *ISerializable* interface is defined in the assembly mscorlib.dll and within the *System.Runtime.Serialization* namespace. When a class is marked with the *SerializableAttribute*, all public members will attempt to be serialized. If the class contains references to other objects, those objects must also be marked with the *SerializableAttribute* or implement *ISerializable*. Implementing *ISerializable* gives you more control over how the serialization and deserialization of your class takes place. For more details on the serialization of objects in Visual Basic .NET, visit *http://www.fawcette.com/ reports/vsliveor/2002/09_18_02/hollis/*.

For the sake of performance, you're better off storing all session state data using only one of the basic data types (numeric and non-numeric types) listed earlier. For example, if you want to store a name and address in session state, you can store them using two *String* session variables, which is the most efficient method; or you can create a class with two *String* members and store that class object in a session variable, which is more costly.

Important   Store only basic data types in session state; avoid storing complex types or custom classes. Storing basic data types will decrease the serialization and deserialization costs associated with out-of-process session as well as reduce the complexity of the system.

Now that you've had an overview of out-of-process session, let's discuss the two out-of-process modes, *StateServer* and *SQLServer*.

StateServer Mode

The *StateServer* out-of-process mode relies on a running Microsoft Windows NT Service as well as changes to the default configuration settings. Code Listing 5-2 shows machine.config with the necessary configuration settings (which appear in boldface) for *StateServer*. Note that the *mode* attribute is set to *State-Server*. The *stateConnectionString* and *stateNetworkTimeout* settings are required values for *StateServer* mode.

Code Listing 5-2 StateServer Session State Configuration

```
<configuration>
    <system.web>
        <sessionState mode="StateServer"
                    stateConnectionString="tcpip=127.0.0.1:42424"
                    stateNetworkTimeout="10"
                    cookieless="false"
                    timeout="20"/>
    </system.web>
</configuration>
```

When ASP.NET is configured to use state server for out-of-process session, it uses a TCP/IP address and port number to send HTTP requests to the state server (which is in fact a lightweight Web server running as a Microsoft Windows Service).

The IP address (in *stateConnectionString*) must be changed to the IP address of the machine running the ASP.NET State Service. The port (the default is 42424), should also be changed unless the state service is running behind a firewall (which it should be). The port number can be configured on the machine running the service by editing the registry and changing the value of the port setting found in the following:

```
HKLM\SYSTEM\CurrentControlSet\Services\aspnet_state\Parameters\
```

As seen in Figure 5-1, the default setting for the port is 0x0000A5B8 in hexadecimal, or 42424 in base 10.

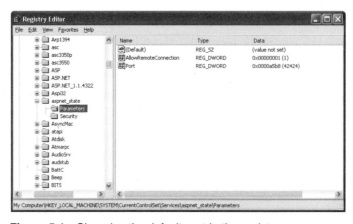

Figure 5-1 Changing the default port in the registry

> **Tip**   If the server running the state service is accessible outside the firewall, the port address of the state service should be changed to a value other than the default. In version 1.1 of ASP.NET, due to security reasons, only local machines can connect to the state server. To allow only non–local host requests in ASP.NET 1.1, open the same registry entry listed earlier for the port setting: *HKLM\SYSTEM\CurrentControlSet\Services\aspnet_state\Parameters*.   Change   *AllowRemoteConnection* to 1.

The value of *stateNetworkTimeout* represents the number of seconds that may elapse between the time ASP.NET tries to connect to the state service and the time the request times out. Although the default value for *stateNetworkTimeout* does not need to be changed, you have the option to make the value higher or lower depending upon your requirements.

Once the server designated to run the state server has been properly configured, it is simply a matter of starting the Windows service. The service can be started from either the command line or the Microsoft Management Console (MMC) for Services.

Starting the state service from the command line is simple. Navigate to the .NET Framework installation directory. For version 1, this is [system drive]\WINDOWS\Microsoft.NET\Framework\v1.0.3705\. Start the server by executing a net start command:

```
net start aspnet_state
```

After starting the service, you should see the following text: "The ASP.NET State Service service is starting. The ASP.NET State Service service was started successfully."

The second option for starting the state service is through the Services MMC snap-in, which you open by navigating to Start\Administrative Tools\Services. Right-click on the ASP.NET State Service option in the list and select Start to start the service. Once the Services MMC is started, you should see a screen similar to Figure 5-2.

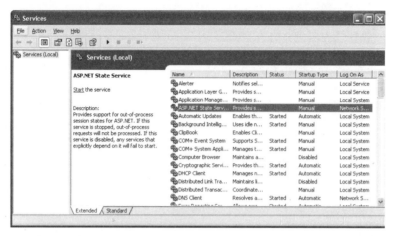

Figure 5-2   Services MMC with ASP.NET state service started

SQL Server Mode

SQL Server is an enterprise-class database solution optimized for managing, storing, and retrieving data quickly and efficiently. It is also capable of replication and clustering. In a clustered environment, SQL Server can be configured to failover. For example, when the clustered production SQL server fails, a backup can take over.

Note that clustered SQL Server scenarios are not supported out of the box for ASP.NET session state. To enable the clustering or replication features of SQL Server, session data must be stored in a non-tempDB table.

Again, you do not need to make any special changes to the code to use SQL Server as the session state store. Code Listing 5-3 shows the necessary configuration file machine.config for SQL Server. (Configuration changes are in boldface code.)

Code Listing 5-3   SQL Server Session State Configuration

```
<configuration>
    <system.web>
        <sessionState mode="SQLServer"
                      sqlConnectionString="database=[ServerName];
                                           Trusted_Connection=true"
                      cookieless="false"
                      timeout="20"/>
    </system.web>
</configuration>
```

The *mode* attribute needs to be *SQLServer*, and the *sqlConnectionString* attribute must point to a server running SQL Server that has already been configured for ASP.NET SQL session state.

> **Tip**   For ASP.NET 1, configure SQL Server for mixed-mode authentication by adding the ASPNET account enabled for the necessary SQL Server permissions (EXECUTE) for ASP.NET session state. (The ASPNET account is the user that the ASP.NET worker process runs as.) For ASP.NET 1.1 running on IIS 6, configure SQL Server for mixed-mode authentication by adding the NT AUTHORITY\NETWORK SERVICE account.

If the account has the necessary permissions, *integrated authentication* should be used. This prevents the need to store a username and password in clear text within the configuration. When integrated authentication is used, ASP.NET accesses SQL Server using the credentials of the Windows user that the worker process runs as. By default, these credentials are ASPNET and NT AUTHORITY\NETWORK SERVICE on Windows Server 2003 running IIS 6.

> **Important**   Use integrated authentication rather than store SQL Server credentials within your configuration file. If you decide to use SQL Server user names and passwords, do not use the system administrator (sa) account. Instead use an account that has only the necessary access to the database object required for the operations (for session state, this account is EXECUTE only). If you must use SQL Server credentials, ASP.NET 1.1 supports storing credentials securely.

To configure SQL Server to support ASP.NET session state, either open the InstallSqlState.sql file in isqlw.exe (Microsoft SQL Server Query Analyzer), or use the command-line tool osql.exe. To use SQL Server Query Analyzer, from the Start menu, navigate to \All Programs\Microsoft SQL Server\Query Analyzer. The SQL Query Analyzer application appears in Figure 5-3.

> **Important** Ensure SQL Server Agent is running before running the SQL Scripts. The agent runs a periodic job to purge expired sessions from the database.

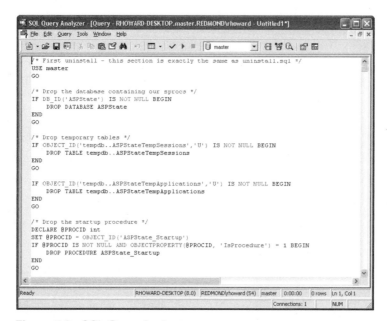

Figure 5-3 SQL Query Analyzer

If you're running ASP.NET 1, from the toolbar select File | Open [system drive]\WINDOWS\Microsoft.NET\Framework\v1.0.3705\ InstallSqlState.sql. If you're running ASP.NET 1.1, navigate to [system drive]\WINDOWS\Microsoft.NET \Framework\v1.0.4322\ directory and open the same file. Execute the script, either by clicking the Play button or by pressing F5. Using the command-line tool (osql.exe), open a command window and then navigate to \[system drive]\WINDOWS\Microsoft.NET\Framework\[ASP.NET version]\.

If integrated authentication is enabled for SQL Server and the current Windows logged-on user has permissions to SQL Server, type the following: **osql -E < InstallSqlState.sql**.

If SQL Server mixed-mode authentication is enabled and the current logged-on user does not have permissions within SQL Server, specify a user name and password using **osql - U [sql user] - P [password] < InstallSqlState.sql**.

After running the SQL Script, SQL Server is configured to support ASP.NET session state. Two tables are created within the tempdb database: *ASPStateTempApplications* and *ASPStateTempSessions*.

> **Note**   Why do we use tempdb? We often get asked why we store session data using tempdb vs. a table. The original design goal was to ensure that SQL Server state was fast, and because tempdb is memory-based, SQL Server state would be very fast. However, since SQL Server is so optimized, storing the data in non-temporary tables proved to be nearly as efficient. (SQL Server is super aggressive about keeping frequently accessed data in memory.) In retrospect, using tempdb probably wasn't necessary.

Session Data in a Web Farm

The major benefit of out-of-process session is that it no longer requires client/server affinity. Servers in an ASP.NET Web server farm can be configured to share session data. (However, individual applications cannot share session data because a session is tied to a single application.)

To configure session support in a Web farm, you must take one additional step regardless of whether a session is even used: you must configure the *machineKey* settings. Machine-wide settings are configured in the machine.config file (\[Windows Directory]\Microsoft.NET\Framework\[Versions]\Config\). The *machineKey* settings store the *validationKey* and the *decryptionKey* attribute values, which are used in many scenarios—for example, *ViewState*, Forms authentication, and session—to provide encryption and validation of values sent back and forth from client to server.

By default, the values for the *validationKey* and *decryptionKey* attributes are set to *AutoGenerate*, which enables the server to randomly create the values. Randomly selected values work well in a single server environment; however, in a Web server farm in which there is no guarantee which server will satisfy the client's request, the values for *validationKey* and *decryptionKey* must be precise and predictable.

Optimizing Out-of-Process Session Use

When using out-of-process session, ASP.NET makes two requests to the out-of-process session store for every one page requested (if the request comes in with a session ID). When the request first starts, the session state module connects to the state store, reads the session state data, and marks the session as locked. At this point the page is executed, and the *Session* object is accessible. When the page completes execution, the session state module connects to the state store, writes the session state data if it changed, and unlocks the session data.

The locking mechanism implemented is a reader-writer lock using the ReaderWriterLock class. Multiple requests can read data simultaneously when the session isn't locked. If the session is locked, read requests are blocked until the write lock is released. This locking strategy guarantees that the *Session* object with which the user is interacting is always an accurate reflection of the data. If you attempt to build a site that uses frames, and each page within a frame requires session state, the pages will execute serially. You can configure session state to be read-only on a page-by-page or even application basis. Configuring a page to use session data in a read-only manner allows the page to be requested without locking the session data and prevents serialized access.

If session is configured as read-only, in out-of-process mode, the session module does not need to go back to the session store to release the lock. Multiple requests can read session data simultaneously without serialized access, which yields better throughput. To configure the read-only option on a page-by-page basis, simply set the page-level directive *EnableSessionState*:

```
<%@ Page EnableSessionState="ReadOnly" %>
```

Another option is to configure session to *enableSessionState="false"* as the default setting (you can change this in web.config or machine.config) and use *EnableSessionState="ReadOnly"* or *EnableSessionState="true"* at the page level. Code Listing 5-4 shows the code for disabling session state.

Code Listing 5-4   Disabling Session State
```
<configuration>
    <system.web>
        <pages enableSessionState="false" />
    </system.web>
</configuration>
```

> **Important** For out-of-process session, set session state to *enableSessionState="false"* within the configuration file and set the *EnableSessionState* page directives to either *true* or *ReadOnly* based on what behavior is needed. Note that the length of the session will still be reset (even when set to *false*).

When you apply this strategy for optimizing out-of-process session, you get fewer requests to the out-of-process session store, which increases the scalability and throughput of the site.

Cookieless Session

Session state, to HTTP purists, is a frowned upon but necessary feature for building real-world Web applications. Session state was designed to work around the limitations of the stateless nature of HTTP. To do so, the browser and the server must share a common piece of data: the *SessionID*. This shared value must be stored somewhere—we're certainly not going to ask the user to re-enter an ID value upon each request to the server! To solve this problem, we take advantage of another HTTP feature known as a cookie, which you learned about briefly earlier in the chapter.

A cookie is a highly contentious, much debated feature supported by all browsers that allows the server to store a small amount of data, private to the server, on the client. Upon each client request to the server, the browser sends along any cookie data belonging to that server.

For both ASP and ASP.NET, the *SessionID* is stored within a cookie. When the client makes requests to the server, the client presents the cookie, giving ASP.NET the opportunity to fetch any associated session data belonging to the presented *SessionID*.

> **Important**   Using the *SessionID* as a key for user data is not recommended. The *SessionID* is randomly generated, and session data—as well as session IDs—do expire. Additionally, although a *SessionID* might be generated on each request, a *SessionID* is set only when a *Session* value is set server side. This means that if no session values are set server side, new *SessionID*s are issued on each request.

Storing the *SessionID* in a cookie works very well except when the client chooses not to accept cookies. (By default, cookies are accepted, and the user has to explicitly disable cookie support to avoid using them.) When cookies are not supported, ASP.NET provides a cookieless option in which the *SessionID* is stored within the URL instead of an HTTP cookie.

An ASP.NET Web application cannot be configured to support both cookie and cookieless *SessionID* storage; that is, the application cannot dynamically choose whether to use cookies. This can be seen as advantageous because designing an application to accommodate various cookie scenarios can be very difficult.

When building applications to take advantage of a cookieless session, you must carefully design navigation in the user interface. Any links within the site that are not relative (those starting with *http://*) will cause the user to lose her session when clicked. For relative URLs (for example, /MyStore/default.aspx), the embedded *SessionID* is automatically added by ASP.NET when generating the page output.

> **Tip**   If you have to develop an application that supports both cookie and cookieless sessions, your best strategy is to write an HTTP module to redirect the browser to the appropriate application or server for the supported browser feature, for example, configure a dedicated application that is used for cookieless sessions.

Using *ViewState* to Store State in the Page Output

As stated earlier in the section on session state, Web application communication takes place over HTTP, a stateless protocol. The ASP.NET session state feature circumvents the stateless nature of HTTP by storing its *SessionID* in an HTTP cookie or embedding it within the URL of the page. This shared session key is then used to associate data stored on the server with the browser making the request.

In some cases, it isn't necessary or desirable to require session state, and a common technique that many developers have used in the past is to store data in hidden form fields like this: *<input type="hidden" value="some value here"/>*. When the client submits the page and causes either an HTTP POST or GET request to the server, this data, along with other *input* form data, is sent to the server in either the POST body or the query string.

ASP.NET has taken this concept of hidden input form fields and utilized them for maintaining state for pages that participate in postback. (All ASP.NET pages that use *<form runat="server"/>* send the contents of the *form* back to the same page. Additionally, the *action* attribute of *form* is ignored when the *form* is marked with *runat="server"*.) This feature is known as view state; data is stored in a special hidden *<input type="hidden" name="__VIEWSTATE"/>* form element. The data stored in the *value* attribute of the *__VIEWSTATE* form element consists of a base-64 encoded string that contains all the serialized *ViewState* data for the current page plus a MAC (Message Authentication Code). When the page is posted back to the server, the ASP.NET page framework deserializes the data in *__VIEWSTATE* and automatically repopulates the *ViewState* state bag. Thus data added to the view state is available when the page is posted back again. View state is very useful for building complex server controls since data not usually sent as a *form* element can be stored in the view state and retrieved when the page is posted back. (For more details on the inner workings of view state, I highly recommend you take a look at Chapter 7 of *Developing Microsoft ASP.NET Server Controls and Components,* written by Nikhil Kothari and Vandana Datye and published by Microsoft Press.)

> **Note**   A MAC is a key-dependent, one-way hash. A MAC is used to verify *ViewState* data by recomputing the MAC on post back and comparing it to the MAC stored in *__VIEWSTATE*. If the MACs match, the data in *__VIEWSTATE* is valid. If they do not match, the *ViewState* data is invalid and an exception is thrown.

Programming *ViewState*

ViewState data is accessible in much the same way that *Session* data is; both use a key to set or retrieve data. However, unlike *Session*, *ViewState* data is available only in pages that utilize *<form runat="server"/>*, which causes the page to perform a postback. The data types that can be stored in *ViewState* are limited to *Int32, Boolean, String, Unit,* and *Color*. Data types other than these incur significant overhead and must first either be converted to a string or be serialized using the same binary serializer used by session state.

The view state can be extremely useful in cases in which there is a costly piece of data to fetch that is necessary for the duration of the page (where duration of the page is equal to the first request and all postbacks). A great example of this is in the source code for the ASP.NET Forums (*www.asp.net/forums*). One of the controls used frequently within the Forums is a server control used for paging data. This server control (Paging.cs) allows the user to page through multiple records of data in SQL Server (as opposed to paging through the data in ASP.NET). One of the paging control's tasks is to keep track of the total number of available records. Using this number and the requested page size, the control can calculate the total number of pages available. The total records available are not computed on each request—instead, this data is fetched once and stored in view state, alleviating the stress on the server from making multiple requests to the database for the same information.

Below is a code snippet from the Paging.cs file that demonstrates this technique—the full source is available as part of the ASP.NET Forums downloadable from *www.asp.net*.

```
/// <summary>
/// TotalRecords available
/// </summary>
public int TotalRecords {
    get {
        // The total records available is stuffed into
        // ViewState so that we don't pay the lookup cost
        // across postbacks.
        if (ViewState["totalRecords"] == null)
            return defaultTotalRecords; // 0

        return Convert.ToInt32(ViewState["totalRecords"].ToString());
    }
    set {
    // Recalculate the total number of pages in case page size changed
    TotalPages = CalculateTotalPages(value, PageSize);

    // set the ViewState
    ViewState["totalRecords"] = value;
    }
}
```

ViewState's Liability

Using *ViewState* does have a liability: it increases the total size of the page that must be created. Although it doesn't affect the UI generated by the page, the HTML payload can dramatically increase depending upon how much view state is used by the page. We recommend that you disable *ViewState* for page or controls that don't require it.

> **Tip** The view state can be disabled in a page by using *<%@ Page EnableViewState="false" %>*, or in a control by specifying *Page.Enable-ViewState="false"* on the server control.

Without disabling view state, the following code sample demonstrates using the *DataGrid* server control bound to a *DataSet* to serialize the XML document BookData.xml to base64 in an XML attribute value:

Code Listing 5-5   Serializetobase64.aspx

```
<%@ Page Language="C#" %>
<%@ Import Namespace="System.Data" %>

<script runat="server">

    public void Page_Load (Object sender, EventArgs e) {

        // Load some data
        DataSet ds = new DataSet();
        ds.ReadXml(Server.MapPath("BookData.xml"));

        // Now databind to the datagrid
        DataGrid1.DataSource = ds;
        DataGrid1.DataBind();

    }
</script>
<form runat="server">
<asp:Button runat="server" Text="PostBack" />
</form>
<asp:DataGrid id="DataGrid1" runat="server" />
```

When this page is requested and the HTML source is viewed, the value for
__*VIEWSTATE* contains this:

```
<input type="hidden" name="__VIEWSTATE"
value="dDwxMzg3MzYyMzg7dDw7bDxpPDI+Oz47bDx0PEAwPHA8cDxsPERhdGFFZLZXlz018hSXRlbUNv
dW5[…30 lines removed…]z47dDxwPHA8bDxUZXh00z47bDxQYXJpcczs+Pjs+Ozs+03Q8cDxwPGw8V
GV4dDs+02w8Jm5ic3BcOzs+Pjs+Ozs+03Q8cDxwPGw8VGV4dDs+02w8RnJhbmN1Oz4+0z470z47Pj47
Pj47Pj47Pj47Phd0PzYb9Lz7N2ZqMReiGAMMnwyz" />
```

In this case, we're not using a view state, so we should disable it by adding an *EnableViewState* attribute to *DataGrid*:

```
<asp:DataGrid id="DataGrid1" runat="server" EnableViewState="false" />
```

Now when this page is requested, the value for __*VIEWSTATE* is more reasonable:

```
<input type="hidden" name="__VIEWSTATE"
value="dDwxMzg3MzYyMzg7Oz6TQ21xg8KTWseIQ341mOOdKXguIw==" />
```

View state is a powerful technique for managing state for pages that participate in post back. However, you need to be aware that view state has an
associated cost that can easily increase the size of your page output, as demonstrated in this code sample.

Using Cookies for Client State Management

The last technique that we'll examine for managing client state is the cookie, which you learned about briefly earlier in the chapter. Unbeknownst to many Web developers, cookies are not an approved standard, although all major browsers support them and all Web application development technologies use them. To review, cookies are small state bags that belong to a particular domain and are stored on the client's machine rather than on the server. ASP.NET utilizes cookies for two tasks:

- **Session state**   The associated cookie is .ASPXSession. The cookie stores the *SessionID* used to associate the request with its session data.

- **Forms authentication**   The associated cookie is .ASPXAUTH. The cookie stores encrypted credentials. Credentials can be decrypted and the user re-authenticated.

You can view all the cookies on your system by opening Microsoft Internet Explorer and selecting Tools\Internet Options to open the Internet Options dialog box. Click the Settings button to open the Settings dialog box. Click the View Files button to open Explorer and access your temporary Internet files directory. You can then sort by type *Text Document* or by items named Cookie. As you can see, you've got lots of cookies!

Cookies are actually a great way to manage state if you can guarantee that your clients use them. They can store multiple name/value combinations as long as the value is of type *string* (or can be converted to string). The only limitation with cookies is the amount of data that can be stored; most browsers support a maximum cookie size of 4 KB (4096 bytes, to be more precise).

Working with cookies in ASP.NET is simple. We use them in many of our sample applications, including the *www.asp.net* Web site, in which we store the roles that a user belongs to. Rather than fetching the user roles on each request from the database, we fetch the user roles only if a specific *UserRoles* cookie doesn't exist. We then create the *UserRoles* cookie and add the roles the user belongs to. On subsequent requests, we can simply open the *UserRoles* cookie, extract the roles, and add them to the roles the current user belongs to. The following code fragment illustrates this.

```
//*********************************************************************
//
// Application_AuthenticateRequest Event
//
// If the client is authenticated with the application, then determine
```

```
// which security roles he/she belongs to and replace the "User" intrinsic
// with a custom IPrincipal security object that permits "User.IsInRole"
// role checks within the application
//
// Roles are cached in the browser in an in-memory encrypted cookie.
// If the cookie doesn't exist yet for this session, create it.
//
//***********************************************************************
void Application_AuthenticateRequest(Object sender, EventArgs e) {
    String[] roles = null;

    if (Request.IsAuthenticated == true) {
        // Create roles cookie if it doesn't exist yet for this session.
        if ((Request.Cookies["userroles"] == null) ||
            (Request.Cookies["userroles"].Value == "")) {

            // Get roles from UserRoles table, and add to cookie
            roles = UserRoles.GetUserRoles(User.Identity.Name);

            CreateRolesCookie(roles);

        } else {

            // Get roles from roles cookie
            FormsAuthenticationTicket ticket =
                FormsAuthentication.Decrypt(
                    Context.Request.Cookies["userroles"].Value);

            // Ensure the user logged in and the user
            // the cookie was issued to are the same
            if (ticket.Name != Context.User.Identity.Name) {

                // Get roles from UserRoles table, and add to cookie
                roles = UserRoles.GetUserRoles(User.Identity.Name);

                CreateRolesCookie(roles);
            } else {
                // convert the string representation of the role
                // data into a string array
                ArrayList userRoles = new ArrayList();

                foreach (String role in
                        ticket.UserData.Split( new char[] {';'} )) {
                            userRoles.Add(role);
                }

                roles = (String[]) userRoles.ToArray(typeof(String));
            }
        }
```

```
            // Add our own custom principal to the request
            // containing the roles in the auth ticket
            Context.User = new GenericPrincipal(Context.User.Identity, roles);
            }
    }


//**********************************************************************
//
// CreateRolesCookie
//
// Used to create the cookie that store the roles for the current
// user.
//
//**********************************************************************
private void CreateRolesCookie(string[] roles) {

    // Create a string to persist the roles
    String roleStr = "";
    foreach (String role in roles) {
        roleStr += role;
        roleStr += ";";
    }

    // Create a cookie authentication ticket.
    FormsAuthenticationTicket ticket = new FormsAuthenticationTicket(
                1,                              // version
                Context.User.Identity.Name,     // user name
                DateTime.Now,                   // issue time
                DateTime.Now.AddHours(1),       // expires every hour
                false,                          // don't persist cookie
                roleStr                         // roles
    );

    // Encrypt the ticket
    String cookieStr = FormsAuthentication.Encrypt(ticket);

    // Send the cookie to the client
    Response.Cookies["userroles"].Value = cookieStr;
    Response.Cookies["userroles"].Path = "/";
    Response.Cookies["userroles"].Expires = DateTime.Now.AddMinutes(5);

}
```

The first method, *Application_AuthenticateRequest*, is an event delegate that gets called when ASP.NET is ready to authenticate the request. Within this method, we check to see whether we have a cookie named *UserRoles* and whether it has a value.

If the cookie isn't found, we load the roles for the user and then call the *CreateRolesCookie* method, passing in a *string[]* of role names. Within *Create-RolesCookie*, we simply format the *string[]* into a semicolon-delimited string, encrypt it using APIs from Forms Authentication, and then store the encrypted data in the *UserRoles* cookie.

If the *UserRoles* cookie is found, we first decrypt the value of the cookie, ensure that the user the cookie belongs to is the same user that is currently logged in, split the roles using a semicolon as the delimiter, and finally create a new *GenericPrinicpal* (authenticated identity), passing in the roles as one of the arguments.

Obviously this code works on each request, but it doesn't go to the database on each request to refetch the roles. The *www.asp.net* site averages about 85,000 unique users per day. If each user made an average of 30 requests, by using cookies for storing the user roles, we would eliminate at least 2,465,000 requests to the database!

Summary

In this chapter, we examined three techniques for managing client state: session state, view state, and cookies. Session state is a powerful tool that you can use to store data associated with individual users. Session state requires a storage location for this user data. By default, user data is stored in the current process's memory space, as was the case with ASP. However, ASP.NET introduces a powerful new concept known as out-of-process session state that allows for all servers in a farm to use a common store such as SQL Server. Additionally, session state requires the use of a session ID. The session ID is a token shared between the client and the server that is used to identify the client's session to the server on subsequent requests.

View state solves a problem that many developers have solved in the past through custom code. Unlike session state, view state never times out, but it is limited to the postback life cycle of a page—once you navigate away from the page, you lose your view state. View state allows for simple types to be stored in the hidden input in the HTML of the page, but caution should be used when using view state because the size of *ViewState* affects the size of the page the client must download.

Cookies can be used to store client state independent of the server. However, cookies are not an approved standard and have data storage limitations.

Choosing the appropriate client state management technique depends on what you need to accomplish within your application. ASP.NET provides you with easy-to-use APIs for working with the three client state management techniques covered in this chapter. In Chapter 6, we'll examine another type of state: application state.

6

Managing Application and Request State

In the previous chapter, we discussed three techniques for managing client state: session, view state, and HTTP cookies. In this chapter, we'll examine four techniques for managing application state and request state: cache, static variables, application, and request. These are described in Table 6-1.

Application state describes any data or state that is shared throughout the application using the Application API, the *Cache* API, or static application variables. *Request state* describes any data or state that is shared throughout the duration of the request, that is, created once and then used multiple times throughout the lifetime of the request.

Table 6-1 Techniques for Managing Application and Request State

Type of State	Applies To	Description
Cache	Application	State stored within the application's memory and available anywhere within the application. *Cache* additionally supports dependencies and other features to expire items from memory.
Static variable	Application	Declared in global.asax or from an *HttpModule* and available anywhere within the application.
Application	Application	State stored within the application's memory and available anywhere within the application.
HttpContext	Request	State stored within *HttpContext* is accessible only for the duration of the request.

Some developers follow the line of thinking that all Web applications should be stateless. Although statelessness is a noble concept, it is unrealistic. In fact, *HttpRuntime*—the underlying plumbing that runs ASP.NET—is not even stateless. When the first request comes into an ASP.NET application, the *HttpRuntime* performs multiple tasks, one of which is parsing and storing the configuration for the application from the web.config/machine.config configuration files. The resulting configuration data gleaned from these files is then stored in the ASP.NET cache (the cache is specialized in-process memory) to alleviate the need to perform multiple requests to the file system. In this chapter, we'll discuss how to use these techniques to improve the scalability and performance of your application.

Caching Overview

One presentation I give frequently at user groups, internal Microsoft presentations, and conferences is "ASP.NET Performance Best Practices." I always make the same statement when starting the talk: "We're going to discuss several areas you should understand to get optimal performance from ASP.NET. The last topic, caching, is the most important."

Caching is the technique of storing frequently accessed data as close as possible to the resource needing the data. In my opinion, aggressively using the caching features of ASP.NET is the most important design decision you can make when building an ASP.NET Web application that must easily scale and perform well under load. Caching is not unique to ASP.NET. Many other technologies, such as the processor for your computer, use caching to increase performance and scalability. However, the implementation of caching within ASP.NET is unique and was developed specifically for Web applications.

Understanding the caching features of ASP.NET and implementing them correctly allows your applications to perform and scale incredibly well—if you can correctly implement a caching scenario, you can potentially increase performance 3–5 times!

Unfortunately, retrofitting an existing application to support caching is difficult. Caching does have some limitations that affect how the program is architected, and you must understand and account for these nuances early in the architecting phase of your application.

Common Questions about Caching

We'll begin by answering some common, frequently asked questions about caching in ASP.NET.

When Should I Use Page Output Caching?   Any content created with ASP.NET that does not need to have its code executed upon each request is a candidate for page output caching. For example, pages that display product details, in which the data comes from the database and changes infrequently, are great candidates for output caching. For pages that require further data transformations or that rely heavily on user personalization, partial page caching or the *Cache* API should be used.

Where Is Cached Data Stored?   Cached data is stored in the memory of the process running the application. It is not stored on disk.

Is Cached Data Shared in a Web Farm?   Unlike session state, data stored within the cache is stored only in the memory of the application in which the data was created. Also, multiple applications on the same server do not share memory and thus cannot share cached data. An application's cache is private to the application that created it.

Because cached data between applications is never shared, there cannot be cache coherency across the server farm. For example, a page or *DataSet* cached on server A might be different from a page or *DataSet* cached on server B. This difference is not a problem, however. Implicitly, you assume that data that can be cached must have some acceptable age limit and that coherency between two or more servers can be loosely controlled through cache dependencies. Additionally, the cache is a feature designed to increase performance, and we know that using an out-of-process session decreases performance by 30–40 percent (mainly due to serialization costs). In version 2 of ASP.NET, you have more control over these dependencies, for example, you can make cache entries dependent upon database tables.

How Long Is an Output Cached Page Stored in Memory?   The duration for which a page can be stored in memory is controlled by several dependencies: time, file, and other cache entries. These dependencies are an inherent feature of the *Cache* API, which is discussed later in the chapter. As they apply to page output caching, these dependencies are controlled by the developer authoring the page.

What Are the Rules for How a Page Can Be Cached?   Two types of rules can be applied to determine how the page output cache behaves: *VaryBy* style caching and HTTP cache policy. The first allows output cached pages to vary by data related to the page, for example, query string parameters or HTTP headers. The second, HTTP cache policy, controls how the output cache follows HTTP rules for document caching.

What Happens When the Cache or ASP.NET Needs More Memory?   The page output cache utilizes the ASP.NET *Cache* API, which implements a least recently used (LRU) algorithm. When ASP.NET has need for more memory, the cache can be asked to evict items to reclaim or free up memory. This eviction process walks through the items stored in the cache and removes items based on two conditions:

- When was the item last used (LRU)
- Which priority was assigned to the item

Internally, the cache sorts the items to be removed first by the least recently used and then by priority. The cache then removes items, removing the lowest priority and least recently used first, and working up based on priority—for example, an item not accessed in a long time but assigned a high priority might never be evicted from the cache. Since the cache manages itself proactively for us, we don't have to worry about managing it.

> **Note**   When using Microsoft Windows Server 2003 and Microsoft Internet Information Services (IIS) 6, it is recommended to configure the IIS 6 worker process to use 60 percent of the physical memory or to limit the total to 800 MB of physical memory.

How Do I Clear or Flush the Cache?   People frequently ask us how to clear the cache. Unfortunately, there is no *Clear* method to simply remove everything from the cache. One reason such a method does not exist is because internally ASP.NET is also using the cache to store all sorts of other data, such as configuration. However, it is possible to both individually remove output cached pages (using the output cache API) and items stored in the cache. To remove pages, you must know the name of the page, and to remove items using the *Cache* API, you must know the name of the key used to retrieve the item.

Now that we've gotten the most common questions out of the way, let's dig into the details of how some of these features work, starting with page output caching.

Page Caching Using the *OutputCache* Directive

The most familiar programming target in ASP.NET is the page, such as default.aspx. The page is the usual target of a request, such as an HTTP *GET* for *http://www.asp.net/default.aspx*, and is responsible for generating the response. Internally, the page executes logic and writes output, such as HTML, WML markup, or XML to a series of memory buffers. It is configurable, but these *memory buffers*, also called *response buffers*, are flushed when the page completes execution. Output buffering can be controlled at the page level using *<%@ Page Buffer="[true/false]" %>* or at the application level by setting *<pages buffer="[true/false]" />* in a configuration file. By default, this is set to *true*.

The page output caching feature of ASP.NET allows for the contents of the response buffers to be written to memory before being sent to the client. When output caching is enabled, the contents are written to memory and the page has been *output cached*. On subsequent requests, rather than executing the page to fulfill the request, the memory from cache can be written directly to the output stream; page buffering settings do not affect the output cache. This process is illustrated in Figure 6-1.

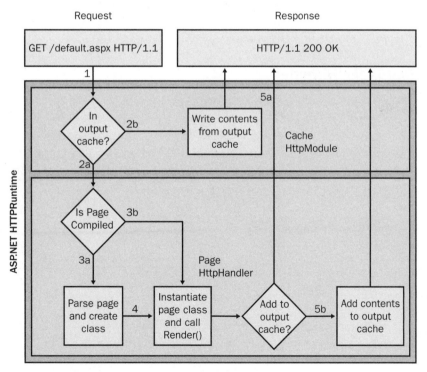

Figure 6-1   *HttpRuntime* request and response

Let's review in detail what is happening in Figure 6-1. An HTTP request is made for an ASP.NET page (1), for example, default.aspx. The request is handled by the ASP.NET *HttpRuntime*. ASP.NET determines whether the request can be satisfied from the output cache: (2a) either the request cannot be satisfied from the output cache; or (2b) the request can be satisfied from the output cache, and the contents from the output cache are written directly back to the response stream. ASP.NET also determines whether the page being requested is already parsed and compiled (3a and 3b).

An instance of the requested page is created, and the *Render* method is called (4) for the page to render its contents. ASP.NET determines whether the contents of the rendered page can be served from the output cache: if it cannot, the response is written back to the response stream (5a); if it can, the response is stored in the output cache and written back to the response stream (5b).

The ability for ASP.NET to write directly to the response stream from memory means that responses served from the cache are incredibly fast—in some ways, this is equivalent to sending static HTML.

To put this scenario in perspective, consider that a common but costly stored procedure used in the ASP.NET forums (*http://www.asp.net/Forums/*) generates about 60 page requests per second (with results simply bound to a *DataGrid*). With page output caching enabled, the number of requests jumps to approximately 480 per second—about 8 times faster!

The *OutputCache* Directive

Page output caching follows a common pattern found in the .NET Framework: *programming model factoring*. A page can be instructed to output cache itself using either the *OutputCache* page directive or the APIs found on *Response.Cache*. The *Response.Cache* APIs are used to programmatically manage page output caching. For example, the page *OutputCache* directives:

```
<%@ OutputCache Duration="60" VaryByParam="none" %>
```

is equivalent to the page output *Cache* API:

```
public void Page_Load(Object sender, EventArgs e) {
    Response.Cache.SetExpires(DateTime.Now.AddSeconds(60));
    Response.Cache.SetCacheability(HttpCacheability.Public);
    Response.Cache.SetValidUntilExpires(true);
}
```

Following are HTTP exchanges for a page that do not use page output caching (the examples include HTTP headers only). These are the HTTP request headers:

```
GET /test.aspx HTTP/1.1
Host: rhoward-laptop
Accept: */*
HTTP Response
HTTP/1.1 200 OK
Server: Microsoft-IIS/5.1
Date: Thu, 17 Apr 2003 15:49:38 GMT
Cache-Control: private
Content-Type: text/html; charset=utf-8
Content-Length: 865
```

The same request with page output caching enabled yields much different results. These are the HTTP response headers:

```
HTTP/1.1 200 OK
Server: Microsoft-IIS/5.1
Date: Thu, 17 Apr 2003 15:53:06 GMT
Cache-Control: public
Expires: Thu, 17 Apr 2003 15:55:05 GMT
Last-Modified: Thu, 17 Apr 2003 15:53:05 GMT
Content-Type: text/html; charset=utf-8
Content-Length: 865
```

Note that the *Cache-Control* header changed from *private* to *public*, an *Expires* header was added, and a *Last-Modified* header was added. So, as you can see, in addition to caching the page in memory on the server, when ASP.NET output caches a page, it sends the appropriate HTTP cache headers. Table 6-2 describes these headers in more detail. You can read more about HTTP in Hypertext Transfer Protocol–HTTP/1.1 (RFC 2616), available at *http://www.ietf.org/rfc/rfc2616.txt*.

Note   For more details on the *Cache-Control* header, see Chapter 8 of *Web Proxy Servers* by Ari Luotonen (published by Prentice Hall).

Important   Use the page directives when possible. There is less risk of introducing bugs in your application because the *OutputCache* directive is declarative.

Table 6-2 HTTP Cache Headers

HTTP Header	Description
Cache-Control	Specifies how servers connected to the network that participate in the process of returning the requested document to the browser participate in caching. The *Location* attribute in the *OutputCache* directive of ASP.NET is used to control this header. (This attribute is discussed later in the chapter.)
	Here are several of the most commonly used values returned by this header:
	■ **public** Any server/browser can cache the response.
	■ **private** Cacheable only by the browser/client that made the request.
	■ **no-cache** Whenever the document is requested, the request must go directly to the server that originated the response.
	Other values returned by this header can be found in RFC 2616, available at *http://www.ietf.org/rfc/rfc2616.txt*.
Expires	If the response can be cached, the *Expires* header specifies a point in time at which the response can no longer be cached. When the *Duration* attribute is set in the *OutputCache* directive of ASP.NET, the setting affects the *Expires* HTTP header.
Last-Modified	This is the point in time at which the document was last modified, for example, when the document was last saved.

The two samples we looked at earlier—the *OutputCache* page directive compared to the *Cache* APIs—accomplish the same page output caching behavior: Both cache the page for 60 seconds and do not use any *VaryBy* parameters. (We'll discuss the *VaryBy* options in a moment.) However, two methods used by the page output *Cache* API achieve parity behavior with the directive:

■ *SetCacheability*

■ *SetValidUntilExpires*

We'll talk about these methods, as well as several others supported by the page output *Cache* APIs, after our discussion of the page *OutputCache* directive.

Using the Page *OutputCache* Directive

The page *OutputCache* directive is designed to be a simple technique for enabling page output caching. It successfully addresses 95 percent of page output caching scenarios. For special cases, such as an *ETag* HTTP header generated by pages, the page output cache APIs should be utilized.

> **Note**   An *ETag*, or entity tag, specifies an HTTP header sent with the served document to uniquely identify a specific version of the page. Cache servers can query the originating cache server to determine whether a cached document is still valid by comparing the cached documents entity tag to the entity tag returned from the origin server.

The following code shows the syntax for the *OutputCache* directives:

```
<%@ OutputCache Duration="[seconds]"
                VaryByParam="[none or parameter list]"
                [Optional attributes] %>
```

The *Duration* and *VaryByParam* attributes are required when using the *OutputCache* directive. If these attributes are not specified, a detailed exception is thrown when the page is compiled that indicates the *VaryByParam* attribute is missing, as shown in Figure 6-2.

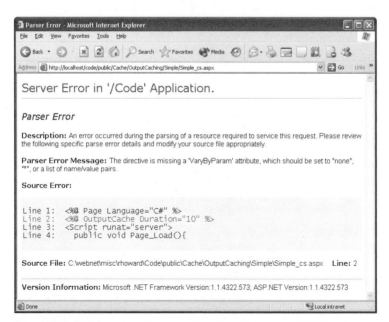

Figure 6-2   Parser error from missing *VaryByParam* attribute

The most common use of the *OutputCache* directive is to output cache a page for a duration of time, for example, output caching a page used to display sales reports for a duration of 12 hours. The following *OutputCache* directive would accomplish this:

```
<%@ OutputCache Duration="43200" VaryByParam="none" %>
```

As stated earlier, the *VaryByParam* attribute is a required attribute that must be set when using the directive. When not used, its value must be set to *none*.

Although we specified *Duration* with 43200 (12 hours), there is no guarantee that the output cached page would remain in the cache for this entire period of time. Earlier we discussed how a cached item could be evicted from the cache when memory needs to be reclaimed. In the case of an output cached page, the page would simply be evicted, and on the next request, the page would fully re-execute and be re-inserted into the cache. No exception occurs when this happens; it's a normal and expected occurrence. Auto-eviction allows the server to optimize itself depending upon the current load. An ASP.NET application performance object is available in the Windows Performance monitor. A *Cache* API misses counter increments when a page marked as cacheable, or other items requested from the cache, cannot be served from the cache.

Storing an output cached page for a period of time is straightforward unless the cache is dealing with more complex requests. For example, a simple HTTP *GET* request (with no querystring parameters) is assumed with the directive here:

```
<%@ OutputCache Duration="43200" VaryByParam="none" %>
```

What happens for HTTP *POST* requests, in which parameters are sent via the *POST* body, or for HTTP *GET* requests, in which parameters are sent via that querystring?

When building dynamic Web applications, the parameters passed via the *POST* body or the querystring represent significant data that might affect how the page is displayed. For example, when looking at the *www.asp.net* site, you'll notice that we pass querystring parameters *tabindex* and *tabid*. The statement */default.aspx?tablindex=0&tabid=1* tells the server to load the controls to display the home page as shown in Figure 6-3.

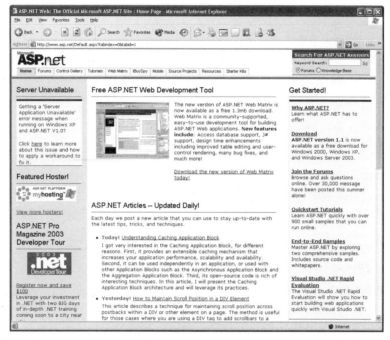

Figure 6-3   The www.asp.net site

Simultaneously, the statement */default.aspx?tabindex=2&tabid=31* tells the server to load the Control Gallery (Figure 6-4):

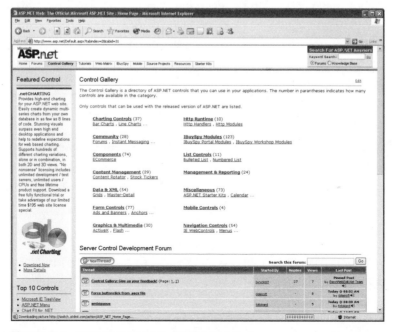

Figure 6-4   The www.asp.net site Control Gallery

Your assumption might be that this page could not be output cached because default.aspx can have different output that is determined by the parameters sent to it. However, this assumption *is totally incorrect* and the ability to vary the cache by request parameters is one of the unique advantages of the ASP.NET output cache. In fact, the ASP.NET page output cache supports several vary by options to support the scenario in which parameters or other data might affect how the page is to be cached.

Varying Cached Pages by Parameters

An output cached page can be varied by a number of different conditions. Internally, when the page output cache is varied, the cache stores different versions of the page in memory, for example, the ASP.NET output cache is capable of storing different contents for a single page by varying parameters:

```
http://www.asp.net/Default.aspx?tabindex=0&tabid=1
http://www.asp.net/Default.aspx?tabindex=5&tabid=42
http://www.asp.net/Default.aspx?tabindex=2&tabid=31
```

To support this scenario, we need to use the *VaryByParam* attribute, which we had previously set to *none*.

> **Important**   If *VaryByParam* is not used, why is it required and why is its value set to *none*? The decision was made to force the developer to add *VaryByParam* with a value of *none* to clearly indicate that the page was not varying by any parameters. Requests with parameters sent to an output cached page using *VaryByParam* with *none* will not be resolved by the output cache and are treated as misses.

```
<%@ OutputCache Duration="43200"
            VaryByParam="tabindex;tabid" %>
```

When you set the *VaryByParam* values to *tabindex* and *tabid*, the output cache will store and retrieve different versions of the requested page from cache, or execute the page if it is not found in the cache. This behavior is shown in Figure 6-5.

> **Note**   A single parameter can be specified, for example, *VaryByParam="tabindex"*. Multiple parameters to be varied by must be semicolon-separated, for example, *VaryByParam="tabindex;tabId"*.

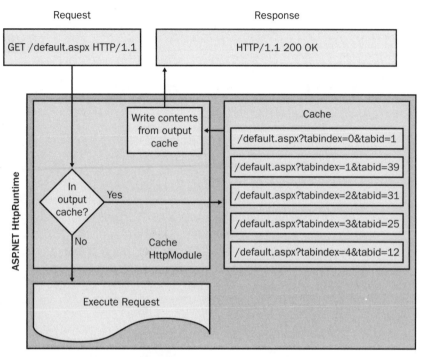

Figure 6-5   Cache in *HttpModule*

Multiple versions of the page reside in the cache, and if the requested version is found in the cache, the contents from the cache are sent back as the response. Otherwise, the request is executed normally as if it were not cached.

The *VaryByParam* attribute is powerful because it allows the developer to author a single page to be output cached, which can further be constrained by the parameters that affect how the page is to be displayed. Using *VaryBy-Param*, we can build highly specialized pages and still guarantee that we can take advantage of the output caching feature for increased performance.

> **Tip**   Varying the output cache by various parameters is very useful. However, here is a good rule of thumb to keep in mind: the more specific the request, the less likely it is that the request can be satisfied from the cache. For example, if the page's output is highly user-specific, for example, an e-commerce check-out page, the output cached page could only be utilized again by that same user in the same condition (in contrast to output caching the page used to display product information). When items are stored in the cache and cannot be utilized again, the cache is a wasted resource.

The *VaryByParam* attribute supports three settings:

- ***None***   Vary by no parameters. Requests with either a query string or *POST* parameters cannot be satisfied from the cache.

- ***[Param1]* or *[Param1;Param2]***   Parameter names are sent in either the query string or the *POST* body of the request. Multiple values are semicolon-separated.

- *******   This is a special option to vary by all parameters (vs. naming each parameter individually).

> **Tip**   Do not use *VaryByParam* with * unless absolutely necessary. Any arbitrary data passed in the query string or *POST* body will affect how many versions of the output cached page are created, potentially filling memory with many pages that can't be used again.

In addition to varying the cache by the query string or *POST* parameters, the output cache allows for two other vary by conditions:

- ***VaryByHeader***   Varies cache entries by HTTP headers
- ***VaryByCustom***   Varies cache entries by the browser type or by user code

Varying by HTTP headers

Varying the output cached result of a page based on parameters sent to the page is very powerful, but the page can also be varied by the HTTP headers that are available when the request is made.

When a desktop browser such as Microsoft Internet Explorer 6 makes an HTTP request for a resource stored on a Web server, the client sends several HTTP headers along with the request. Following are the applicable headers Internet Explorer 6 sends for a standard HTTP *GET* request:

- *Accept-Language*
- *User-Agent*
- *Cookies*

The *Accept-Language* header is used by the client to set the language that the client is using. In the case of my browser, the language set is EN-US, which means United States English. A request from the United Kingdom might be EN-GB, from France FR-FR, from Japan JP-JP, and so on.

Applications are often developed to support globalization and localization, that is, changing content or display based on the locale or language native to the user. Users can specify their language interactively through the application, such as selecting an option from a drop-down list, or the application can intelligently choose which language to use based on the *Accept-Language* client header.

The *www.asp.net* site does not support various languages, but if it did have its content stored in both French and Japanese, the site could still output cache its pages varying by the *tabindex* and *tabid* parameters and also varying by the *Accept-Language* header:

```
<%@ OutputCache Duration="43200"
                VaryByParam="tabindex;tabid"
                VaryByHeader="Accept-Language" %>
```

The total number of pages that can be stored in the output cache based on the current settings follows this formula:

```
[occurrences of tabindex] * [occurrences of tabid] * [Supported Languages]
```

As you can clearly see, the output cached version of the page is becoming more and more specific; also more and more entries must be kept in the cache. Keep in mind that an entry is created only after it is first requested, so if no requests are made for FR-FR, for example, no entry would appear in the cache.

The second HTTP header of interest, *User-Agent*, is used to identify the type of browser to the server, for example, the user agent string for Internet Explorer 6:

```
Mozilla/4.0 (compatible; MSIE 6.0; Windows NT 5.1; .NET CLR 1.0.3705)
```

> **Note**   If you have the .NET Framework installed and are using Internet Explorer, a *.NET CLR [version #]* string will be added as part of the *User-Agent* header. This can be useful for users who are downloading .NET applications because you can determine whether they also need to download the .NET Framework.

Earlier we said that the more specific the request, the less likely it is that the request will be satisfied from the cache. Constraints such as *Accept-Language* are common. We can expect multiple requests to specify EN-EN. However, many different browsers types (versioned by both major and minor version numbers), and in some cases the *User-Agent*, can contain even more data, such as which version of .NET Framework the client has installed. The cache varies by the entire contents of the header, so using *User-Agent* as a *Vary-ByHeader* option is a poor choice for varying by header since the value is unique.

However, just because using *VaryByHeader* with *User-Agent* is a bad choice for varying the output cached by browser type does not mean we can't vary by browser type! To vary by browser type, we use a special vary by option: *VaryByCustom*.

Varying by Browser Type

ASP.NET supports a rich server control model that allows developers to declaratively add programmable elements to their page using special XML tags. These server controls go through a life cycle, shown in Figure 6-6.

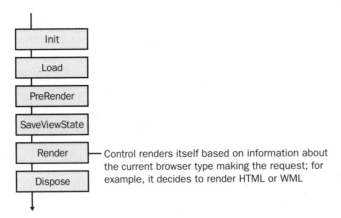

Figure 6-6   Server control rendering events

Server controls have an event life cycle and eventually render contents into the response stream to be sent back to the client. Part of this life cycle involves ASP.NET providing the server controls with information about the request, such as the type of browser, for example, Internet Explorer 6; or type of device, for example, a phone supporting WML. The server control then uses this information to determine what markup should be rendered.

For example, a server control might posses the ability to render standard HTML, DHTML, or WML based on the browser or device requesting the page that the control is used within. To successfully cache this page, we need to vary the output based on the type of device requesting the page. We already have this information in the *User-Agent* header, but we concluded that the *User-Agent* header is not a good vary-by candidate. Knowing this, and still wanting to vary by the browser type, a special *VaryByCustom* attribute was created.

The *VaryByCustom* attribute can be used to either vary the output cache entries by browser type and major version or allow the user to specify a custom vary by option. To vary by the browser type and major version, we simply specify the following:

```
<%@ OutputCache Duration="43200"
               VaryByParam="tabindex;tabid"
               VaryByHeader="Accept-Language"
               VaryByCustom="browser" %>
```

> **Tip**   Page output cache directives are additive, and you should plan to use more than just the required *VaryByParam* for pages containing server controls that behave differently for different browser types. Otherwise, inconsistencies will occur, as Internet Explorer DHTML could potentially be sent to a Netscape 4 browser (if the output cache is not being varied by browser type).

Varying By User-Defined Conditions

So far we've examined three distinct vary by options supported by the *Output-Cache* directive. It was our team's belief when designing this feature that the *OutputCache* directive would address the majority of output caching scenarios developers would face. However, one last piece of vary-by extensibility was added just in case we didn't cover all the scenarios: the ability to override the behavior of *VaryByCustom*.

VaryByCustom accepts a string, just as the other vary by conditions do. However, with *VaryByCustom*, we stated that if the string was *browser*, ASP.NET would vary the cache by browser type and major version. Under the covers, however, ASP.NET is calling a method in the output cache API:

```
virtual HttpCachePolicy.GetVaryByCustomString(HttpContext, string)
```

It is the responsibility of this method to perform the appropriate actions when *browser* is specified. However, this API is marked as *virtual* and thus can be overridden, allowing the developer to customize the output cache *VaryBy-Custom* behavior.

Overriding the default behavior of *VaryByCustom* means that we can vary by any custom condition. For example, we could vary our cache by browser minor version as well.

The following syntax is used when overriding *GetVaryByCustomString* in C#. This code could be within an *HttpModule* or within global.asax:

```
override public string GetVaryByCustomString(HttpContext context,
                                             String arg) {
    // Implementation
}
```

The following syntax is used when overriding *GetVaryByCustomString* in Microsoft Visual Basic .NET:

```
Overrides Public Function GetVaryByCustomString
                (context As HttpContext, arg As String) As String
    ' Implementation
End Function
```

When *GetVaryByCustomString* is overridden, ASP.NET uses the overridden method instead of the default implementation. The method accepts two parameters. The first is an instance of *HttpContext*, which contains all the details about the current request. The second parameter is the string value set in the *VaryByCustom OutputCache* directive.

To vary by a custom scenario, such as caching the page based only on the minor version of the requesting browser, you would use this code:

```
<%@ OutputCache Duration="60"
                VaryByParam="none"
                VaryByCustom="MinorVersion" %>
--- Page Content Here (not shown) ---
```

To vary by a custom scenario in global.asax, you would use this code:

```
<script runat="server" >
    override public string GetVaryByCustomString(
        HttpContext context, String arg) {
            string[] varyByArgs;
            string customVaryByString = null;

    // Assume the string follows a similar pattern
    // using a semi-colon as a separator.
    //
    varyByArgs = arg.Split(';');

    // Now process each string
    //
    foreach(string varyByArg in varyByArgs) {
        // Case each string separately
        //
        switch (varyByArg) {
            case "MinorVersion":
```

```
            return "minorVersion=" +
                context.Request.Browser.MinorVersion.ToString()
            break;
        }
    }
}
</script>
```

This code must reside either within global.asax or within an ASP.NET *Http-Module*, and *GetVaryByCustomString* must return a unique string value. The returned string value is used to create the key to the output cached page.

Controlling Where the Page Is Cached

The final *OutputCache* attribute, *Location*, is used to control who can cache a copy of the response generated by ASP.NET. It is shown in the next code snippet. Note that you are unlikely to use this attribute unless you are using other caching hardware within your network.

```
<%@ OutputCache Duration="43200"
                VaryByParam="none"
                Location="Client" %>
```

Valid values for *Location* are as follows:

- **Any**   Indicates that any downstream caching application is allowed to cache the generated response from ASP.NET. *Any* is the default value for *Location*.

- **Client**   Indicates that the browser can store the page in its local browser cache. When the user navigates using the Back and Forward buttons, the browser can satisfy these requests without a request to the server.

- **Downstream**   Indicates that downstream clients, such as browsers or proxy caches, can cache the document, however, the document is not cached by the server. This setting is useful when you want to guarantee that any requests to the origin server are generated dynamically. However, if the request was made through a proxy server, the proxy server has the first chance to satisfy the request.

- **Server**   Indicates that the response is cached only by the server and no downstream caching clients or proxies can cache the response. This setting is useful when you want to ensure cache consistency throughout the network by not allowing any proxy servers to cache the contents of the request.

- **None**   Indicates that only the page cannot be stored in any caches.

> **Tip**   Don't use the *Location* attribute unless you completely understand how it works. In the majority of cases, it is unnecessary.

Now that we've covered how to use page output caching through the *OutputCache* directive, let's examine how to use page output caching using the page output *Cache* APIs surfaced from *Response.Cache*.

Output Cache APIs

The page *OutputCache* directive, as stated earlier, should address 95 percent of your page caching needs. For the other 5 percent, the page output *Cache* API is used. The page output *Cache* API is incredibly powerful, albeit a bit more complex, and is surfaced through the *HttpCachePolicy* class in the System.Web.dll assembly in the *System.Web* namespace. An instance of this class is exposed as the *Cache* property on the *Response* class within the Page, that is, as *Response.Cache*.

Obviously the page output *Cache* API supports all the same capabilities offered by the page *OutputCache* directive. However, how these features are used is distinctly different. As demonstrated earlier, the *OutputCache* page directive code is equivalent to the output *Cache* API code. The output *Cache* API still requires you set an expiration (*Duration* in the *OutputCache* directive) for the time when the page is to be removed from the cache.

> **Tip**   Do not use the page *OutputCache* directive on a page that also uses the output *Cache* APIs. If used together, the more restrictive setting is applied. Thus, if the page *OutputCache* directive has a duration of 60 seconds but the output *Cache* API sets a duration of 30 seconds, the page will be cached for only 30 seconds. (The same is true of the other settings as well.)

Setting the Expiration

The page *OutputCache* directive allows us to set a *Duration* attribute to control how long the page's response can be stored in the cache before being expired. However, in the page *OutputCache* directive, this is always a sliding expiration—that is, the response expires from the time the page was requested plus the time in seconds specified in the *Duration* attribute. For example, if the *Duration* is 120 and the request for the page occurs at 11:29:03 PM, the page would expire at 11:31:03.

Our customers often request to have the output cached page expire at a fixed point in time. Although this is not possible using the page *OutputCache* directive, you can create a fixed expiration using the output *Cache* API.

SetExpires Method

The output *Cache* API exposes a single method for controlling how long a document is to be cached: *SetExpires*. (Note that the value set in the *SetExpires* method directly affects the value of the Expires HTTP header generated with the page.) The *SetExpires* method accepts a single parameter of type *DateTime* and returns *void*. To mirror a behavior similar to the *Duration* attribute in the *OutputCache* directive, we simply need to set this value using the *DateTime* class:

```
Response.Cache.SetExpires(DateTime.Now.AddSeconds(120));
```

This follows the same sliding expiration programming model that is the default for the page *OutputCache Duration* attribute. The document will expire at the current time plus 120 seconds.

We can additionally specify a fixed point in time, for example, invalidating the cached response at midnight:

```
Response.Cache.SetExpires(DateTime.Parse("12:00:00AM"));
```

This will instruct the cache to purge the response from the cache at exactly midnight. It doesn't matter whether the document is first requested at 8:00 AM or 11:59:59 PM, the cached page is guaranteed to be evicted at precisely the time specified.

> **Tip**   Sliding expiration is usually the recommended approach simply because setting all the pages to expire simultaneously, such as at midnight, would cause the server to re-execute all those pages at midnight, potentially putting an unnecessary load on the server.

Setting the Cacheability

The output *Cache* API also supports a way to configure how the output cached page behaves for downstream proxies or browsers that desire to cache the output. The *SetCacheability* method accepts a single parameter of type *HttpCacheability*. *HttpCacheability* is an enumeration that supports the values in Table 6-3.

Table 6-3   *HttpCacheability* Values

Member Name	Description
NoCache	Sets the HTTP *Cache-Control* header to *no-cache header* and indicates that only the server is allowed to cache a copy of the page. This is equivalent to *Location="none"* using the *Output-Cache* directive.
Private	Sets the HTTP *Cache-Control* header to *Private*. Indicates that only the client is allowed to cache the page in its browser cache. This is equivalent to *Location="Client"* using the *Out-putCache* directive.
Public	Sets the HTTP *Cache-Control* header to *Public*. Indicates that downstream clients, such as browsers or proxy caches, can cache the document, but the document is not cached by the server. This is equivalent to *Location="Downstream"* using the *OutputCache* directive. If not set, *Public* is the default.
Server	Sets the HTTP *Cache-Control* header to *Server*. Indicates that the response is cached only by the server and no downstream caching clients or proxies can cache the response. This is equivalent to *Location="Server"* using the *OutputCache* directive.
ServerAndNoCache	Sets the *Cache-Control* header to *no-cache* but allows the document to be cached on the server. The goal of this is to still allow programmatic output caching while sending the HTTP header *Expires: -1* to force the client to always pull a new copy from the server. This value is new in ASP.NET 1.1.
ServerAndPrivate	Sets the HTTP *Cache-Control* header to *Private* but still allows the response to be cached on the server. This value is new in ASP.NET.

Unfortunately, the page output *Cache* API gets more complicated when we want to accomplish vary by behavior. First we'll examine how the page output *Cache* API allows us to use vary by syntax, and then we'll examine some of the other unique capabilities of the page output *Cache* API.

Vary By Options with the Output Cache APIs

The behavior of varying by parameters is the same for both the *OutputCache* directive and the output *Cache* APIs; however, the syntax is different.

VaryByParams is a property of *HttpCachePolicy*. Programmatically this is accessed as follows:

```
Response.Cache.VaryByParams["[string]"] = [true/false];
```

Using the example we examined earlier of the *http://www.asp.net* site with the *tabindex* and *tabid* query string or *POST* parameters, the page output *Cache* APIs would look as follows:

```
Response.Cache.VaryByParams ["tabindex"] = true;
Response.Cache.VaryByParams["tabid"] = true;
```

To vary by headers, we use the *VaryByHeaders* property, which has a similar syntax to *VaryByParams*:

```
Response.Cache.VaryByHeaders["Accept-Language"] = true;
```

This syntax is very unlike the *OutputCache* directive that allows us to specify these items in a semicolon-separated list. However, the end result is the same.

> **Tip**   Setting the Boolean value to *true* for *VaryByParams* or *VaryBy-Headers* indicates that the output cache is to be varied by the parameter or header. Programmatically, you can decide not to vary by that particular parameter or header later in the processing of the page execution, and *false* could be set to indicate this behavior.

Varying by Browser

Varying the output cached page by browser type by passing in the *browser* string can still be accomplished using the output *Cache* APIs. However, unlike the other vary by options, this method is virtual:

```
Response.Cache.SetVaryByCustom("browser");
```

This method can be overridden, as you learned earlier in this chapter.

Honoring or Ignoring Cache Invalidation Headers

One last method shown in all the code samples that deserves some attention is the *SetValidUntilExpires* method. The default behavior of the page *Output-Cache* directive and the output *Cache* APIs is not identical due solely to the existence of the *SetValidUntilExpires* method. The *SetValidUntilExpires* method controls a nuance of how the ASP.NET page output cache honors the HTTP cache invalidation headers.

Cache invalidation headers are sent by browsers, such as Internet Explorer, Netscape, and Opera. Browsers send HTTP headers for certain browser actions such as when the Refresh button is clicked. When the Refresh button is clicked, the browser sends instructions with its HTTP request, effectively stating that any cached versions of the document being requested are not to be served from any cache.

Sample Browser/Web Server Session

Let's take a look at a sample browser/Web server HTTP session with *http://www.asp.net* (only the client headers are shown). Here is the initial request:

```
GET http://www.asp.net/ HTTP/1.0
Accept-Language: en-us
User-Agent: Mozilla/
4.0 (compatible; MSIE 6.0; Windows NT 5.1; .NET CLR 1.0.3705)
Host: www.asp.net
Proxy-Connection: Keep-Alive
```

This is the code generated when the Refresh button is clicked in the browser:

```
GET http://www.asp.net/ HTTP/1.0
Accept-Language: en-us
Pragma: no-cache
User-Agent: Mozilla/
4.0 (compatible; MSIE 6.0; Windows NT 5.1; .NET CLR 1.0.3705)
Host: www.asp.net
Proxy-Connection: Keep-Alive
```

The important HTTP header relevant for caching sent by the client is *Pragma: no-cache*. This HTTP header indicates that the origin server is to be contacted and the page requested anew. The goal of this HTTP header is to ensure that in complex caching scenarios, where caching hardware potentially has invalid copies of the requested page, the client can override any cached versions of the page and re-request the document from the server that originally created the page.

> **Note**   The *Pragma: no-cache* HTTP header is not officially an HTTP version 1 behavior and is replaced in HTTP 1.1 with the *Cache-Control* header. However, like many characteristics of HTTP, the standard is only loosely followed. Nearly all browsers still use *Pragma: no-cache* and thus ASP.NET must know how to process it.

When *SetValidUntilExpires* is *false*, the *Pragma: no-cache* browser headers invalidate the output cached page from ASP.NET's cache because ASP.NET honors HTTP cache invalidation headers. When *SetValidUntilExpires* is *true*,

ASP.NET ignores the request to invalidate the page output cache, keeping the output cached page in memory.

> **Tip**   When using the page output *Cache* APIs, always set *SetValid-UntilExpires* to *true* unless you want clients to be able to remove your output cached pages from memory. The output cache is a performance enhancement, and if clients can arbitrarily remove pages from the cache, performance suffers.

When you use the page output *Cache* APIs and *SetValidUntilExpires* is not specified, the method defaults to *false*. Conversely, when using the page *OutputCache* directive, *SetValidUntilExpires* defaults to *true!* (In fact, you cannot control the behavior of *SetValidUntilExpires* using the page *OutputCache* directive.)

Although the default between the two is inconsistent, the belief is that it is more common to want the page to remain in cache when using the page *OutputCache* directive. However, when using the page output *Cache* APIs, more consistency with HTTP cache semantics is the default.

> **Note**   Why have differing default behaviors for the page *OutputCache* directive and the page output *Cache* API? The HTTP specification mandates that documents with HTTP *GET* (querystring) or *POST* parameters not be cached. However, we felt that the developers writing the application were more qualified to decide whether the page should be cached. Most developers desire the document to remain in the cache when that behavior is specified, rather than allow a client browser to evict the page from the output cache by simply refreshing the page in the browser.

Thus, to mirror the behavior of the *OutputCache* directive that caches a document for 60 seconds, we need to—at a minimum—specify the following:

```
Response.Cache.SetExpires(DateTime.Now.AddMinutes(60));
Response.Cache.SetValidUntilExpires(true);
```

> **Note** Several additional methods are supported by the page output *Cache* API but are not covered in this book. Many of these have more to do with the nuances of HTTP cache behaviors than caching content, and thus are rarely used by most developers. For more information about these APIs, the product documentation provides excellent coverage.

Deterministically Serving Pages from the Cache

Now that we've discussed achieving parity behavior with the *OutputCache* directive, let's look at some of the APIs offered only by *Response.Cache*:

- Validation callback

- Dependencies

- Programmatically removing output cached pages

- *SetAllowResponseInBrowserHistory* method

We can deterministically serve pages from the cache by utilizing a less-known feature of the page output cache API: validation callbacks. A *validation callback* allows us to wire in some code that is called before an output cached page can be served from the output cache. This wire-up is done using the *Response.Cache.AddValidationCallback* method and allows us to specify a delegate method that will be called through.

The delegate method must follow the method prototype defined by the *HttpCacheValidateHandler* constructor:

```
public void Validate(HttpContext context,
                Object data,
                out HttpValidationStatus status) {

}
```

We can then wire up the delegate by specifying the *Validate* method as the parameter of the *Response.Cache.AddValidationCallback* method:

```
public void Page_Load(Object sender, EventArgs e) {
    Response.Cache.SetExpires(DateTime.Now.AddSeconds(60));
    Response.Cache.SetCacheability(HttpCacheability.Public);
    Response.Cache.SetValidUntilExpires(true);
    Response.Cache.AddValidationCallback(Validate);
}
```

Now whenever the page is served from cache, the *Validate* method is called through. Within the method, we can perform the necessary logic to determine whether the requested page is still valid. We simply need to set the *status out* parameter to one of three possible values of the *HttpValidationStatus* enumeration:

■ **IgnoreThisRequest**   Leave the output cached page in the cache and execute the page.

■ **Invalid**   Remove the output cached page from the cache and execute the page.

■ **Valid**   Serve the request from the output cache.

For example, if we were running a reporting service that provided time-critical information, we might decide that we never serve cached content to paying customers, but to anonymous customers, we always serve from the cache when it's available. Here's the validation callback method:

```
public void Validate(HttpContext context,
                     Object data,
                     out HttpValidationStatus status) {

    // Is the request from an anonymous user?
    //
    if (!context.Request.IsAuthenticated) {
        status = HttpValidationStatus.Valid;
        return;
    }

    // Request must be from a paying customer
    //
    status = HttpValidationStatus.IgnoreThisRequest;

}
```

This code checks the *Request.IsAuthenticated* property to determine whether an authenticated user is making a request. (An authenticated user is one who is signed in; we would likely want to base this authenticated user status on a user role in your actual program.) If the request is not authenticated, the request can be served from the cache. If the request is authenticated, we guarantee that the page requested is executed while leaving the output cached version in memory.

Removing Pages with Dependencies from the Cache

As it applies to page output caching, dependencies allow us to remove output cached pages when external but related dependent items change. For example, the output cached page is automatically made dependent upon the file or files used to create it, including the page (.aspx file) as well as any associated user controls or include files. If any of these files change, the output cached page is automatically removed from the cache. (We'll look more at dependencies later in this chapter when we examine the *Cache* API.)

In many cases, it is desirable to make pages dependent upon other files or other types of resources. You can do this by using APIs found on the *Response* object:

```
AddFileDependencies(ArrayList filenames)
AddFileDependency(string filename)
AddCacheItemDependencies(ArrayList cacheKeys)
AddCacheItemDependency(string cacheKey)
```

> **Note** In version 2 of ASP.NET, we'll add a *AddCacheDependency* method to allow you to add an instance of *CacheDependency* directly.

The first set of APIs allow the output cached page to be made dependent upon any file. For example, if the page relies on several XML files used as persistent data stores, the output cached page could be made dependent upon these files:

```
public void Page_Load(Object sender, EventArgs e) {

    // Make dependent upon files
    ArrayList files = new ArrayList();
    files.Add(HttpServer.MapPath("Products.xml"));
    files.Add(HttpServer.MapPath("Customers.xml"));
    files.Add(HttpServer.MapPath("Sales.xml"));

    // Setup to output cache this page
    Response.AddFileDependencies(files);
    Response.Cache.SetExpires(DateTime.Now.AddSeconds(60));
    Response.Cache.SetCacheability(HttpCacheability.Public);
    Response.Cache.SetValidUntilExpires(true);
}
```

If any of these files change, the page is evicted from the output cache.

> **Note**   No race condition exists when creating a dependency. If the dependent item changes before the item is inserted into the cache, the insert fails and the item is not added to the cache.

> **Tip**   If the page you are output caching relies upon file resources other than those used to execute the page, use the output *Cache* APIs and make the page dependent upon those files. If the files change, the output cached page will be evicted from the output cache.

Another, more powerful, technique is to make the output cached page dependent upon other cache entries. If these other cache entries change, the output cached page is evicted from the output cache. This approach is more powerful because a relationship can be made between multiple cached items. For example, an item can be added programmatically to the cache and a page can then be made dependent upon it. This code snippet stores some product details:

```
public void Page_Load(Object sender, EventArgs e) {

    if (Cache["ProductDetails"] == null) {

        // Store product details in the Cache API
        DataSet ds = GetProductDetails();

        Cache["ProductDetails"] = ds;
    }
}
```

The second bit of code depends on the first:

```
public void Page_Load(Object sender, EventArgs e) {

    // Setup to output cache this page
    Response.Cache.SetExpires(DateTime.Now.AddSeconds(60));
    Response.Cache.VaryByParam["ProductId"] = true;
    Response.Cache.SetCacheability(HttpCacheability.Public);
    Response.Cache.SetValidUntilExpires(true);

    // Make dependent upon ProductDetails cache entry
    // if it exists
    //
```

```
if (Cache["ProductDetails"] != null)
    Response.AddCacheItemDependency("ProductDetails");

}
```

The first snippet stores a *DataSet* in the *Cache* using the key *ProductDetails*. The second snippet is then made dependent upon the *"ProductDetails"* cache entry if it exists.

Cache key dependencies allow you to build cascading removal of entries in the cache, as shown in Figure 6-7. In the figure, there are three cached *DataSets* and three cached pages. If the *SalesReport* cache entry were changed or removed, all dependent entries would be removed. However, if the *Products* cache entry were changed or removed, only the cache entries dependent upon *Products* would also be removed.

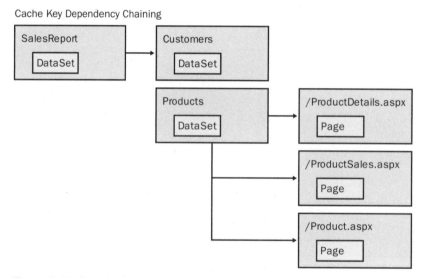

Cache Key Dependency Chaining

Figure 6-7 A cache key dependency relationship

> **Tip** Use cache key dependencies where caching is used to enforce behaviors throughout your application. Dependencies do have additional overhead, but for scenarios such as those described thus far, dependencies allow for some powerful behaviors. For example, every page could theoretically be dependent upon a common cache key. When an administrator wanted to flush the cache, she would simply need to invalidate the common key. This would then evict all output cached pages from memory.

Programmatically Removing Output Cached Pages

It is possible to force the eviction of any output cached page using the static *HttpResponse.RemoveOutputCacheItem* method. This little-known method allows for easy removal of any output cached page. For example, if we wanted to evict the output cached page /Products/ProductDetail.aspx, we could simply call the following:

```
HttpResponse.RemoveOutputCacheItem("/Products/ProductDetail.aspx");
```

This would evict the named page (and all of its associated pages) from the ASP.NET output cache.

> **Tip**   The technique we just described works well in a single server environment. In a Web farm environment, however, the static method *HttpResponse.RemoveOutputCacheItem* would need to be called on each server since the cache is not shared.

Controlling Whether the Page Can Live in the Browser's History

Here is a new method added in ASP.NET 1.1:

```
Response.Cache.SetAllowResponseInBrowserHistory
```

This API allows the page developer to control whether the output cached page can be stored in the browser's history, for example, when you navigate using the browser's Back and Forward buttons.

The default value is *true*, meaning that the browser can store the output cached page in browser history, honoring the value set in the HTTP *Expires* header. However, if the value is set to *false*, ASP.NET will set the HTTP *Expires* header to *-1*. The *Expires: -1* setting simply tells the browser that any request for the page must be directed back to the server because the page does not have a future expiration value.

SetAllowResponseInBrowserHistory is a method that allows you to ensure that the browser can never cache a version of the page in the browser's history. This is useful for scenarios in which data, such as stock quote information, can change significantly.

Caching Parts of the Page

Output caching the contents of a page is very powerful but not always possible. For example, in many cases, content (such as advertisements or user-specific information) must be dynamic. Page output caching can't be used in these scenarios, so ASP.NET supports partial page caching technology, which allows only part of the page output to be cached.

Partial page caching allows for regions of a page to be cached while other regions are executed dynamically. The ASP.NET control gallery (found at *http://www.asp.net*), shown in Figure 6-8, is an example. Areas within Figure 6-8 that are grayed-out represent content that is output cached; areas that are not grayed-out represent areas that are not output cached.

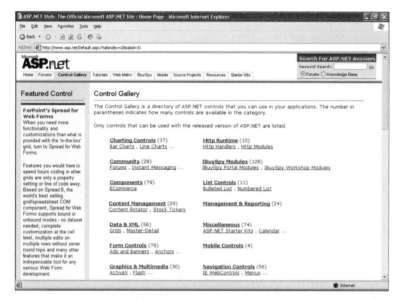

Figure 6-8 The ASP.NET control gallery, with only some content output cached

As you can clearly see, a lot of content is cached, but a large percentage of the content is also not cached. Content that can be shared for multiple users, such as top 10 lists, featured controls, or the list of the available controls, are not cached. However, content that is personalized, such as the displayed tabs or the discussion forum, are rendered dynamically on each request.

This ability to partially cache content on the page is incredibly useful because we can still derive the benefits of not doing unnecessary work on each request. Partial page caching employs user controls to divide regions of the page. In Figure 6-8, the page is divided into several user controls, each identified within a black-bordered rectangle.

User controls, which are server controls, are best thought of as pages that can be reused in other pages. For example, you can think of the Top 10 Controls as a stand-alone page capable of displaying just this data. This page can then be composed with other pages to present a single unified view. User controls use the special extension .ascx, and nearly all user control can have their extension renamed to .aspx and run as normal pages. The beauty of user controls is that they are programmed in a way that is similar to programming pages, but they can be reused as server controls by other pages. Code Listings 6-1 and 6-2 represent the source code to the 10 Ten Controls user control from the *http://www.asp.net* Control Gallery.

Code Listing 6-1   MostPopularControls.ascx

```
<%@ Control language="C#" EnableViewState="false" %>
<%@ OutputCache Duration="60" VaryByParam="none" %>
<%@ Import Namespace="System.Data" %>
<%@ Import Namespace="System.Data.SqlClient" %>
<script runat="server">
    public void Page_Load(Object sender, EventArgs e) {
        SqlConnection connection;
        SqlCommand command;

        // Initialize connection and command
        connection = new SqlConnection([connection string]);
        command = new SqlCommand("CG_Top10Controls", connection);
        command.CommandType = CommandType.StoredProcedure;

        connection.Open();
        ControlList.DataSource = command.ExecuteReader();
        ControlList.DataBind();
        connection.Close();

    }
</script>

<span class="normal">
Below are the top 10 most popular controls today.
</span>
<p>
<asp:datalist id="ControlList" runat="server" class="Normal" >
    <itemtemplate>
        <li>
            <a href="/ControlGallery/
ControlDetail.aspx?control=<%# DataBinder.Eval(Container.DataItem, "Id") %>&t
abindex=2"><%# DataBinder.Eval(Container.DataItem, "Name") %></a>
    </itemtemplate>
</asp:datalist>
```

Code Listing 6-2   Page Using a User Control

```
<%@ Register TagPrefix="ControlGallery"
             TagName="MostPopular"
             Src="MostPopularControls.ascx" %>
<Font size=3>Top 10 Controls</Font>
<ControlGallery:MostPopular id="MostPopular1" runat=server />
```

To enable the partial page output caching feature, we simply add output cache directives to the user control instead of to the page. For example, to output cache the Top 10 Control list, we simply add the following directive to the MostPopularControls.ascx user control:

```
<%@ OutputCache Duration="60" VaryByParam="none" %>
```

When the page is requested, ASP.NET builds what is known as a *control tree*. The page is the top node, and controls are added in order beneath the appropriate parent controls, as shown in Figure 6-9. In the figure, the literal content *<Font size=3>Top 10 Controls</Font>* is stored in a literal control, and the user control is stored as a *UserControl*.

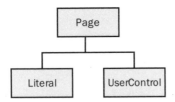

Figure 6-9   Control tree

When a user control is found that supports caching, ASP.NET does a bit of trickery whereby it inserts a special control, shown in the following code and in Figure 6-10.

```
System.Web.UI.PartialCachingControl
```

In Figure 6-10, the *UserControl* that is marked as output cached is replaced with a *PartialCachingControl*. When the control tree is created, the *Partial-CachingControl* retrieves it's output from the cache. If the output is not found, the original user control is rendered and the contents are added to the cache.

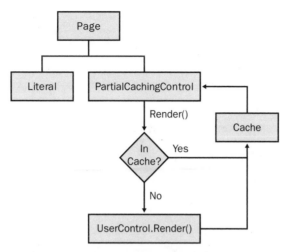

Figure 6-10   Control tree with *PartialCachingControl*

This control is inserted into the control tree where the output cached control should be. The *PartialCachingControl* represents a cached view of the user control. If the *PartialCachingControl* finds contents in the cache for the user control, it uses that as its output; otherwise, it calls *Render* on the user control, stores its contents in the cache for subsequent use, and then renders itself.

Although this scenario sounds complex, the good news is that programming partial page output caching feels very similar to programming page output caching. The bad news is that partial page output caching supports only page directives and has no programmatic API.

Partial page output caching does support two concepts not found in the output cache directives for pages:

- Varying by control state
- Shared user control cache entries

Varying By Control State

Partial page caching supports the concept of varying by parameters using the standard vary-by syntax, which allows the output cached user control to vary its content by HTTP *GET* (querystring) or HTTP *POST* parameters:

```
<%@ OutputCache Duration="60" VaryByParam="tabindex" %>
```

However, user controls can also participate within a *<form runat="server" />*, whereby the user control might contain an input element, such as a drop-down list, which can be posted back to the server. For example, when using the Control Gallery at *http://www.asp.net*, you can view multiple control summaries simultaneously, such as Form Controls, as shown in Figure 6-11.

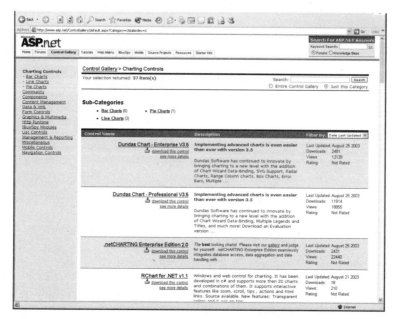

Figure 6-11 Viewing multiple control summaries simultaneously

The display in Figure 6-11 is an output-cached user control and by default is shown filtered by *Date Last Updated*. However, when the user filters by a different option, such as *Most Downloads*, the list re-sorts itself according to this new criteria. This newly filtered output is also served from the cache.

However, no *VaryByParam* option is used, because the name of the parameter that is sent via *HTTP POST* cannot be easily deduced. (The name of the control cannot be easily deduced because it is a subcontrol of *<form/>*, which is a naming container and prepends information to contained control IDs so that it can uniquely identify controls within that naming container.) Instead, the *VaryByControl* option is used, naming the control to vary by. In this case the control is a *DropDownList* control with an ID of *FilterControls*:

```
<% OutputCache Duration="600"
            VaryByParam="none"
            VaryByControl="FilterControls" %>

<asp:DropDownList ID="FilterControls" runat="server" >

</asp:DropDownList>
```

When the control is rendered in the browser, its name value is as follows:

```
<select name="_ctl2:ControlList:_ctl0:FilterControls" >
```

When the control is posted back to the server, it won't be named *FilterControls*. If we attempt to specify *VaryByParam="FilterControls"*, we wouldn't get the desired behavior—since that's not the control's name!

Rather, the *VaryByControl* is simply aware of how the name of the contained controls is changed to guarantee uniqueness within the page. So instead of having to decode the name, we can rely upon the *VaryByControl* attribute to give us the correct behavior.

> **Tip**   Don't use *VaryByParam="*"*, which would also resolve to an unknown *HTTP POST* parameter name. Instead use the *VaryByControl* option.

Shared User Control Cache Entries

In ASP.NET 1.0, the user control caching model created a separate entry in the cache for each use of a user control. Thus, if the same cached user control is used to generate a navigation menu and it is used on 50 pages, 50 entries would appear in the cache for this user control.

In ASP.NET 1.1, we added a new *Shared* attribute that can be specified in the directive. This attribute instructs ASP.NET to share any instances of the user control rather than create new entries in the cache for each control. In ASP.NET 1.1, then, you could specify the following:

```
<%@ OutputCache Duration="60" VaryByParam="none" Shared="true" %>
```

This directive instructs ASP.NET to share the cached version of the control across all pages.

Cache and the Application API

The output cache and partial page output cache both rely upon common infrastructure for their storage of output cached data. This common infrastructure is the *Cache* API, which is responsible for managing dependencies and the memory used by all caching features.

The *Cache* API is a dictionary-based API, which means we can use string keys to set and retrieve items similar to *Session* or *Application*. If you are familiar with programming *Session* or *Application*, you will understand the *Cache* API. For example, to store a *DataSet* in *Session*, *Application*, and *Cache*, you would use the code in Code Listing 6-3.

Code Listing 6-3   Session, Application, and Cache

```
// Name a common key
string key = "ProductsKey";

// Use some custom business logic class to create the DataSet
//
DataSet products = ProductsDB.GetProductsDataSet();

// Store in the user's Session - available on for this user
//
Session[key] = products;

//·Store in Application and Cache - available to entire application
//
Application[key] = products;
Cache[key] = products;
```

Storing the *products DataSet* in *Session* stores a copy of the *DataSet* for each user for which that *Session[key]* is called. Additionally, as we discussed in Chapter 5, you can configure *Session* such that all servers in the Web farm have access to a common session store.

> **Note** We're using a *DataSet* for consistency in the sample code. If you are using out-of-process *Session*, store only as little information as is required. Storing an entire *DataSet* for each user can get expensive quickly, especially if you have a very active site.

Storing the *products DataSet* in *Application* or *Cache* stores a copy of the *DataSet* for all users in the memory space of the current application (this data is isolated from any other running applications)—if the user browses to another server in the server farm, that server has the responsibility to either execute code or fetch the item from its *Cache* or *Application*. An item stored in *Cache* or *Application* is not replicated between servers in the server farm, and neither of these features supports an out-of-process mode similar to *Session*.

> **Note**   Why doesn't ASP.NET provide a common *Application* or *Cache* out-of-process option similar to *Session*? Unlike *Session*, which is tied to a specific user, *Application* and *Cache* contain application-wide settings that apply, or are available to, all users. Thus, changes to *Application* or *Cache* must be propagated immediately. However, there are several problems with this: managing contentions when two applications simultaneously modify the same data; and decreased efficiency with replication—as the number of servers grows, the data gets exponentially more difficult to replicate between servers.

Deciding to Use *Cache* or *Application*

Application and *Cache* both store data locally in the memory of the running application. Both, in effect, provide identical functionality. So the question is which to use. It is recommended that any time you need to store application-wide data, use *Cache* instead of *Application*.

> **Note**   *Cache* supersedes all the functionality provided by *Application* and both simplifies it (because it requires no locking to modify) and provides more advanced functionality (such as expiration, dependencies, and purging of data when necessary). This chapter does not contain any direct discussion of *Application*. *Application* exists primarily for backward compatibility with Microsoft Active Server Pages, or ASP.

Here is a summary of *Cache* functionality:

- Automatic eviction of infrequently used items
- Pinning items in the cache to prevent automatic eviction
- Method callback when an item is removed from the cache
- Cache dependencies to control evictions

What to Store in the Cache

We commonly are asked, "what should be stored in the cache?" The answer really depends on what the application is doing. Common objects such as *DataSets* are excellent objects to store in the cache because they can be used as is for data binding and other scenarios. Any custom class that represents data is also a good candidate. Take a look at the source code for the ASP.NET Forums (*http://www.asp.net/Forums/*). We have business classes that represent forums, forum groups, threads, posts, and so on, many of which are stored and retrieved from the cache for anonymous user requests—for known users we don't cache, but for anonymous users we do cache.

We should also address what should not be stored in the cache. An item such as a *DataReader* is an excellent example of what should *not* be stored in the cache. A *DataSet* and a *DataReader* are both classes provided by ADO.NET and used for working with data. A *DataSet* is a disconnected snapshot of the data, whereas a *DataReader* holds a cursor in the database. A *DataReader* shouldn't be stored in the cache since the *DataReader* has an open connection to the database. Storing a reference to a *DataReader* instance would keep that connection open, and keeping the connection open prevents it from being sent back to the connection pool. Eventually, all available connections would be used and you would start to get exceptions.

Setting and Retrieving Values from the *Cache*

Adding and retrieving items from the cache is easy. You can accomplish both in several ways, the most common of which is using the dictionary-style API, shown in Code Listing 6-4.

Code Listing 6-4   Cache Dictionary API

```
// Name a common key
string key = "ProductsKey";

// Use some custom business logic class to create the DataSet
DataSet products = ProductsDB.GetProductsDataSet();

// Add the DataSet to the Cache
Cache[key] = products;

// Get a DataSet 'products' from the Cache
DataSet ds = (DataSet) Cache[key];
```

In addition to using the dictionary-style API, which is easy to work with but doesn't present the full capabilities of the cache, you can store items in the cache using two methods: *Insert* and *Add*.

You use these methods slightly differently. The *Insert* method stores an item in the cache and replaces an existing named item if it already exists. The *Add* method stores an item in the cache but doesn't replace an existing item.

Inserting an Object into the *Cache*

The *Insert* method is overloaded and has four signatures.

■   `Insert(string key, object value)`

■   `Insert(string key, object value, CacheDependency dependency)`

■   `Insert(string key, object value,`
`            CacheDependency dependency,`
`            DateTime absoluteExpiration,`
`            TimeSpan slidingExpiration)`

■   `Insert(string key, object value,`
`            CacheDependency dependency,`
`            DateTime absoluteExpiration,`
`            TimeSpan slidingExpiration,`
`            CacheItemPriority priority,`
`            CacheItemRemovedCallback callback)`

The *Insert(string key, object value)* overload is identical in behavior to the dictionary-style API. It accepts a key or a name of the cache item to add as well as an object type for the item to store.

Inserting an item with a dependency into the cache   The second *Insert* method implementation also accepts a *CacheDependency* parameter This parameter indicates that the item added to the cache will be dependent upon external conditions. When these external conditions change, the item is automatically removed from the cache. These external conditions are configured through the *CacheDependency* class.

The *CacheDependency* class is used to make *Cache* entries dependent upon either files or other cache entries. An instance of this class is created using one of the eight constructors it supports:

■   `CacheDependency(string filename)`

■   `CacheDependency(string[] filenames)`

■   `CacheDependency(string filename, DateTime start)`

- ■ `CacheDependency(string[] filenames, DateTime start)`

- ■ `CacheDependency(string[] filenames, string[] cachekeys)`

- ■ `CacheDependency(string[] filenames,`
         `string[] cachekeys, DateTime start)`

- ■ `CacheDependency(string[] filenames,`
         `string[] cachekeys,`
         `CacheDependency dependency)`

- ■ `CacheDependency(string[] filenames,`
         `string[] cachekeys,`
         `CacheDependency dependency, DateTime start)`

Using the constructors in the preceding list, we can create *CacheDependency* objects for a file or files. Here is the code for file dependency with a single file:

```
// Create the dependency
CacheDependency c = new CacheDependency(Server.MapPath("products.xml"));

// Insert into the Cache
Cache.Insert("products", productsDataSet, c);
```

Here is the code for multiple file dependency:

```
// Create the files we are dependent upon
String[] files = new String[2];
files[0] = Server.MapPath("products.xml");
files[1] = Server.MapPath("sales.xml");

// Create the dependency
CacheDependency c = new CacheDependency(files);

// Insert into the Cache
Cache.Insert("products", productsDataSet, c);
```

In addition to monitoring files, we can create *CacheDependency* objects for existing *Cache* keys. Dependencies that reply upon existing *Cache* entries are very powerful because we can essentially extend the cache to support a dependency of our choice. For example, when a manager updates the sales history, we can remove the *Sales* cache item, which can remove related and dependent items through cascading. Following is an example single key dependency:

```
// Keys we are dependent upon
String[] keys = new String[1];
keys[0] = "Sales";
```

```
// Create the dependency
CacheDependency c = new CacheDependency(null, keys);
```

```
// Insert into the Cache
Cache.Insert("products", productsDataSet, c);
```

Here is an example of code for multiple key dependency:

```
// Keys we are dependent upon
String[] keys = new String[2];
keys[0] = "Sales";
keys[1] = "Products";
```

```
// Create the dependency
CacheDependency c = new CacheDependency(null, keys);
```

```
// Insert into the Cache
Cache.Insert("products", productsDataSet, c);
```

We can also specify when we want monitoring of the files to start by using the *DateTime start* parameter:

```
// Create the dependency
CacheDependency c = new CacheDependency(Server.MapPath("products.xml"),
                                        DateTime.Now.AddSeconds(15));
```

```
// Insert into the Cache
Cache.Insert("products", productsDataSet, c);
```

Delayed monitoring of the file for changes is a nice feature—since we know that operations on the file will occur within a certain period of time, we can delay any removal from cache until past the time specified.

Lastly, *CacheDependency* also provides a way to aggregate a new dependency with an existing dependency. Aggregate dependency basically means this: "The following dependency is dependent upon these conditions plus the included existing dependency." Aggregate dependency is shown here:

```
// ... early in the code execution
// Create the dependency
CacheDependency d = new CacheDependency(Server.MapPath("products.xml"),
                                        DateTime.Now.AddSeconds(15));
```

```
// ... later in the code execution
// Keys we are dependent upon
String[] keys = new String[1];
keys[0] = "Sales";
```

```
// Create the key dependency
CacheDependency c = new CacheDependency(null, keys, d);
```

```
// Insert into the Cache
Cache.Insert("products", productsDataSet, c);
```

Removing items from the *Cache* at a point in time   The fourth overloaded *Insert* method allows us to control time-based eviction of items from the cache using a *DateTime* parameter and a *TimeSpan* parameter:

```
Insert(string key, object value,
               CacheDependency dependency,
               DateTime absoluteExpiration,
               TimeSpan slidingExpiration)
```

Scavenger hints and the removal callback   The final overloaded method for *Insert* lets us set a *CacheItemPriority* parameter and a *CacheItemRemovedCallback* parameter:

```
Insert(string key, object value,
               CacheDependency dependency,
               DateTime absoluteExpiration,
               TimeSpan slidingExpiration,
               CacheItemPriority priority,
               CacheItemRemovedCallback callback)
```

The *CacheItemPriority* parameter allows us to instruct the cache as to which priority the inserted item should receive. For example, underused items within the *Cache* with a low priority are the first to be evicted when ASP.NET is under memory pressure. *CacheItemPriority* is an enumeration. Its values are shown in Table 6-4, in order of precedence:

Table 6-4   *CacheItemPriority* Values, in Priority Order

Member Name	Description
Low	First items to be removed.
BelowNormal	Items that are removed after low priority items.
Normal	Default priority when the priority is not specified. This is the default used by output caching.
AboveNormal	More important than regular items.
High	Last items to be removed.
NotRemovable	Items that cannot be removed. Don't use this option unless you are fully confident that the item has to remain in memory no matter what load the server is under. Configuration data is a good example for this value.

How should these priorities be used? If you have multiple, large, but easily created items stored in the cache, assigning them a *Low* priority would ensure that the items would be the first evicted. Conversely, if you had an item that was small but very expensive to create, you would want to assign it a *High* priority so that it would be evicted only under extreme circumstances.

The last parameter of *Insert* is an instance of *CacheItemRemovedcallback*. It allows us to pass in a delegate method that is called when an item is removed from the cache.

Finally, for items that should never be removed from the cache—and to mirror the behavior of *Application*—use the *NotRemovable* value. Items added to the cache with *NotRemovable* will not be removed from the cache unless code is used to remove them, or they have a dependency that is enforced.

Add Method

The *Add* method accepts the same parameters as the last overloaded *Insert* method. The only difference is that *Insert* always replaces an existing *Cache* item and has no return value, and *Add* will not only insert an item into the cache if it doesn't already exist but also return the item from the cache.

Removing Items from the Cache

Entries within the cache can be removed by using the *Remove* method:

```
// Remove a key named 'products'
Cache.Remove("products");
```

Static Application Variables

The *Cache* is the recommended location to store frequently used application data. However, using static application variables is another technique for efficiently storing frequently used data. An ASP.NET application consists of files and resources authored by you, and files and resources provided by ASP.NET. One of the characteristics of ASP.NET is that it truly is an application in the sense that there are application-level events and methods such as those defined in global.asax or in instances of *HttpModule*, and that we can also define application-level static variables.

A static variable, as related to object-oriented programming, is a variable shared by all instances of a class. For example, suppose you authored an ASP.NET page that defined a static variable:

```
static string backgroundColor = "blue";
```

All instances of that page would share the same string vs. creating their own copies of the string. The same concept can be applied to the entire application.

For example, if we populate a *DataSet* to store all the URLs used in our site, we could perform this work within global.asax when the application starts:

```
<script runat="server">
public void Application_OnStart (Object sender, EventArgs e) {

    // Get the dataset from our custom business object
    DataSet siteUrls = SiteUrls.GetSiteURLs();

    // Store the dataset in the cache to never expire
    //
    Cache.Insert("SiteURLs",
                siteUrls,
                DateTime.MaxValue,
                TimeSpan.Zero,
                CacheItemPriority.NotRemovable,
                null);
}
</script>
```

We could then request this *DataSet* from anywhere within our application:

```
DataSet siteUrls = (DataSet) Cache["SiteURLs"];
```

Easy enough, right? Yes, and no. Every time we fetch the item, we're incurring a hashtable lookup and casting to the correct data type.

An alternative approach to handling this problem would be to define a static application variable, as shown in the following code. (This is only one alternative. You will get no noticeable performance gains or other improvements from using this technique instead of using the cache.)

```
<%@ Application Classname="MyApplication" %>
<script runat="server">
static DataSet siteUrls;

public void Application_OnStart (Object sender, EventArgs e) {

    // Get the dataset from our custom business object
    // and assign to the static application variable
    siteUrls = SiteUrls.GetSiteURLs();

}

</script>
```

Notice that we made a few changes to the global.asax file. We added a static variable *siteUrls* of type *DataSet*, set the *Classname* attribute of the *Application* directive, and removed all the code to insert into the cache.

To access the value of the *siteUrls* static variable defined in global.asax from anywhere within the application, we simply need to remember the name of our application, in this case *MyApplication*:

```
DataSet siteUrls = MyApplication.siteUrls;
```

Using static application variables allows us to skip the hashtable lookup and also does not require us to cast to the type. It's definitely a handy technique!

Per-Request Caching

It is sometimes desirable to cache data or information only while the request is being processed independent of the component, server control, or page.

The ASP.NET Forums makes heavy use of personalization. In fact, each server control is responsible for checking the identity of the user and personalizing its display based on data relevant to the user. For example, users can define their own date and time display formats.

All user data is stored in a database. To guarantee consistency, user data is fetched on each request. All personalization data is accessible through a *User* class, which is retrieved from *Users.GetLoggedOnUser*. Any functionality within the application needing personalization can call this API. Internally, it will either return a per-request cached instance of the *User* class or connect through the data provider and populate a *User* instance.

The beauty is that all calls to *GetLoggedOnUser* are guaranteed to work, but the caller is completely unaware of whether it is receiving the *User* from the per-request cache or the data provider is creating a new *User*. Not creating a new *User* for each call saves on round trips to the database. For example, a page might have eight controls that need to access the *User*. Seven of those calls will be satisfied from the per-request cache; only the first will connect to the data store directly.

Implementing Per-Request Caching

Per-request caching is very easy to implement. Code Listing 6-5, from the ASP.NET Forums, shows how it is done.

Code Listing 6-5   Per-Request Caching

```
public static User GetLoggedOnUser() {
    if (!HttpContext.Current.Request.IsAuthenticated)
        return null;

    return Users.GetUserInfo(HttpContext.Current.User.Identity.Name, true);
}


public static User GetUserInfo(String username, bool updateIsOnline) {
    string userKey = "UserInfo-" + username;

    // Attempt to return the user from Cache for users not online to save
    // us a trip to the database.
    if (updateIsOnline == false) {
        if (HttpContext.Current.Cache[userKey] != null)
            return (User) HttpContext.Current.Cache[userKey];
    }

    // Let's not go to the database each time we need the user's info
    if (HttpContext.Current.Items[userKey] == null) {
        // Hang on to the data for this request only
        HttpContext.Current.Items[userKey] =
                DataProvider.Instance().GetUserInfo(username,
                                                    updateIsOnline);
    }

    // Do we need to add the user into the Cache
    if (updateIsOnline == false) {
        if (HttpContext.Current.Cache[userKey] == null)
            HttpContext.Current.Cache.Insert(userKey,
                                        HttpContext.Current.Items[userKey],
                                        null,
                                        DateTime.Now.AddMinutes(1),
                                        TimeSpan.Zero);
    }

    return (User) HttpContext.Current.Items[userKey];
}
```

Per-request caching simply makes use of *HttpContext.Items* for data storage. *HttpContext* is a class that ASP.NET uses for the life cycle of a request/response, and internally it is the class that many APIs forward to. For example, when you call *Response.Write*, you're actually calling *HttpContext.Response.Write*.

The *Items* property is simply a name/value collection within which we can store arbitrary data. The data is available only for the life type of the *HttpContext* instance. The instance of *HttpContext* is created at the beginning of the request and destroyed at the end of the request. Once *HttpContext* goes out of scope (that is, it's no longer needed because ASP.NET sent the response), all associated memory is released—including data stored in *Items*. Thus, *HttpContext.Items* is a perfect data store for per-request caching.

Summary

ASP.NET provides some powerful APIs for managing state within your application. Features such as page output caching and partial page caching take advantage of the ASP.NET *Cache* to store frequently requested pages, or parts of a page, rather than execute them on each request. Output caching not only yields better performance, 2–3 times in most cases, but also makes your application more scalable since it can take the load off of other areas, such as the database. To take advantage of output caching and partial page caching, you need to consider both before you build your application; bolting them on later can be problematic.

Programmatically, ASP.NET provides three options for managing application state: *Cache*, *Application*, and static application variables. The *Application* API is redundant and replaced by the more feature-rich *Cache* API. *Cache* has many features that give you more control over how application state is managed. *Cache* API features such as dependencies and callback allow you to control how your state is being managed.

7

Configuration

Configuration refers to any settings or data required by an application to run. This information can be as simple as the connection string used to connect to a database, or as complex as the number of threads the running process requires. Techniques for configuring applications come in many forms, from using the original system.ini of Microsoft Windows to using the Windows registry. Each approach has advantages and disadvantages.

ASP.NET's configuration system is XML file–based. Many first-time ASP.NET developers expect to configure ASP.NET using the Microsoft Internet Information Services (IIS) Manager, just as they would with ASP. ASP.NET does not, however, rely on the IIS metabase at all, even though the IIS metabase is also now XML file–based. The ASP.NET configuration system does not require any proprietary tools to update or manage it since an XML-based configuration system easily lends itself to manual editing and updating. You simply open the XML file, make changes, and save the file, and the changes are applied immediately. Again, this is unlike ASP, which required you to stop and start the Web server for the changes to affect the running application.

The ASP.NET configuration was designed to be simple. Following is a sample ASP.NET configuration file used to change the timeout of ASP.NET Session state from 20 minutes to 30 minutes:

```
<configuration>
    <system.web>
        <sessionState timeout="30" />
    </system.web>
</configuration>
```

Saving this file as web.config in the root of your application will immediately cause ASP.NET to change the default Session state timeout value from 20 minutes to 30 minutes—without requiring you to restart your application.

If your site runs across multiple servers, changing configuration is equally as easy. Simply copy the web.config configuration file to each of the application directories requiring the modification, and the application will apply the changes as soon as the file update is complete.

Unlike other books that cover all the various configuration settings, this book does not examine the individual configuration settings in detail. Plenty of books address that topic. (Our favorite reference is the machine.config file, which is extensively documented.) Instead we will focus on how the ASP.NET configuration works and how to use the ASP.NET configuration system to store custom settings.

How Configuration Works

The ASP.NET configuration system is simple to work with but offers complex functionality. Two types of configuration files are used in ASP.NET:

- **machine.config**   Used to configure settings that are global to all .NET applications across the computer. This file can be found in C:\Windows\Microsoft.NET\Framework\[version]\CONFIG\, where [version] is replaced by the exact version number of the .NET Framework. Settings made in this file set the default behavior for all ASP.NET applications.

- **web.config**   Used to override defaults, change inherited configuration settings, or add new configuration settings. Whereas only one copy of the machine.config file exists for each installed version of the .NET Framework, many different web.config files can exist for the Web applications you run. Each Web application can have its own web.config file, and each subdirectory within the Web application can also have its own web.config. The next section explains how all this works.

> **Important**   You might find that you have more than one machine.config on your computer. The .NET Framework is designed to allow multiple versions to run side by side. Each version has its own separate machine.config file. The version of the .NET Framework your Web application is using is determined by the extension mappings, for example, .ASPX, in Internet Information Services. Be sure you edit the correct machine.config file if you want to change global settings.

.NET Framework Versions

Figure 7-1 demonstrates a system that has two installations of the .NET Framework, version 1.0 and 1.1. Each separate version has its own subdirectory within the C:\Windows\Microsoft.NET\Framework directory.

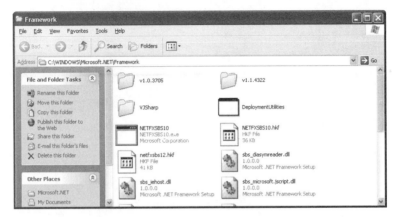

Figure 7-1   A server with multiple installed .NET Framework installations

Two subdirectories are of interest in the C:\Windows\Microsoft.NET\Framework directory: v1.0.3705, which contains all the files for the 1.0 version of the .NET Framework; and v1.1.4322, which contains all the files for the 1.1 version of the .NET Framework.

To view the version of ASP.NET your application is running, open Microsoft Internet Information Services (IIS) Manager, right-click the Default Web Site option, and select Properties. Next, click on the Home Directory tab, and click the Configuration button. A listing of the extension mappings used by ASP.NET appears. Figure 7-2 shows the extension mapping for .ASPX, which maps to aspnet_isapi.dll in the .NET Framework version 1.1 directory. Changes made to the machine.config file in the v1.1.4322\CONFIG\ subdirectory are applied to this application.

> **Tip**   You can change mappings to allow your application to use a different version of the .NET Framework by using the aspnet_regiis.exe tool. This tool is found in the version-specific .NET Framework directory.

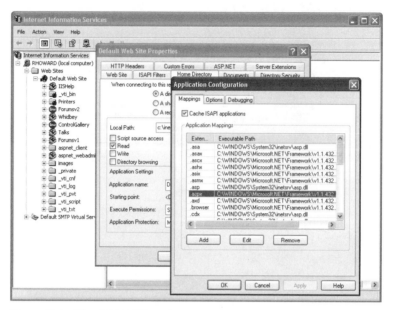

Figure 7-2   The ASP.NET application mapping for IIS

It's uncommon to need to change machine.config settings. In fact, the only setting for ASP.NET that must be configured in machine.config is the *<process-Model />* section. Settings in *<processModel />* are used to control the behavior of the ASP.NET worker process.

The ASP.NET worker process is relevant only to Microsoft Windows 2000 Server and Microsoft Windows XP Professional. Microsoft Windows Server 2003 uses the new Microsoft Internet Information Services 6 worker process model.

Important   Don't modify the machine.config file unless you absolutely have to, such as changing settings to purposely affect all applications. Changes to machine.config affect the entire server. Instead, use web.config in your application to specify desired behavior and configuration options. The web.config file is the recommended location for specifying all your configuration settings.

Using web.config

The web.config file is used to override configurations inherited from machine.config or other parent web.config files. The web.config file is also used to add new settings not already defined, such as custom configuration settings. This file can reside in one of two locations:

- **Web application or Web site root directory**   The web.config file can be placed at the root of your Web site or Web application. A Web application is determined through IIS. By default, all virtual directories are Web applications. Further, any directory in your Web site can be made into a Web application by right-clicking on the directory within the IIS MMC, selecting Properties, and clicking the Create button on the Directory tab.

- **Subdirectory within your Web site or Web application**   Any directory or folder within your Web site or Web application might contain a web.config file. However, some settings are allowed only in a web.config file that resides in the Web application or Web site root directory.

> **Note**   An easy way to tell whether you are working with the root directory for either a Web site or Web application is to look for a bin subdirectory. The bin subdirectory is allowed only in the root directory of a Web site or Web application.

Knowing the location of your web.config file is important. Some configuration settings, such as *<authentication />*, are allowed only at the root directory level, whereas other settings, such as *<authorization />*, are allowed within any directory.

Figure 7-3 shows the IIS MMC snap-in browsing a default Web site. A web.config file could be placed within any of the folders shown in the figure. However, only Default Web Site and ForumsV2 would be considered applications.

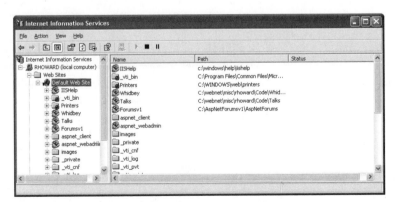

Figure 7-3   Internet Information Services MMC snap-in browsing a default Web site

The actual configuration applied to your application is a merged view of all inherited configuration settings. In the default Web site shown in Figure 7-3, settings made in machine.config are inherited by the Default Web Site and merged with its web.config. Further, those configuration settings are merged with the web.config settings in the ForumsV2 directory. Later in the chapter we'll discuss how to control which settings can be overridden.

Table 7-1 lists the various ASP.NET configuration sections that are allowed in a Web site and Web application or subdirectory. Note that all these settings are allowed in the machine.config file.

Table 7-1   ASP.NET Configuration Sections

Section	Web Site or Application	Subdirectory	Purpose
<authentication />	Yes	No	Determines how HTTP requests are authenticated
<authorization />	Yes	Yes	Allows or denies access based on user identity or role membership
<browserCaps />	Yes	Yes	Enumerates browser capabilities
<clientTarget />	Yes	Yes	Defines alias for a rendering agent
<compilation />	Yes	Yes	Controls how pages and other related ASP.NET resources are dynamically compiled
<customErrors />	Yes	Yes	Overrides default ASP.NET error pages
<deviceFilters />	Yes	Yes	Filter used for specific devices to control rendering of mobile content
<globalization />	Yes	Yes	Controls encoding and related globalization settings
<httpHandlers />	Yes	Yes	Maps HTTP requests to the appropriate classes
<httpModules />	Yes	Yes	Configures modules that participate in an HTTP request/response
<httpRuntime />	Yes	Yes	Controls max request length, number of threads, and other settings related to the ASP.NET HTTP Runtime

Table 7-1   **ASP.NET Configuration Sections**

Section	Web Site or Application	Subdirectory	Purpose
<identity />	Yes	Yes	Windows identity to use when processing HTTP requests
<machineKey />	Yes	No	Keys used for encryption and hashing
<mobileControls />	Yes	Yes	Lists settings specific to mobile controls
<pages />	Yes	Yes	Configure page-specific settings for the application
<processModel />	No	No	Configures the ASP.NET worker process, present only in machine.config
<securityPolicy />	Yes	No	Defines security policy for the application
<sessionState />	Yes	No	Session state options such as in-process and out-of-process
<trace />	Yes	Yes	Enables tracing at the application or page level
<trust />	Yes	No	Defines trust levels regarding what the application can or can not do
<webControls />	Yes	Yes	Identifies the location of the client script JavaScript files
<webServices />	Yes	Yes	Controls behavior of ASP.NET XML Web services

Changing Configuration

Whenever an application-level configuration file or machine.config is modified and saved, several important things happen:

1. Settings are applied immediately.

2. All existing requests are completed against the old configuration settings. A new instance of the application is started, and new requests are directed to the new application.

When running a live application, you will notice a 2 to 10 second delay between the time you save or update your CONFIG file and the time the settings are actually applied to your application. When the application is restarted, all pages are recompiled and the application reinitializes itself, which takes a few seconds.

> **Tip**   When updating a live site, perform all web.config changes locally and upload the new configuration file to the running site. This approach is much more efficient than changing and saving multiple times on the live web.config file.

This update process is slightly different when changes are made to the *<processModel />* section when running Windows 2000 Server and Windows XP Professional—you will need to stop the Web server and restart it for the changes to take effect.

Anatomy of the .CONFIG File

The machine.config and web.config files are identical in structure, which is shown in the following code:

```
<configuration>

    <!-- XML comments are allowed -->
    <configSections>
        <section name="[name]" type="[type]"
            allowLocation="[true/false]"
            <sectionGroup name="[name]" />
    </configSections>

    <[Section Group Name]>

        <[Section Name] [Settings] />

    </[Section Group Name]>

</configuration>
```

All .CONFIG files require the root XML element *<configuration />*. Following *<configuration />* is the *<configSections />* element. Configuration sections, such as *<sessionState />*, as shown in the following code, are used to process configuration data (which is found in machine.config).

```
<section name="sessionState"
    type="System.Web.SessionState.SessionStateSectionHandler,
```

```
System.Web, Version=1.0.5000.0, Culture=neutral,
PublicKeyToken=b03f5f7f11d50a3a"
allowDefinition="MachineToApplication" />
```

Additionally, within **, *<sectionGroup name="[name]" />* is defined. The *<sectionGroup name="[name]" />* section allows for groups of common settings so that you can better organize the configuration file. For example, ASP.NET settings such as *sessionState* are grouped in the *system.web* group. Unless you are creating custom configuration sections, you will not use the ** element or any of its child elements.

The next configuration section contains the actual settings. The opening element is the section group that the settings belong to, for example, *<system.web>*. Within this element are the actual settings, such as **. Figure 7-4 illustrates the configuration mappings when using section groups and system.web settings.

```
<configuration>

  <configSections>

   <sectionGroup name="system.web">

     <section name="sessionState"
        type="System.Web.SessionState.SessionStateSectionHandler,
              System.Web,
              Version=1.0.5000.0,
              Culture=neutral,
              PublicKeyToken=b03f5f7f11d50a3a"
        allowDefinition="MachineToApplication"
     />

   </sectionGroup>

  </configSections>

  <system.web>

    <sessionState timeout="30" />

  </system.web>

</configuration>
```

Figure 7-4   Mapping of sections and groups

Centralized Configuration Settings

Although the generally recommended approach is to place all configuration settings in a web.config file for each individual Web application, you can also define configuration settings in a parent web.config file that will be applied to resources in subdirectories or subapplications.

You specify settings in parent web.config files—or only in machine.config—through the *<location />* element:

```
<location path="[web path]">
    <[sectionGroup]>
        <[section] />
    </[sectionGroup]>
</location>
```

The *<location />* element is most commonly used for security purposes in Web sites with complex directory structures. Rather than creating a web.config file for each directory and specifying the authorization requirements, you can use the *<location />* element to store authorization requirements centrally in the application's root web.config file, as shown in the following code example. This is perhaps the best use of the *<location />* element.

```
<configuration>
    <!-- Other application configuration settings not shown -->
    <location path="Forums/EditPost.aspx">
        <system.web>
            <authorization>
                <deny users="?" />
            </authorization>
        </system.web>
    </location>
</configuration>
```

In this sample web.config file, a single comment line reflects that more configuration settings have likely been specified but are not shown in the sample. We also find the *<location />* element used to deny access to anonymous users. This is accomplished through *<deny users="?" />* applied to *path="Forums/EditPost.aspx"*. This is the setting we use on the *www.asp.net* site to prevent unauthorized users from accessing the *edit post* functionality of the ASP.NET Forums (*www.asp.net/Forums*).

Locking Down Configuration

Earlier in this chapter, we discussed how the configuration for the application is computed by merging the machine.config and web.config settings for the application. Sometimes it is not desirable to allow the settings to be overridden by the application, as in hosted environments. The ASP.NET configuration system accounts for this through a special *allowOverride* attribute that is optionally defined with the *<location />* element:

```
<configuration>
    <location path="MyApplication" allowOverride="false">
        <system.web>
            <sessionState timeout="30" />
        </system.web>
    </location>
</configuration>
```

If not specified, the default value for the attribute is *allowOverride="true"*. You can use the *allowOverride* attribute to lock down ASP.NET settings in parent applications and prevent child applications from changing the values. The following example demonstrates how this can be accomplished in machine.config:

```
<configuration>
    <!-- Additional machine.config settings not shown -->
    <!-- Override Session defaults for Application 1 -->
    <location path="Application1" allowOverride="false">
        <system.web>
            <sessionState timeout="30" />
        </system.web>
    </location>

    <!-- Override Session defaults for Application 2 -->
    <location path="Application2" allowOverride="false">
        <system.web>
            <sessionState mode="StateServer" />
        </system.web>
    </location>
</configuration>
```

Any attempts to change *<sessionState />* settings via a web.config in *Application1* or *Application2* would result in an exception.

Storing Custom Configuration Data

One design philosophy of ASP.NET was to create an architecture that allowed a problem to be solved in two ways. This design philosophy is evident in the configuration system in that you have two options for storing configuration data for your own applications: *<appSettings />*, which is a special configuration section that allows you to store string name/value pairs for easy access in your application; and the custom configuration section handler, which allows you to author a custom configuration section handler capable of reading and processing your own custom configuration sections.

Using Application Settings

Application settings allow you to store commonly used data such as connection strings within the configuration and to access that data through a simple, easy-to-use API.

> **Tip** Customers often ask us whether they should store data in web.config or global.asax. We recommend you store the data within the configuration file. Storing settings in files such as global.asax implies code. The configuration file allows you to make simple changes without having to recompile your application. Simply add the settings and update the web.config file on your running server.

The following code demonstrates storing data in the *<appSettings />* section of configuration:

```
<configuration>
    <appSettings>
        <add key="DSN"
            value="server=.;database=pubs;uid=sa;pwd=00password" />
    </appSettings>
</configuration>
```

The next code example shows accessing the data from within an ASP.NET page:

```
<%@ Imports Namespace="System.Data" %>
<%@ Imports Namespace="System.Data.SqlClient" %>
<%@ Imports Namespace="System.Configuration" %>

<script runat="server">
Public Sub Page_Load (sender As Object, e As EventArgs)
    Dim connectionString As String

    ' Fetch the connection string from appSettings
    connectionString = ConfigurationSettings.AppSettings("DSN")

    Dim connection As New SqlConnection(connectionString)

    ' Additional data access code…
End Sub
</script>
```

In the preceding sample, we use the *ConfigurationSettings.AppSettings* property to request the value of the key *DSN* and use value this for our constructor of a new *SqlConnection* class instance. We also had to include this:

```
<%@ Imports Namespace="System.Configuration" %>
```

Without it, we would have received compile errors when attempting to use the *ConfigurationSettings* class.

As you can see, application settings are very powerful, and you can use them to store just about any configuration data you can think of. However, you might want something a little more customized, possibly to support nesting or some other structural organization not supported by the flat *<appSettings />*. In that case, you'll want to write a custom configuration section handler.

Custom Configuration Section Handler

The role of the custom configuration section handler is to parse configuration data and populate a class instance in which configuration settings can be accessed programmatically in a type-safe manner. The class instance can be retrieved using the *ConfigurationSettings.GetConfig* method. For example, if we had a custom configuration section handler named *ForumsConfiguration*, we could access it through a custom handler. Here is the web.config containing our configuration details:

```
<configuration>
    <configSections>
        <sectionGroup name="forums">
            <section name="forums"
                type="ForumsConfigurationHandler,
                    AspNetForums.Components" />
        </sectionGroup>
    </configSections>

    <forums>
        <forums defaultProvider="SqlForumsProvider"
            defaultLanguage="en-en" >
            <providers>
                <add name="SqlForumsProvider"
                    type="AspNetForums.Data.SqlDataProvider,
                        AspNetForums.SqlDataProvider"
                    connectionString="[your connection string]"
                    databaseOwner="dbo" />
            </providers>
        </forums>
    </forums>

</configuration>
```

This configuration file contains a *<sectionGroup>* for *forums* as well as defines a new section named *forums*. We then see the configuration data for the *forums*. This is the exact configuration system used by the ASP.NET forums.

Here is sample code (written in Visual Basic .NET) showing how we can use the custom configuration section handler to read the configuration data and then use it in a type-safe manner:

```
Dim configSettings As Object
Dim forumsConfig As ForumsConfiguration
Dim language As string

' Get configuration settings as an object
configSettings = ConfigurationSettings.GetConfig("forums/forums")

' Cast to the ForumsConfiguration data type
forumsConfig = CType(configSettings, ForumsConfiguration)

' Get the default language
language = forumsConfig.DefaultLanguage
```

The magic happens through a special mapping in web.config:

```
<section name="forums"
    type="AspNetForums.Configuration.ForumsConfigurationHandler,
        AspNetForums.Components" />
```

This entry in the *<configSections>* of the configuration file instructs ASP.NET to load a configuration section handler in the namespace *AspNetForums.Configuration* with a class name of *ForumsConfigurationHandler*. The class is found in the *AspNetForums.Components* assembly.

Here is the source for the *ForumsConfigurationHandler* class, which is provided in C# because it is the same source used in the ASP.NET Forums. (You can download it from *www.asp.net*.)

```
namespace AspNetForums.Configuration {

    // *****************************************************************
    /// <summary>Class used to represent the configuration data for
    /// the ASP.NET Forums</summary>
    // ****************************************************************/
    public class ForumConfiguration {
        Hashtable providers = new Hashtable();
        string defaultProvider;
        string defaultLanguage;

        public static ForumConfiguration GetConfig() {
            return (ForumConfiguration)
```

```
            ConfigurationSettings.GetConfig("forums/forums");
}


// ************************************************************
/// <summary>Loads the forums configuration
/// values. </summary>
// ************************************************************/
internal void LoadValuesFromConfigurationXml(XmlNode node) {
    XmlAttributeCollection attributeCollection
        = node.Attributes;

    // Get the default provider
    defaultProvider
        = attributeCollection["defaultProvider"].Value;

    // Get the default language
    defaultLanguage
        = attributeCollection["defaultLanguage"].Value;

    // Read child nodes
    foreach (XmlNode child in node.ChildNodes) {
        if (child.Name == "providers")
            GetProviders(child);
    }
}


// ************************************************************
/// <summary>Internal class used to populate the
/// available providers. </summary>
// ************************************************************/
internal void GetProviders(XmlNode node) {
    foreach (XmlNode provider in node.ChildNodes) {
        switch (provider.Name) {
            case "add" :
                providers.Add(
                    provider.Attributes["name"].Value,
                    new Provider(provider.Attributes));
            break;

            case "remove" :
                providers.Remove(
                    provider.Attributes["name"].Value);
            break;

            case "clear" :
                providers.Clear();
            break;
        }
```

```
            }
        }

        // Properties
        public string DefaultLanguage {
            get { return defaultLanguage; } }
        public string DefaultProvider {
            get { return defaultProvider; } }
        public Hashtable Providers {
            get { return providers; } }
    }

    public class Provider {
        string name;
        string providerType;
        NameValueCollection providerAttributes
            = new NameValueCollection();

        public Provider (XmlAttributeCollection attributes) {

            // Set the name of the provider
            name = attributes["name"].Value;

            // Set the type of the provider
            providerType = attributes["type"].Value;

            // Store all the attributes in the attributes bucket
            foreach (XmlAttribute attribute in attributes) {

                if((attribute.Name!="name")
                    &&(attribute.Name!="type"))
                    providerAttributes.Add(attribute.Name,
                        attribute.Value);
            }
        }

        public string Name {
            get { return name; }
        }

        public string Type {
            get { return providerType; }
        }

        public NameValueCollection Attributes {
            get { return providerAttributes; }
        }
    }
```

```
// ***************************************************************
/// <summary>Class used by ASP.NET Configuration to load ASP.NET
/// Forums configuration. </summary>
// ***************************************************************/
internal class ForumsConfigurationHandler :
    IConfigurationSectionHandler {
    public virtual object Create(Object parent,
        Object context, XmlNode node) {
        ForumConfiguration config = new ForumConfiguration();
        config.LoadValuesFromConfigurationXml(node);
        return config;
    }
}
}
```

When a request is made for *ConfigurationSettings.GetConfig("forums/ forums")*, either the results are read from cache—if they've been requested before—or a request is made to the appropriate configuration section handler. In the previous code example, an instance of the *ForumsConfigurationHandler* was created and a populated instance of *ForumConfiguration* returned.

As you can see, the code for *ForumConfiguration* is simply reading and processing the raw XML from the configuration file and returning a strongly typed class.

Securing Configuration Data

Storing commonly used data within configuration is exactly what configuration is designed for. For example, the settings necessary to support out-of-process Session state, such as the connection string, are stored within configuration. Your own application resources, such as connection strings, are also recommended for .config storage. As you know, configuration provides a central, easy-to-manage repository for this type of information. However, this data storage is not secured by default. If the system were compromised, system information could be taken from the configuration file. Fortunately, by default, the .CONFIG extension is blocked, so you can't simply download someone's web.config!

Version 1.1 of ASP.NET introduced a new capability that allows for the encryption of some part of configuration, such as *<processModel />* and *<session-State />*, that can potentially contain data to be secured. (Knowledge base article 329290 has more extensive and recent details.) Support for secure storage of connection strings and other configuration data is a planned addition for ASP.NET 2.0.

Encrypting Data

Information stored in the following configuration sections can be encrypted and stored securely in the registry:

- **<*identity/*>** Windows identity (username and password) to impersonate

- **<*processModel* />** Windows identity to use when running the process

- **<*sessionState* />** Connection string used to connect to out-of-process state server

To enable this encryption capability, you first need to download a special tool, aspnet_setreg.exe, from *http://download.microsoft.com/download/2/9/8 /29829651-e0f0-412e-92d0-e79da46fd7a5/Aspnet_setreg.exe*. After you download this file, extract it, and store it in the following version-specific directory, which also contains other ASP.NET-related command-line utilities, for example, C:\Windows\Microsoft.NET\Framework\v1.1.4322\. Visit the following site for instructions about how to use this tool: *http://support.microsoft.com/default .aspx?scid=kb%3ben-us%3b329290*.

Summary

ASP.NET's configuration system provides a simple configuration that does not require special tools to edit or manage the file. Instead, XML is used to store the various configuration options required by ASP.NET. The configuration system is very flexible in that it allows for fine-grained control at various application levels as well as provides switches that allow or deny the overriding of sections.

Storing custom configuration data can be accomplished either by using the *<appSettings />* section or by authoring a custom configuration section handler. Although *<appSettings />* is the easiest approach to use, authoring a custom configuration section handler provides the highest degree of flexibility. Note that in the next version of ASP.NET, we will provide graphical tools as well as more APIs for programming and managing the ASP.NET configuration system.

8

ASP.NET Security

We've all seen the aftermath of various worms and viruses. Given the huge number of systems affected and their global reach, you've probably already dealt with this sort of disruption firsthand. Fortunately, keeping a server updated with the latest fix might be all that's necessary to prevent a problem, and recovering from an infected system has been relatively straightforward so far. But these high-profile episodes are just part of the overall security story. The more insidious attacks are less publicized: the system compromises that result in corrupted or stolen data. In these cases, keeping a server updated with the latest security fix won't help. You have to be prepared before the damage is done. You must design, write, and deploy the applications with security always in mind.

In this chapter, we'll cover the features of version 1.1 of the .NET Framework that make writing secure applications easier. We will look at the mechanisms available for limiting access to parts of a Web application and consider what you can and should do to limit the risk when dealing with sensitive data. We will also cover the basic steps to hardening a Web server.

Introducing ASP.NET Application Security

First, let's establish what we mean by authentication, authorization, and impersonation. (We'll introduce them here but talk about each in more detail later in this chapter.) These terms can be confusing, so let's define them in a more concrete way by using the metaphor of securing an office building.

Authentication is simply establishing the identity of the user. In the secure office building, every person must have an ID badge. Each person who works in the building might be issued a cardkey or badge to display, and a visitor might be asked to wear a temporary ID.

Authorization is a set of rights granted to particular users. Once the ID is established through authentication, security isn't improved beyond the ability to log an individual's actions unless we enforce that only certain users can access certain resources. In the secure office building, we might limit specified groups to accessing only certain parts of the building. For example, only those individuals working on a top-secret project would be authorized to enter the project lab.

Impersonation is assuming the identity of someone else. In our example, impersonation would be using the cardkey issued for someone else's authentication. When impersonating, all actions appear to be carried out by the assumed identity.

Figure 8-1 shows how Microsoft Internet Information Services (IIS) acts as the front line in establishing user permissions, and how ASP.NET builds on top of it later in the request.

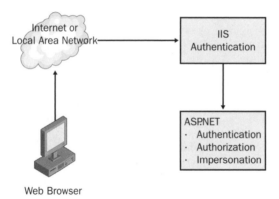

Figure 8-1   IIS and ASP.NET authentication and authorization

These key security concepts are the basis for creating a secure Web site. IIS and Microsoft ASP.NET work together closely to authenticate and impersonate users, authorize requests, and delegate credentials to gain access to the required resources. ASP.NET goes beyond these security primitives to validate input and perform dynamic role checking.

The security role IIS performs is driven primarily by configuration data, using Microsoft Windows accounts and certificates for authentication, and NTFS (file permissions) for authorization.

Authenticating Users

IIS offers several approaches for authenticating users, and ASP.NET works with all of them. The choices that we will discuss are anonymous, certificate, and Windows Authentication. These comprise the top-level choices in IIS for securing resources. First we'll discuss what these options are and examine how they are configured, and then we'll look at how ASP.NET fits in.

IIS Authentication

ASP.NET requests are first handled by the Web server, which usually means IIS. The dialog box in which IIS security settings can be set and viewed is accessed from the Computer Management application for managing local and remote computers by following these steps:

1. Expand the Services And Applications area of the Computer Management, part of the Microsoft Management Console.

2. Click on Internet Information Services.

3. Right-click the Web site (such as Web Sites or Default Web Site) or application root, and select the Properties option.

4. Click the Directory Security tab.

5. Click the Edit button for Anonymous Access And Authentication Control. Figure 8-2 shows the Authentication Methods dialog box.

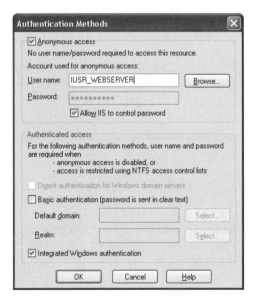

Figure 8-2   Authentication Methods dialog box

> **Tip**   To launch the Computer Management application from the command prompt, enter **start compmgmt.msc**. You can also launch the Internet Information Services Management snap-in directly by entering **start inetmgr**.

Anonymous Access

The default mode in IIS is *anonymous access*, meaning that all users are allowed access to the site and are assigned the *IUSR_WebServer* identity, where *WebServer* is the machine name of the Web server. The *IUSER_WebServer* identity is a real user account on the Web server machine, but it has very limited permissions; although we've assigned the user's identity, we haven't authenticated who he is.

Client Certificates

Another option for authentication is the use of *client certificates*, in which the Windows accounts are mapped to certificates as part of user management and application configuration. Then, during authentication, the certificate is presented by the browser and validated by the Web server. The client does not need to present user credentials (the user name and password) because the certificate exchange happens automatically. (You can find more information on mapping certificates at *http://www.microsoft.com/technet*. Search for the topic "Mapping Certificates.")

Windows Authentication

The other main option for authentication in IIS is referred to as *Integrated Windows Authentication*. Windows Authentication also has several other suboptions: basic and digest. Both authenticate credentials presented by the user or the user's browser are verified against a Windows account on the server. *Basic Authentication* allows the user name and password to be sent without encryption and must be used on a user account that is defined explicitly on the Web server machine. Someone capturing network traffic would be able to see the user name and password.

> **Important**   Never use Basic Authentication without requiring Secure Sockets Layer (SSL) so that user credentials are sent in an encrypted form. Using basic authentication without encrypting communications is referred to as sending credentials "in the clear" and is a very bad practice.

Digest Authentication looks like Basic Authentication to the user but requires that the user account be a domain account. The user is presented with a dialog box that enables her to enter her user name and password. Digest Authentication encrypts the credentials before transmitting them to the Web server so that they are not sent in the clear, that is, their transmission requires an SSL connection.

Integrated Authentication utilizes the credentials the user obtained when she logged on to the machine. The user is not presented with another dialog box, and the password is not sent to the Web server. Depending on the environment, integrated authentication will use either Kerberos or NTLM to establish the domain identity of the user.

Before a request is handed over to ASP.NET, it is authenticated using one of these Windows authentication options by IIS. When ASP.NET receives the request, IIS always passes the identity of the Windows user along with it. This identity might be the anonymous user account (*IUSER_WebServer*), a local machine account, or a domain account.

> **Tip**   A Windows user account is always associated with an executing request. A good way to review the security of a Web application is to walk through what identity is being used by Windows when executing any part of the request.

ASP.NET Authentication

Once the request is handed over to ASP.NET along with the user credentials provided by IIS, the additional authentication options of ASP.NET come into play. These options are driven primarily by scenarios in which having a Windows account for each user of the Web application is not feasible. The ASP.NET authentication options are set in the *authentication* element of the web.config file. Settings in the web.config file will override the default settings in the machine.config file. An example of using the *authentication* element is seen in Code Listing 8-2. There are four possible values for the *mode* attribute of the configuration element: Windows, Forms, Passport, and None.

The default ASP.NET authentication mode is Windows, meaning that File Authorization and URL Authorization are carried out using the Windows user account provided by IIS. (See the section in this chapter titled "Authorizing Users" for more information). Access to backend resources, such as databases and registry entries, is performed using the identity of the worker process. (See the section titled "Using Impersonation" later in this chapter.)

When the authentication mode is Passport, the user is denied access to the directory until he has been authenticated by the Microsoft Passport Authentication service. This service essentially wraps the calls with the Passport SDK for you, automating the process of logging the user into Passport. (For more details on the .NET Passport authentication service, go to *http://www.microsoft.com/net/services/*.)

The Forms Authentication mode of ASP.NET is the most popular for enabling authentication that doesn't require a Passport login or a separate Windows account to be maintained on the server. We'll discuss it in more detail in the "Using Forms Authentication" section later in this chapter.

Using Impersonation

The choice you make for authentication in IIS is closely related to your choices about authorization and impersonation. As mentioned earlier in this chapter, no matter what authentication option you choose, a Windows user account will be associated with the request by IIS. Exactly how ASP.NET utilizes the associated account depends on whether impersonation is enabled. Without impersonation, the page is executed with the identity of the worker process handling the request.

In IIS 5, ASP.NET applications run in a worker process called aspnet_wp.exe with a default identity of ASPNET, a special account created for ASP.NET. The *processModel* element of the web.config file allows us to control the identity that is used for the *aspnet_wp* worker process. When the *userName* attribute is set to *Machine* by default, the worker process runs as ASPNET; when it is set to *SYSTEM*, the worker process runs as the more trusted *LocalSystem* account. You can also specify a different account altogether, but you must specify the password in the *processModel* element of machine.config file as well.

> **Tip** Do not run the worker process as an account other than *ASPNET* unless absolutely necessary. Compromising the worker process that is running as *SYSTEM* would give an attacker much higher level permissions than the *ASPNET* account. Any page will execute as this user unless impersonation is enabled.

IIS 6 uses a set of worker processes called w3wp.exe that allow pooling and isolation of the application processing. By default, these processes run as the Local Network account, but they too can be configured to use a different identity in the Internet Services Manager. If you changed the identity for the worker process in IIS 5, your application might not run as the expected identity in IIS 6 because the *processModel* settings are not applied when using w3wp.exe worker processes.

> **Tip**   You can force IIS 6 on Windows Server 2003 to use the version 5.0 behavior in the Internet Services Manager by right-clicking the Web Sites folder, selecting Properties, and selecting Run WWW Service In IIS 5.1 Isolation Mode on the Services tab.

Enabling ASP.NET Impersonation

To enable impersonation, set the *impersonate* attribute of the *identity* element to *true*. Code Listing 8-1 causes the pages of a Web application to run as the identity of the user provided by IIS. When anonymous access is allowed for the Web application and impersonation is enabled, pages execute as the *IUSER_WebServer* account.

Code Listing 8-1   Impersonate Web.config

```
<configuration>
    <system.web>
        <identity impersonate="true" />
    </system.web>
</configuration>
```

There are two other options for impersonating in ASP.NET. You can set up impersonation to use either a specific user from the configuration or the Web service Logon identity. In some scenarios, they might be useful, but be aware that page code will execute as the impersonated user. If you impersonate a more powerful user, you might be granting more access than you intend. By setting the value of the *username* and *password* attributes to an empty string, ASP.NET impersonates the Logon user of the Web service. By default, this is the *LocalSystem* account, which has a powerful set of permissions. You can also specify a specific user by including his credentials, but note that the user's name and password are being placed directly in the web.config file. Code Listing 8-2 shows the identity configuration that would cause all pages of the application to run as *joeuser*, as long as *joesPassword* is correct.

Code Listing 8-2   Impersonate User Web.config

```
<configuration>
    <system.web>
        <authentication mode="Windows" />
        <identity impersonate="true"
                  username="joeuser"
                  password="joesPassword" />
    </system.web>
</configuration>
```

Impersonation can be particularly useful when used in conjunction with IIS non-anonymous authentication. To work correctly, however, ASP.NET must be configured for Windows Authentication as well. The page executes as the authenticated user. Access to resources is checked against the permissions of the user. For example, when you apply this scenario, a database query runs as the authenticated user, and log files accurately reflect user activities. This can be ideal in scenarios in which managing user accounts and permissions is feasible and Windows Authentication can be used. For large-scale Internet scenarios, it might be more feasible to use anonymous authentication in IIS without impersonation so that you can take advantage of ASP.NET Forms Authentication.

Using Forms Authentication

Forms Authentication allows you to authenticate the user against synthetic accounts. In other words, it liberates authentication from the Windows user accounts and lets the user information be centralized in a backend database or even placed directly in config files in the application. You can still take advantage of the kind of role management available with Windows accounts. (See the section "Working with Roles" later in this chapter).

Configuring Forms Authentication

To enable Forms Authentication with the defaults, simply set the value of the *mode* attribute of *authentication* to *Forms*. Code Listing 8-3 demonstrates enabling Forms Authentication and setting a custom cookie name.

Code Listing 8-3   Forms Auth Web.config

```
<configuration>
    <system.web>
        <authentication mode="Forms" >
        <forms name="CookieName" loginUrl="login.aspx" />
    </system.web>
</configuration>
```

When using ASP.NET Forms Authentication, each request is checked against authentication tickets from a *FormsAuthenticationTicket* object. In mobile pages, the ticket might be carried in the query string (the string at the end of the URL preceded by a *?*); otherwise, it is carried in the cookies. If it is not found or has expired, the user is redirected to the *loginUrl* specified in the *forms* element. The default value of *loginUrl* in machine.config is *login.aspx*. The purpose of the *loginUrl* page is to ask the user for the user name and password, and if satisfied, issue a ticket. Just like Basic Windows Authentication, ASP.NET doesn't provide any means for automatically encrypting the credentials supplied by the user, so it is up to you to implement SSL in conjunction with Forms Authentication to secure passwords against being captured in network traffic.

> **Tip**   Always use SSL in conjunction with ASP.NET Forms Authentication to secure the transmission of user names, passwords, and during transmission between the browser and string.

Authenticating the User

Although a default path is provided for the *loginUrl*, the page itself is not created by ASP.NET. Code Listing 8-4 is a simple page that takes a user name and password from the user and authenticates them. In this example, we hardcoded just one acceptable user name (*TheUsername*) and password (*ThePassword*) into our *AuthenticateUser* method. Once the correct credentials are received, we issue the ticket and get the user back to where she started by calling the static *RedirectFromLoginPage* method of the *FormsAuthentication* class.

Code Listing 8-4   Login.aspx

```
<%@Page language="C#" %>
<script runat="server">
protected void Page_Load(object o, EventArgs e) {
    if(IsPostBack) {
        if(AuthenticateUser(username.Text, password.Text)) {
            FormsAuthentication.RedirectFromLoginPage(
                "TheUsername", false);
        }
        else {
            instructions.Text = "Please try again!";
            instructions.ForeColor = System.Drawing.Color.Red;
        }
```

```
    }
  }
  bool AuthenticateUser(string username, string password) {
      if((username == "TheUsername") && (password == "ThePassword")) {
          return true;
      }
      return false;
  }
  </script>
  <form runat="server">
  <asp:Label runat="server" id="instructions" Text="Please input your credentia
  ls:" /><br>
  Username: <asp:Textbox runat="server" id="username" /><br>
  Password: <asp:Textbox runat="server" id="password"
                  TextMode="Password" /><br>
  <asp:button runat="server" Text="LOGIN" />
  </form>
```

The login page can be seen in Figure 8-3. With just a few lines of code, we are authenticating users. The identity of the worker process hasn't been affected, and we didn't have to coordinate the creation of a new Windows user account. Notice that the call to the *RedirectFromLoginPage* method passes *false* as the second parameter (the Boolean *createPersistentCookie*), which indicates that the authentication ticket should be a session cookie only and not a durable cookie, that is, one that persists past the time the user closes the browser.

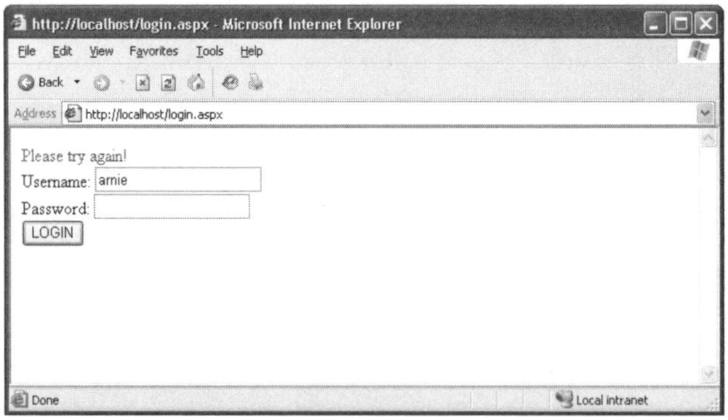

Figure 8-3   A simple login form

> **Note**   *RedirectFromLoginPage* relies on the user having been redirected to the login page with a query string to know where to redirect them back to. For example, in the URL *http://www.contoso.com/login.aspx?ReturnUrl=mypage.aspx*, mypage.aspx is the return URL that the user is redirected to. If the user requests the login page directly, he will be sent to the page configured as the default for the Web application in the Internet Services Manager, usually default.aspx.

Storing Passwords

ASP.NET supports storing user names and passwords directly in the *credentials* element of either the web.config or machine.config file. Because storing the passwords in clear text is not a good idea, the *FormsAuthentication* class provides the *HashPasswordForStoringInConfigFile* method using a hash algorithm. There is still a downside to storing the hashed versions of passwords in the web.config file. Updating the web.config file causes the application to restart. This might be bothersome if the application is forced to restart every time a new user is created or updates his password. So you'll probably use a back-end data store for managing Forms Authentication credentials.

You can still take advantage of the *HashPasswordForStoringInConfigFile* method. When adding a user, hash the password but store only the hash, not the password. To authenticate the user, hash the password again and compare the hash to what is stored. If they match, the user supplied the correct password. The odds of having two separate passwords hash to the same value is mathematically infeasible. This approach prevents anyone who has or gets access to the database from getting access to the user passwords. The hash process, for all intents and purposes, is a one-way function, meaning that you can't get the password from the hash. You have to guess the password and hash it for confirmation, which is infeasible.

> **Important**   Never store user passwords in clear text.

Forms Authentication scales easily to thousands of users when working against a database backend. You can store user preferences and personal information for the user as well as additional security for use in role management, which is discussed in the next section.

Working with Roles

Most security decisions do not focus on the rights of the individual user. Instead, a user belongs to a group, and application security focuses on authorizing these group roles for access to information and functionality. The application can customize the data displayed based on the groups to which the authenticated user belongs. Role management is driven by examination of the object stored by ASP.NET in the *HttpContext.User* property. This object implements the *IPrincipal* interface, which has just two members: the *Identity* of the user; and the *IsInRole* method, which checks for group membership.

Using Roles with Windows Authentication

When the authentication mode is Windows Authentication, ASP.NET creates a *WindowsPrincipal* object that is available in the *HttpContext.User* property. The *WindowsPrincipal* object is used to access the identity of the authenticated user. The identity can get you more information about the user, including access to the Windows account token, which can be used to access resources on behalf of the user. This *IsInRole* method takes the name of a role and returns a Boolean value indicating whether the user is a member of the role.

Group membership can be used to customize an application as well as restrict access. Code Listing 8-5 demonstrates programmatically retrieving the *IPrincipal* object and using it to customize the output when the user is in the Windows Administrators group. For the customization to work, both IIS and ASP.NET must be configured correctly. If IIS is configured to allow anonymous access, the *IPrincipal* object will correspond to the *IUSER_WebServer* account, which should not be a member of the Administrators group. If the authentication mode in the ASP.NET configuration is not Windows Authentication, the cast from *HttpContext.User* to *WindowsPrincipal* will fail. Notice that the code sample does not guard against the *WindowsPrincipal* object being null. A null value indicates that the configuration is incorrect.

Code Listing 8-5   CheckWindowsPrincipal.aspx

```
<%@Page language="C#" %>
<%@Import Namespace="System.Security.Principal" %>
<script runat="server">
protected void Page_Load(object o, EventArgs e) {
    WindowsPrincipal principal =
        (WindowsPrincipal)HttpContext.Current.User;
        if(principal.IsInRole(WindowsBuiltInRole.Administrator)) {
          message.Text = "Secret message for administrators only!";
        }
```

```
}
</script>
<form runat="server">
<asp:Label runat="server" id="message"
    Text="Text that everyone can see!" /><br>
</form>
```

Using Roles with Forms Authentication

ASP.NET Forms Authentication and Windows Authentication both make the *IPrincipal* object available from the *HttpContext.User* property; however, this object is just a *GenericPrincipal* object, and it doesn't use the Windows operating system as a back end for validating roles. Instead, role management is implemented as part of the application. In the example that follows, we modify the way that the *FormsAuthenticationTicket* object is constructed in the login page so that it includes a role for the user. Then we add code to the global.asax file so that when subsequent requests come in for the authenticated user, the code creates *GenericPrincipal* with the role that we get back from the ticket. The *GenericPrincipal* object is then made available through the rest of the request processing.

Code Listing 8-6 is like Code Listing 8-4 except that the call to *Redirect-FromLoginPage* is replaced with our own code (the differences are highlighted in the code listing). First, we create the ticket. Notice that the last argument to the *FormsAuthenticationTicket* constructor is user-defined data, our *superusers* role for this user. Then we encrypt the ticket and place it in the *Response* cookie collection and perform the redirect.

Code Listing 8-6   PrincipalLogin.aspx

```
<%@Page language="C#" %>
<script runat="server">
protected void Page_Load(object o, EventArgs e) {
    if(IsPostBack) {
        if(AuthenticateUser(username.Text, password.Text)) {
            FormsAuthenticationTicket ticket =
                new FormsAuthenticationTicket(
                    1,
                    username.Text,
                    DateTime.Now,
                    DateTime.Now.AddMinutes(30),
                    false,
                    "superusers"
                );
            string encryptedTicket =
                FormsAuthentication.Encrypt(ticket);
```

```
                Response.Cookies.Add(new
                    HttpCookie(FormsAuthentication.FormsCookieName,
                    encryptedTicket));
                Response.Redirect(FormsAuthentication.GetRedirectUrl(
                    username.Text, false));
            } else {
                instructions.Text = "Please try again!";
                instructions.ForeColor = System.Drawing.Color.Red;
            }
        }
    }

bool AuthenticateUser(string username, string password) {
    if((username == "TheUsername") &&
        (password == "ThePassword")) {
        return true;
    }
    return false;
}
</script>

<form runat="server">
<asp:Label runat="server" id="instructions" Text="Please input your credentia
ls:" /><br>
Username: <asp:Textbox runat="server" id="username" /><br>
Password: <asp:Textbox runat="server" id="password"
            TextMode="Password" /><br>
<asp:button runat="server" Text="LOGIN" />
</form>
```

Unless we also take over creating the *GenericPrincipal* class (which implements *IPrincipal*) on subsequent requests, the role will not be populated. Code Listing 8-7 provides an *EventHandler* for the *AuthenticateRequest* event. Because global.asax, when installed at the application root, responds to application-level events, ASP.NET raises this event at the beginning of every page request. This example neglects error handling completely while extracting the ticket from the Forms Authentication cookie. It constructs the *GenericPrincipal* used throughout the request by using a *FormsIdentity* object created with the ticket and the role that was stored in the ticket's user data.

Code Listing 8-7   Global.asax
```
<%@import namespace="System.Security.Principal" %>
<script runat="server" language="C#">

protected void Application_AuthenticateRequest(object o, EventArgs e) {
    HttpCookie cookie = Request.Cookies[FormsAuthentication.FormsCookieName];
    if(cookie != null) {
        FormsAuthenticationTicket ticket =
            FormsAuthentication.Decrypt(cookie.Value);
        string[] role = new string[]{ticket.UserData};
        Context.User = new GenericPrincipal(new FormsIdentity(ticket), role);
    }
}
</script>
```

For completeness, Code Listing 8-8 is included. Its use of the *Windows-Principal* is nearly identical to the use of *IPrincipal* object in Code Listing 8-5, except that Code Listing 8-8 no longer relies on built-in Windows groups for role management. Rather, it uses an arbitrary role that we created when the user was logging on and persisted during the authentication phase of each request. For the cast to this *GenericPrincipal* object to work, you must have the global.asax file in the application's root directory and change the *authentication mode* attribute in web.config to *Forms* as it was in Code Listing 8-3. Also, the PrincipalLogin.aspx page must be used for authentication, which can be configured by renaming it to the default login.aspx value or by setting *loginUrl* attribute of the *forms* element to the page name in the web.config.

Code Listing 8-8   FormsAuthRoles.aspx
```
<%@Page language="C#" %>
<%@Import Namespace="System.Security.Principal" %>
<script runat="server">
protected void Page_Load(object o, EventArgs e) {
    GenericPrincipal principal =
        (GenericPrincipal)HttpContext.Current.User;
    if(principal.IsInRole("superusers")) {
        message.Text = "Message for forms auth superusers.";
    }
}
</script>

<form runat="server">
<asp:Label runat="server" id="message" Text="Text the everyone can see!" /
><br>
</form>
```

Authorizing Users

Windows Authentication provides a familiar model for working with user accounts that extends to authorization as well. Windows Authentication works both with and without impersonation enabled, but in slightly different ways.

As mentioned earlier, requiring that a user be authenticated is only part of the story in securing a Web application. Once the identity is established, this identity can be used to determine whether the user is authorized to visit parts of the application or carry out certain functions. The application can be customized easily so that sensitive data is not shown to users without clearance. The choices available for authorization follow along the same lines as those available for authentication. In fact, some authorization features work only when used in conjunction with the appropriate authentication mechanism.

File Authorization

In the "Windows Authentication" section earlier in this chapter, you learned that a request is handled by a worker process. It follows, then, that access to the .aspx files is controlled by setting access control lists (ACLs) for the identity of the worker process. ASP.NET can take this one step further by enforcing the NTFS file permissions for the authenticated user. This enforcement requires Windows Authentication but not impersonation. Recall that when using impersonation, the page code will execute as it would with the authenticated user; however, this authentication is independent of access to the file. One of the modules installed by default in the processing pipeline is the *System.Web.Security.FileAuthorizationModule*. It takes the credentials for the request that are passed from IIS and validates that the user has authorization to load the .aspx file before executing that request. If access has not been granted for that user account, ASP.NET returns an access denied message.

> **Tip** File Authorization works only against file types that are mapped in the Internet Services Manager to ASP.NET. File types that are not handled by ASP.NET will be subject to the IIS authorization checks.

URL Authorization

A different module in the pipeline is responsible for authorizing users for the requested URL based on configuration data. In many scenarios, this authorization can free us from adding explicit role membership checks in code. The *System.Web.Security.UrlAuthorizationModule* does not require that you specify any type of authentication. It examines the user and makes a decision based on the rules in the *authorization* element of machine.config and web.config. Code Listing 8-9 is a web.config file that overrides the machine.config default of allowing all users access. It uses the special wildcard *?* to represent non-authenticated identities. If you haven't enabled Windows Authentication in both IIS and ASP.NET, the user will simply get an access denied message. If you are using Forms Authentication, the user will be redirected to the *loginUrl*.

Code Listing 8-9   DenyAnonymous_Web.config

```
<configuration>
    <system.web>
        <authorization>
            <deny users="?" />
        </authorization>
    </system.web>
</configuration>
```

Of course, denying the anonymous user access just enforces the rule that the user must be authenticated. The configuration system will provide the authorization settings from individual directories to the *UrlAuthorizationModule* object. Whole directories of content can easily be restricted to individual groups in this way.

In addition to *?*, the *** is used as a wildcard to represent all users. The format for the users and role strings depends on the type of authentication being used. For Windows Authentication, you specify users as a comma-separated, domain-qualified list, such as "Domain\User1, Domain\User2." Roles are specified the same way: "Windows\Administrators." When using Forms Authentication, the user names and role names should match the identities stored in the *HttpContext.User* class.

> **Caution**   *Allow* and *deny* tags are processed sequentially by ASP.NET. The first match found is used, so if you allow a user with one statement and deny them with another, the order of elements will determine whether the user gains access.

Code Listing 8-10 is a web.config file that demonstrates denying access to all users except users belonging to the *superusers* group and a person named Bob. The anonymous user or all users must be denied access in order to take advantage of authentication.

Code Listing 8-10 Authorization_Web.config

```
<configuration>
    <system.web>
        <authentication mode="Forms" />
        <authorization>
            <allow roles="superusers" />
            <allow users="Bob" />
            <deny users="*" />
        </authorization>
    </system.web>
</configuration>
```

Validating Input

Before we start talking more about identity primitives and role checking, let's look at a new feature of ASP.NET version 1.1 that makes it easier to avoid an entire category of security problems. The problem is generally called *cross-site scripting* and refers to inadvertently presenting client-side script to the user. Cross-site scripting occurs when invalidated user input is returned in the page. One example of this would be an attacker presenting the user with a link to a trusted Web site that has script embedded in the query string of the URL. If the site uses the *QueryString* variable in the response, the browser will try to execute the script, and the user will think the script is being sent by the trusted Web site. The attacker gets the user to execute her code by making it appear as though the script comes from somewhere else.

By default, ASP.NET parses the data submitted by the browser, looking for potentially dangerous strings. This helps guard against the user forgetting that it's not a good idea to simply return user input directly in the response. Many books about Web programming include a Hello World example that is vulnerable to exactly this sort of threat. The user is asked to enter her name and when the form is submitted, the name is returned to her. Figure 8-4 shows the error that happens when submitting potentially dangerous form data. It is relatively straightforward for a hacker to construct a link to a page that has script included as part of the input. When the script comes back as part of the response, the user thinks the page is coming from the target site. Figure 8-5 illustrates the interactions that occur in a cross-site scripting attack. The user follows a link from the malicious site to the trusted site and gets a page with script provided by the malicious site.

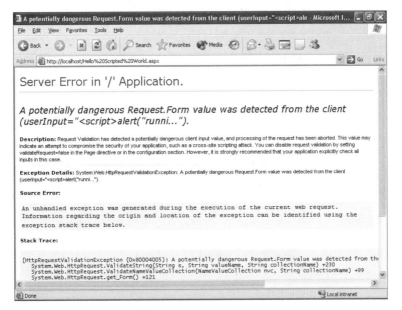

Figure 8-4   Validation failure

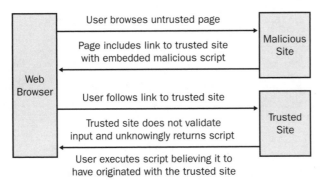

Figure 8-5   Cross-site scripting

Input validation is controlled in several ways. The *pages* element of machine.config includes a *validateRequest* attribute that is set to *true* by default. It can also be controlled in a page directive with the same name or in a web.config file at the application level. It is also possible to cause input validation on demand by calling the new *ValidateInput* method of the *System.Web.UI.Page* class. In most scenarios, leaving the default input validation configuration intact should suffice.

> **Tip** Do not set *validateRequest="false"* in the page's *configuration* element unless absolutely necessary. The better option is to set *validateRequest= "false"* in the page directive for those pages where validation will be handled in your custom code. Such a page directive is shown on the first line of Code Listing 8-11.

If you need to allow the user to submit markup, be sure to encode it with HTML before displaying it in a page. In Code Listing 8-11, we turned off validation in a simple Hello Scripted World.aspx page. The user is allowed to submit anything, but the content is encoded before being displayed.

Code Listing 8-11   Hello Scripted World.aspx

```
<%@Page language="C#" validateRequest="false" %>

<script runat="server">
void Page_Load(object o, EventArgs e) {
    if(IsPostBack) {
        message.Text = "Hello!  Your input was: " +
            Server.HtmlEncode(userInput.Text);
    }
}
</script>

<form runat="server">
<asp:label    runat="server"
        id="message"
        text="Please input your name, or some malicious script." /><br>
<asp:textbox runat="server"
        id="userInput" /><br>
<asp:button  runat="server"
        text="submit" /><br>
</form>
```

Most applications will not need to disable the automatic validation for pages and will benefit from the added protection provided by ASP.NET. If any pages require input that is blocked, be sure to encode all that input before displaying it to the user.

> **Tip** Call the *Server.HTMLEncode* method on all user input before displaying it.

Hardening the Server

I recall a description of a machine that adhered to a strict security policy as having no network connection, no floppy disk drive, and no keyboard or mouse. Obviously, a server like this wouldn't be worth much, but this image does help to illustrate a point about security: reduce the avenues for possible compromise. The last time I heard about a worm compromising systems worldwide, my first question asked which service it was using to get to the machine. Sure enough, it was a service that is enabled by default, but I breathed a sigh of relief knowing that I had long since disabled that service on my machine. It takes some time and some effort to identify and disable the services not required in a particular environment, but it's worth it in the long run.

> Tip   Disable services on the Web server that aren't being used. For example, if you type **net start** at the command prompt, you will probably be surprised at the number of services running on the server. You might not need Simple Mail Transfer Protocol (SMTP), Infrared Monitor, or a DHCP client running on the server. Look at the demands of the Web application, and be sure that the running services are needed to make the server and the application run correctly.

My next advice might seem obvious, but it gets ignored all the time: when operating system, Web server, and database security patches are released, install them! Malicious users and security professionals are constantly looking for new ways to compromise systems. When a hole is found, patch it. Often when system compromises occur, they exploit a vulnerability that was found and fixed in a release long before the attack on your system occurred.

Summary

Designing and implementing Web application security is much easier and more robust with ASP.NET than in the past. In this chapter, we looked at the available options in ASP.NET and how they work hand-in-hand with IIS to authenticate users and authorize their actions.

Think of security first when designing a Web application instead of trying to inject it into the written application. Microsoft has more information online than is provided in this chapter, including a description of several scenarios and the associated step-by-step instructions for implementing your chosen security model. See *http://www.msdn.microsoft.com/library/default.asp?url=/library /en-us/dnnetsec/html/secnetlpMSDN.asp* for more information.

9

Tuning ASP.NET Performance

Let's be honest: performance tuning doesn't sound like fun. It's probably the last thing on your list of things to do when developing an application—if it's even on the list at all. Many developers ignore performance work until they are faced with a critical problem. Maybe this is because so many things contribute to the overall performance of an application that it's difficult to know where to begin. Or maybe developers have difficulty knowing when they have reached the end of the performance work.

In this chapter, we explore how to analyze the performance of an ASP.NET application, discuss what steps can be taken to identify and solve performance issues, and walk through some development best practices that can help you avoid bottlenecks. *Performance tuning*, in which you analyze and measure the behavior of the application as it is being developed, can be interesting, challenging, and very rewarding because it allows you to fully see the results of your work, as long as you don't get caught up in minor details. Look first for the biggest performance issues where your work will pay off the most. This chapter will help you sort out where you can get those payoffs.

Analyzing ASP.NET Applications

Performance tuning is an iterative process. The first step is to analyze the performance of the application. You can't know where to focus your efforts until the behavior of the application is understood. Also, you can't accurately gauge the impact of your changes without being able to reproduce the measurements again and again.

Once you gather performance data about an application, you might be tempted to implement multiple changes simultaneously. However, you might find that when you implement a large set of changes and then repeat the performance analysis, you actually see less improvement than you originally expected. Even if you do get significant improvements, you won't know which changes contributed to them. The iterative process is important because it enables you to understand the impact of each change and validate each change separately. A bad change made at the same time as a good one won't be recognized if both changes are measured together.

You can measure the performance of an ASP.NET application using three primary means: performance counters, profiling, and throughput measurements. These approaches generate solid and reproducible data, so we can measure the behavior of an application through multiple iterations. For all of them, the basic requirements are the same: you must load the application with requests and measure the results.

Controlling the Test Environment

You must have a controlled test environment so that changes in performance measurements reflect the changes you made to the application, not other demands being placed on the server during your testing. You don't want to spend hours chasing down a dip in performance, only to find that the test machine is getting abnormally high file-sharing traffic from peers on the network.

First, establish a set of hardware dedicated to the task. Of course, the ideal is to work on hardware that is exactly the same as the production systems, but you don't have to as long as the architecture is the same. For example, if the production environment consists of front-end Web servers that utilize a back-end database, your test environment should, too. When the hardware is not the same, there is room for error when you extrapolate the capabilities of the deployment environment using numbers gathered in the test environment. Do not use a lack of duplicate hardware as an excuse for not testing, but understand that the results will not be exact when using different processor speeds and quantities of memory.

The hardware dedicated to performance testing should include enough machines acting as clients to generate a significant amount of load. For Web applications that face the Internet instead of internal corporate traffic, make sure you include a variety of user agents and include some random requests. The amount of garbage requests that bombard a publicly accessible server can be staggering. All popular load-generation tools include options for specifying various user-agent strings.

> Tip   When simulating real-world load, use various pseudo-random user-agent strings and completely random requests with large query strings and quantities of posted data. Live servers must endure this type of load, so accurate analysis should include malformed requests along with the valid ones.

Measuring Throughput

The raw throughput number is the key metric used to gauge Web application performance. This metric is the average number of requests per second that the Web server can manage effectively. The other number that is central when discussing throughput is the response time. How long does it take for the request issued by the browser to return results? To really understand response time, you typically divide the measurement into two separate measurements: time-to-first-byte, and time-to-last-byte. *Time-to-first-byte* is calculated as the number of milliseconds that elapse from the moment the client browser makes a request to the moment the first byte of the response is received. Add to that number the time that passes between the first byte and last of byte of the received response and you have *time-to-last-byte*. Figure 9-1 shows the round trip between client and server.

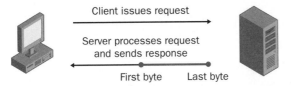

Figure 9-1   Round trip between client and server

You might assume that the time between the first byte and the last byte is very short. Normally it will be, so having large time-to-first-byte or time-to-last-byte times should be investigated. When output is buffered, the time between the first byte and last byte is a rough measure of output size. This timing can also be affected by network bottlenecks. Some performance measuring tools allow you to specify that a selection of clients behave as though they are on slow links to better simulate the real-world mix of connection speeds. A long time-to-first-byte measurement can indicate that the page is performing extensive processing, is blocking on back-end resources, or that the server is in an overloaded state and is undergoing excessive context switching.

> **Note**   The time-to-first-byte throughput metric translates directly into how the user perceives the performance of the Web application. Even when throughput numbers look adequate, the user might feel that the response time is inadequate. The user is not concerned with how many requests the server can manage; she just notices how fast her request is handled.

Using Load Generating Tools

To measure the way an application performs under load, you obviously must subject it to real-world activity. We can't very well enlist hundreds of friends and co-workers to help out, so we use load generating tools. The cost for these software packages varies significantly. The free tools lack some of the features available in the more expensive retail performance analysis software, but we won't take the time here to dissect the various features of each tool. For many applications, using free tools, like Microsoft Web Application Stress Tool, will suffice. This tool is available at *http://www.microsoft.com/technet/treeview /default.asp?url=/technet/itsolutions/intranet/downloads/webstres.asp*. The Web Application Stress Tool is particularly suited for static and relatively static sites where client-side manipulation of variables for subsequent pages is not central to the application. After the Web Application Stress Tool was released, Microsoft went on to incorporate load generation directly into the Application Center Test program, which better handles recording of user actions and managing *ViewState* round trips between client and server.

> **Tip**   Become proficient at using the load generating tool you choose. This might seem like obvious advice, but we can't emphasize it enough. Almost all test packages include various parameters that can be customized to vary the mix of client connection speeds, SSL connections, user-agents, and security credentials. To effectively utilize the tool and thus measure Web application performance accurately, you must understand how to vary the settings in accordance with your application requirements.

The better load generation tools can gather performance counters and log data to give an accurate reporting of how the server and application behaved for a given set of requests. The scripts used to generate the load can be replayed. This is very useful in achieving a controlled test environment after you make adjustments to the application.

When you are finished with a session of throughput measurements, you should have a set of numbers with average time-to-first-byte and time-to-last-byte measurements for all pages of your application. Does that include those rarely used error pages or privacy policy description pages? Yes. After all, the impact of a single poorly behaving page, however infrequently it is requested, can be serious on overall application performance. A user won't care that filling the shopping basket is easy if performance issues during checkout prevent him from completing the transaction. Obviously, the focus of your performance tuning will be on the mainstream process and the most frequently requested pages, but the data for the other pages should be collected so that you don't have any surprises later on.

Using Performance Counters

For the most part, Microsoft Windows performance counters operate in one of two ways: they report a total count of a particular piece of data over time, or they keep running averages of samples provided by the application or service. If an accumulated counter returns to zero and starts climbing again, it's potentially indicating that the associated service failed and re-started. If an averaging counter deviates significantly from the other values for a brief period, even if that variance is short-lived, some resource might have become constrained. These types of anomalies must be investigated because they can be evidence of a stress in the application and can translate into poor user experiences.

The Microsoft common language runtime (CLR) includes a feature referred to as *side-by-side support*, which allows multiple versions of an application to run on the same machine using different versions of the same library. This feature is surfaced in the performance counters. Performance counter objects are supplied by the operating system and by individual processes as well as by the common language runtime. Each performance object provides a set of counters that can include a list of object instances as well as a total counter that provides an aggregated number of all such instances. Both ASP.NET and CLR performance counters include object names that correspond to the last version installed and do not provide the explicitly stated versions. Also present are the full names that include the specific version numbers. In most scenarios, you will be focusing on the latest version, but you might find that you need to work in a side-by-side environment, so you'll need to be aware of this distinction in the names. In the following sections, we describe some of the key counters to collect when examining the performance of an ASP.NET application.

Processor CPU Utilization

In the Performance console, the *Performance Processor* object provides the *% CPU Utilization* metric that indicates what percentage of CPU time is spent actively processing data. (For information on using the Performance console, search for Performance in Help and Support.) In the normal operations of a desktop PC, the CPU is used a relatively small percentage of the time. When you use tools to put stress load on a Web server, the utilization of the CPU can easily be driven to 100 percent. If requests are becoming queued with low CPU utilization, there might be contention for a back-end or operating system resource.

Requests/Sec

The *Requests/Sec* counter, available under the ASP.NET Applications performance object in the Performance console, indicates how many ASP.NET requests per second are handled by the Web server. You can generate enough load to get the requests-per-second counter to a fairly steady state. Then you can gradually add more load to gain an understanding of where the CPU or other resource will become a bottleneck when the number of requests that can be serviced per second is increased.

Errors Total

The *Errors Total* counter, also available under the ASP.NET Applications performance object in the Performance console, tracks the total error count. Check it to ensure that the application is behaving as expected and that stress scripts are generating load correctly. It's amazing how fast some error paths execute when compared with fully functioning pages. A change to configuration or stress scripts can leave you inadvertently measuring how fast the Web server can return a cached error message, which is probably not what you set out to count.

Exceptions Thrown

The *# Of Exceps Thrown* counter keeps a running total of the exceptions. This counter is available under the .NET CLR Exceptions performance object in the Performance console. Some code within ASP.NET includes exception handling logic; the application logic might include some exceptional, but not unheard of, conditions as well. However, if the number is growing rapidly, you should understand why. Perhaps exceptions are being used too heavily within the code, or redirections and transfers (which are handled by the runtime with exceptions) are being used excessively.

Application Restarts

In the ideal world, the Application Restarts counter, under ASP.NET in the Performance console, remains at zero, but remember that modification to config files, compilations exceeding the limit set by the *numRecompilesBeforeAppRestart* attribute of *compile* in configuration data, and modifications to the *bin* directory will cause restarts. An application restart can have a short-term effect on performance that is easily visible to the user.

Page Tracing

Page tracing is a feature of ASP.NET that makes it easy to get some in-depth information about the structure and execution of application pages. In this section, we'll talk briefly about how to turn on tracing and gather information useful for analyzing performance. (See Chapter 10 for more information about using the tracing feature.) When you enable tracing for a page, you can track and view execution time for its various stages. Tracing tracks creation of the server controls along with how they are nested in the control tree, as well as the bytes used to render a particular control and the amount of view state information that control is providing so that it can be round-tripped to the client.

You can enable and view tracing information in two ways: first, via the web.config and machine.config files (which allow you control at the application and machine level); and second, via the *Page* directive. In the former approach, the *trace* element of the system.web configuration section controls the behavior of page tracing. By setting the enabled attribute to *true*, the information is gathered for all application requests. Code Listing 9-1 is a sample web.config file for enabling page tracing for an application.

Code Listing 9-1   Tracing Web.config

```
<configuration>
    <system.web>
        <trace enabled="true"
               localOnly="true"
               pageOutput="false"
               requestLimit="10"
               traceMode="SortByTime"/>
    </system.web>
</configuration>
```

The enabled setting turns tracing off and on. The *localOnly* attribute controls whether the trace information is displayed in response to requests not made directly from the local machine. The *pageOutput* attribute controls whether the trace information should be shown at the end of each page requested, or retrieved via a separate request to the trace handler. The trace handler is accessed by making a request to the trace.axd handler for the application root being traced. For example, if page a.aspx is accessed with *http://localhost/someApplicationRoot/a.aspx*, the trace handler is accessed at *http://localhost/someApplicationRoot/trace.axd*. The *requestLimit* specifies how many page requests' worth of information should be stored. Because a significant amount of data is accumulated in the trace information, consuming valuable server resources, we need to limit the amount of information stored. And finally, we can specify the default *traceMode* of *SortByTime* to retrieve the output in the sequence that the events occurred, or we can switch to *SortByCategory* to have the data grouped. Grouping is particularly useful when adding custom categories of tracing information.

You don't have to enable tracing for an entire application to gather trace information for a page or set of pages. The *Page* directive also allows us to turn on tracing for a single page and is our second approach for viewing and enabling tracing information. By using this setting on a set of pages, we have a great approach for comparing the behavior of our pages on a fixed set of hardware.

Code Listing 9-2, TracingOutput.aspx, demonstrates adding custom information to the trace output by calling the *Trace.Write* method. The first parameter is the category name, and the second parameter is the message. *Trace.Warn* has the same effect, except that the output is red to draw attention to it.

Code Listing 9-2   TracingOutput.aspx

```
<%@Page trace="true" %>
<%@Import namespace="System.Threading" %>
<script language="C#" runat="server">
protected void Page_Load(object o, EventArgs e) {
    Trace.Write("MyInfo", "started Page_Load");
    for(int i = 0; i < 20; i++) {
        Thread.Sleep(100);
        Response.Write(i + "<br/>");
        Trace.Write("MyInfo", "loop iteration number " + i);
    }
    Trace.Write("MyInfo", "ending Page_Load");
}
</script>
```

The output from a page being traced gives us a better understanding of where the page spends its time while executing and how it is composed of server elements. Figure 9-2 is an example of the page output from Code Listing 9-2. In the figure, you can quickly see by looking at the *FromLast* column that the Render phase took the most time for this request. We can also see that although the page shown in the figure has only a label, text box, and button (this is the Hello Scripted World.aspx code from Chapter 8), it does have several other literal server control elements present in the tree, resulting in several hundred bytes of view state.

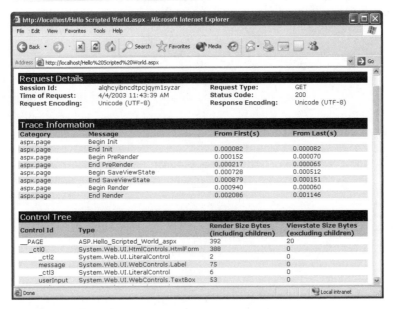

Figure 9-2 Traced output

Once a page is identified as needing performance work, look closely at the data in the trace output. Are controls being created that aren't used? Perhaps a panel contains controls that are used only in certain circumstances. These could be moved to a separate page so that they aren't created until needed. Perhaps output could be cached for portions of the page (see the "Using the Cache" section later in this chapter). Determine what stage of the page processing is taking the most time. Could some repeated work be done less frequently? Identify what about the page is contributing most to the slowdown and focus your efforts there. Take note of the view state size. When databinding controls, you can easily end up with a much larger view state than expected being passed between client and server. It might be more efficient to retrieve the data from the database and store it in *Session* or in the cache and redo the databinding than to round-trip all the data.

Throwing Exceptions

Application error handling can take significant amounts of code. Common practice in many programming languages is to train developers to centralize the error-handling code in one location and automatically go to that code to handle any error conditions. The error-handling code then determines what has gone wrong and deals with it so that the application can resume. At the broadest level, the large amounts of code required to account for many different error conditions when little contextual information is available can be cumbersome and verbose. Beyond that, the error constructs that move execution to the central error-processing code is not as efficient as the try-catch construct. A try-catch can be a more efficient means for dealing locally with exceptional conditions in cases where some context to the possible problems is more readily available.

Throwing and catching exceptions still adds a cost to error management. I recently saw an example illustrating the advantages of try-catch in which the problem was a divide-by-zero error. Even though catching a divide-by-zero error might be simpler than deferring to global error-handling code, checking for problems in code without a try-catch block is actually far more efficient. Remember, however, that an exception is generally used for exceptional conditions. Why pay the performance price of throwing exceptions when simple parameter validation will suffice?

Code Listing 9-3 shows the use of the try-catch construct to handle the case in which the divisor is not valid. In this code, suppose the invalid value comes from user input, not because it is hardcoded. In such a case, it is an error and not really an exceptional condition, so we are using exceptions for error detection. Code Listing 9-4 replaces the try-catch with a simple if-statement to check for the condition and handles the problem in the same way, that is, with a *Response.Write*. Although the try-catch is better than the alternatives such as using a simple *throw*, specific error checks are a better programming practice and can lead to improved performance in many circumstances.

Code Listing 9-3   DivideByZeroWithException.aspx

```csharp
<script language="C#" runat="server">
protected void Page_Load(object o, EventArgs e) {
    try {
        int x;
        int y;
        x = 5;
        y = 0;
        int result = x / y;
        string message = "result is: " + result;
        Response.Write(message);
    }
    catch(DivideByZeroException) {
        Response.Write("divisor can't be zero");
    }
}
</script>
```

Code Listing 9-4   DivideByZeroWithChecking.aspx

```csharp
<script language="C#" runat="server">
protected void Page_Load(object o, EventArgs e) {
    int x;
    int y;
    x = 5;
    y = 0;
    if(y != 0) {
        int result = x / y;
        string message = "result is: " + result;
        Response.Write(message);
    }
    else {
        Response.Write("divisor can't be zero");
    }
}
</script>
```

The overhead of throwing exceptions will probably not be a major factor in most cases, but the accumulated effects of throwing many exceptions can add up. Also, using exceptions instead of handling normal conditions in code, such as with simple statements, might be unnecessary and can lead to overall difficulties in maintaining code. Avoiding unnecessary exceptions is a coding practice that is better for performance and readability.

Compiling ASP.NET Applications

When an .aspx page is first requested, code is generated for a class that derives from the *System.Web.UI.Page* object. That derived page class is then compiled into an assembly and preserved for future requests for the same page. The code doesn't need to be generated and compiled again, but the assembly that holds the class has a certain amount of overhead associated with it. For a single assembly, the amount of overhead is certainly not overwhelming, but an assembly for each page multiplied by hundreds or thousands of pages can lead to unnecessary drag on resources and strained performance. The cumulative effect of all that overhead can take a toll.

When the first request for a Web application is received, ASP.NET can batch compile all the pages in that directory into a single assembly, eliminating the need for multiple assemblies. The *compilation* element in the config files controls how the batch compilation is performed. By default, batch compilation is enabled and limits the number of pages to compile into a single assembly to 1000. These settings are fine for most Web applications as well as the *batchTimeout* setting that limits the batch compilation effort to 15 seconds. If the batch compilation exceeds the timeout, the attempt will be aborted to service the page request that triggered the compilation. You want to avoid losing out on batch compilation, but you also don't want the first request to the Web application to suffer a long delay while the batch compilation occurs. The approach many sites undertake is to trigger the compilation explicitly when bringing a server or updated content online initially. This can be automated by putting together a small application that makes this initial long-running batching request automatically.

> **Tip** Keep batch compilation enabled, but make requests to each Web application while bringing a site online so that the first user to issue a request to the site does not see the delay of batch compilation and the whole directory can be batch compiled.

Code Listing 9-5 takes a static list of URLs, and a single page from each Web application on the local server, and requests them each in turn. This allows us to avoid showing the first user the delay of batch compilation while still enjoying the run time performance benefits.

Code Listing 9-5   TriggerBatchCompile.cs

```
using System;
using System.Net;
using System.IO;
using System.Text;

class TriggerBatchCompile {

private static string[] urls = {
"http://localhost/page.aspx",
"http://localhost/anotherApplication/page.aspx",
"http://localhost/yetAnotherApplication/page.aspx"
};

    public static void Main(string[] args) {
        WebResponse result = null;
        for(int i = 0; i < urls.Length; i++) {
            try {
                Console.WriteLine(urls[i]);
                WebRequest request = WebRequest.Create(urls[i]);
                result = request.GetResponse();
                Stream receiveStream = result.GetResponseStream();
                StreamReader streamReader =
                    new StreamReader(receiveStream);
                char[] read = new Char[256];
                int count = streamReader.Read( read, 0, 256 );
                while (count > 0) {
                    count = streamReader.Read(read, 0, 256);
                }
            }
            catch(Exception e) {
                Console.WriteLine(e);
            }
            finally {
                if ( result != null ) {
                    result.Close();
                }
            }
        }
    }
}
```

The batch compilation has directory granularity, so pages that are updated can cause an assembly to be invalidated and cause additional compilations. But once an assembly is loaded, it can't be unloaded until the application is unloaded. Instead, new assemblies are created for the updated content. Plan accordingly on sites with a high rate of churn. Pages that are updated frequently should be separated from relatively stable pages so that the number of recompilations is limited.

Using the Cache

The ASP.NET cache offers a means for achieving great improvements in performance. The ability to cache output and data for use in subsequent requests that would otherwise have to be created again can result in those later requests running much faster. Caching is covered in detail in Chapter 6, so we'll just review here which cache options can be leveraged to improve performance.

Caching Page Output

When a page is executed, the entire output can be stored in the cache. Subsequent requests for the same page can be handled by the ASP.NET run time by retrieving the output from the cache and returning it. The page itself is not executed again if a match is found in the cache. To get the output from a page to be cached, use the *OutputCache* directive at the top of the page. You can also utilize the cache by writing code directly as detailed in Chapter 6.

The *OutputCache* directive requires a *duration* attribute. An item is removed from the cache when the number of seconds specified in the *duration* attribute passes. Use the *OutputCache* aggressively to increase performance by eliminating page executions. Even caching page output for just a few minutes can have a dramatic impact on performance.

Another attribute required by the *OutputCache* directive is *VaryByParam*. This attribute gives us more control over how ASP.NET looks for items in the cache. If *VaryByParam* is set to *none*, requests with post data or query string data will not be retrieved from the cache. More often, the output is a function of some specific variable in the post data or query string. The *VaryByParam* attribute should then be set to a semicolon-separated list of the variables to use in storing and retrieving the page output.

In some situations, parts of a particular page should be executed on each request but other parts of that page should be cached. The cacheable part of the page can be placed in a separate user control with the *OutputCache* directive specified. This part of the page is then cached even though the rest of the page must be executed for each request. This is called *fragment caching* and can also be a significant factor in improving page execution time.

Caching Objects

The ASP.NET cache provides a rich set of functionality for storing data and objects. It supports setting dependencies for purging an item from the cache as well as for setting priorities to free memory and setting the time when cached output expires. Objects that retain handles and resources, like an open connection to a database, should not be stored in the cache to avoid having other requests deprived of the resources necessary to complete.

> **Tip**   Store application-wide data in the *cache* object instead of the *application* object. The *cache* object does not have the same locking semantics and provides more flexibility.

Consider the cacheability of pages, user controls, objects, and data as the application is designed and developed. Using the cache effectively can have more benefit to application performance than many other performance-coding techniques. After all, code that doesn't have to execute again is much faster than the most optimized running code.

Using COM Objects

The world of Web development has embraced COM as a means for packaging pieces of functionality. Companies have been built on selling COM objects for use in Web applications. ASP.NET and the CLR allow us to continue using COM objects. However, there is a cost associated with using COM objects from an ASP.NET Web application. When you have control of the functionality, make it a priority to rewrite COM objects in managed code to avoid the overhead of COM Interop.

Many COM objects have multiple APIs for accomplishing the same tasks. Perhaps one method call with an extra parameter accomplishes the same thing as several separate calls to different methods. Parameters and return results must be marshaled between the native code world of the COM object and the managed code environment of ASP.NET. Opt for making the single larger call to minimize the number of Interop calls and separate instances of parameter marshalling.

ASP.NET has to take special action in order to run single-threaded apartment (STA) COM objects from within a page. To enable this functionality, you must set *ASPCompat="true"* in the *Page* directive. The page will run from a specially created STA thread pool in which the context and page intrinsics are made available in a fashion compatible with legacy COM objects. When running in ASPCompat mode, be sure to create all COM objects and operating system resources as late as possible and release them as soon as they are no longer needed. This will reduce contention for the resources. If the page constructor creates an STA COM object, this object will be created on a separate thread from the thread that will run the page, automatically requiring all calls to the object to be marshaled across threads, which has an unnecessary and significant performance cost.

> **Tip**   Do not create COM objects in a page constructor, either explicitly or by declaring the object as a page-scoped variable. If you must use legacy COM objects, create them when they are needed and release them as soon as you are finished with them.

Buffering Content

At the lowest level, Web applications are receiving data from the client browser, and formatting and sending data back. In several places during the page execution while the content is being put together, buffering pieces of the output into large pieces can be advantageous. In this section, we'll talk about how buffering works and how to optimize for it. Some developers attempt to accomplish their own optimizations, which can ultimately work against performance, so we'll look at when to leave well enough alone.

Use Response Buffering

ASP.NET is configured to buffer content by default. Data written back to the output is coalesced into larger chunks to avoid the performance penalties associated with sending many small pieces of content through the Web server to the client. You can send fewer TCP packets containing more data, thus reducing the overall percentage of communication overhead. Unless you have specific reasons to turn off buffering, leave it on. One of the few reasons you might consider changing the *buffer* attribute of the pages config setting to *false* is for an extremely long running request. In this case, you would need to be sure that you had a complete piece of content that could be rendered by the browser so that the user could see a visual response. It would be better to break this sort of page, which has intense processing, into multiple requests that conduct smaller pieces of work and provide status updates to the client. Consider queuing work for offline processing or pre-processing where possible.

Avoid String Concatenation

As content is built up for the client, in some cases, you'll need to append strings to an already existing string. You probably have the inclination to write methods that build up a final self-contained piece of content and call *Response.Write* with the complete string. However, this tendency can actually work against performance. In addition to the small substrings, separate larger strings are also created to hold the concatenated string. The substrings in this case are really just temporary memory consumers that must be allocated, copied into the larger string, tracked, and ultimately garbage-collected. If you don't have a compelling reason to concatenate the strings before passing them to *Response.Write*, don't. Remember that ASP.NET will buffer the output, so it's better to create the string once and pass it on to avoid the overhead of concatenation.

Loops of string concatenation are particularly destructive to performance. A single part of a string used in a loop of concatenation can end up in multiple strings that are never actually rendered. Where possible, replace the loop with iterative code or replace the concatenation with separate *Response.Write* calls and let ASP.NET do the buffering.

Use *StringBuilder*

By definition, string instances in the common language runtime are immutable. They can't be changed. When you call an API that results in a modified string, you are really getting a new copy of the string with the change. When strings are concatenated, the original strings still exist, along with a new string that contains copies of the original strings. When code needs to concatenate strings repeatedly, use a *StringBuilder* object to enhance performance. Here's a good rule of thumb: when you have six or more modifications or concatenations to a single string instance, change the code to use *StringBuilder*. The *String-Builder* object acts more like an array of characters. Long chains of concatenation are still associated with performance costs, but the *StringBuilder* class is better equipped to deal with this concatenation.

Minimizing Session State

In this section, we'll highlight the performance tradeoffs inherent in your three choices for using session state services. (We covered session state in detail in Chapter 6.) We'll also talk about a couple of ways to maximize performance. The three options for session state are inproc, out-of-process, and SQL Server.

Inproc refers to session data being stored directly in the same address space as the worker process. This is the fastest option of the three for utilizing session state services. No process hop is required, and object references can be held directly. To use session state effectively in a Web farm scenario requires session-to-machine affinity. The load-balancing technology must be able to recognize the session cookie or browser source address on subsequent requests and have it handled by the same server, which can have performance implications. Fundamentally, it complicates effective load-balancing because the option to utilize the least busy machine is compromised.

Out-of-process state management can be used in a Web farm scenario but the ASP.NET run time must serialize all session data between process and even machine boundaries to communicate with the separate session state process. This option scales well but is still limited by the memory constraints of the state service process.

Using *SQL server* scales beyond the process limits of the out-of-process state service, but it has the biggest cost to performance of the three options. ASP.NET must serialize the session data to store it out-of-process or in SQL server. For the simple types, like strings and numbers, the serialization is relatively fast, but extra overhead is associated with serializing arbitrary user objects.

Generally, even when using in-proc session state, storing data in session has a cost. Still, it can make a world of difference when writing rich Web applications, so use it but be aware that everything stored in session takes up memory and won't be released until the session expires. When storing large amounts of data in session, consider reducing the *SessionState* timeout attribute from its default of 20 minutes to a smaller number.

When the ASP.NET run time manages the *Session* object, the processing of each page has associated overhead. If session is not being used in your application, turn it off. Code Listing 9-6 disables session state functionality at the application level. If any page tries to use the *Session* object, an exception will be thrown.

Code Listing 9-6   No Session State Web.config

```
<configuration>
    <system.web>
        <sessionState mode="Off" />
    </system.web>
</configuration>
```

If a subset of pages in the application utilizes session state, session state can be turned off globally and then enabled only in the pages where it is needed. The *Page* directive includes the *EnableSessionState* attribute, which can override the global application setting. Code Listing 9-7 turns on session state and simply stores the time of the request for later use.

Code Listing 9-7   EnableSessionState.aspx

```
<%@Page EnableSessionState="true" %>
<script runat="server" language="C#">
protected void Page_Load(object o, EventArgs e) {
    Session["enableSessionStateTime"] = DateTime.Now.ToString();
    theLabel.Text = (string)Session["enableSessionStateTime"];
}
</script>
<asp:Label runat="server" id="theLabel" />
```

Finally, there is a potential for race conditions when accessing session data simultaneously from multiple browser instances or when using client-side frames. To manage this, ASP.NET imposes some reader and writer locking semantics around access to session variables. If a page is accessing session state but not storing any new or updated values in session, use the *EnableSessionState Page* directive to enable session state for read-only access. This causes ASP.NET to use a reader lock for session access on the page, which can provide a performance boost. Code Listing 9-8 retrieves the time stored by the EnableSessionState.aspx page and displays it but has read-only access to the *Session* object. Any attempt to write results in an exception being thrown.

Code Listing 9-8   ReadOnlySessionAccess.aspx

```
<%@Page EnableSessionState="ReadOnly" %>
<script runat="server" language="C#">
protected void Page_Load(object o, EventArgs e) {
    string theTime = (string)Session["enableSessionStateTime"];
    if (theTime != null) {
        theLabel.Text = theTime;
    }
}
</script>
<asp:Label runat="server" id="theLabel" />
```

Judicious use of session state avoids the need to put everything in hidden fields and have it carried back and forth between client and server, but once again there is a cost. Examine your application and deployment architecture and pick the session state mode that will satisfy your application needs without sacrificing performance.

Using View State

The use of view state by ASP.NET allows us to easily build sophisticated Web applications that have state information carried between requests while using the stateless HTTP protocol. As with the session state feature, using view state has a price. The state information is stored in a hidden field of the form and posted back to the server with the form. The view state information is then parsed and the data restored to the controls. The trace information, discussed earlier in this chapter, allows us to see the size of the view state for individual controls. Databound controls in particular can have very large quantities of view state information.

As the size of the view state grows, so does the time it takes to send the data to the client, receive the data back from the browser, and parse the data. Examine the view state requirements for the pages on your site. Consider server caching of datasets and perform the databinding again when view state size becomes large.

For pages that do not rely on view state information, disable the view state altogether by setting the *EnableViewState Page* directive attribute to *false*. For pages that take advantage of view state, you can disable it for user controls separately by setting the *@Control EnableViewState* property or by setting the *EnableViewState* attribute on individual controls.

Summary

Performance tuning should not be postponed until you're faced with a serious problem on a live site. Instead, you should consider the issues throughout site development, starting with application design. Performance tuning is an iterative process. The first iteration should be to ascertain the exact behavior of the application. You do this using load-generation tools in a controlled environment while monitoring performance counters and examining page-tracing information. Time-to-first-byte and time-to-last-byte measurements are indicators of application responsiveness and the duration of page execution.

After you assess the problems and make changes to the application, gather performance data again to accurately ascertain the effects of your modifications. Employ caching where possible to eliminate unnecessary code execution and database work. You can make additional gains by improving your coding techniques and eliminating unnecessary view state and session data.

10

ASP.NET Debug and Trace

Trace is a great aid in debugging unexpected application behavior. In Chapter 9, we talked briefly about using the trace feature of ASP.NET to better understand the performance of an application. In this chapter, we'll look at debugging and trace options in more detail. For example, you'll learn how to send your own debug information directly to the trace output or even to an external debugger or monitoring tool. We'll also look at how the compilation system works with trace and debugging—when you know some details about how the ASP.NET compilation system works, you can isolate problems more readily and be better able to leverage the ASP.NET platform.

Before we jump into enabling trace, let's talk a little more about what we mean by debug and trace. As you know, ASP.NET generates code from .aspx pages and .ascx files. These objects derive from the *Page* and *UserControl* base classes and are compiled automatically by ASP.NET. When the page and user control code executes, the output is sent back to the browser. Information about the page and its contents, along with trace and debug information, can be gathered while the page executes. Data about the control tree that makes up the page as well as where the CPU cycles are spent during page execution is important to troubleshooting problems. We said that the debug information could be gathered, but it's important to note that compilation of the generated code actually avoids the performance cost associated with debugging and tracing unless each is explicitly enabled. The trace information can be displayed at the bottom of the page, or an aggregated view can be made available by making requests to a separate trace handler.

Enabling Trace

Trace information can be gathered for an entire application or enabled on a per-page basis. When included on the page, the trace output is appended at the bottom of the regular page output, as a set of tables. To enable trace for a single page, add *Trace="true"* to the *Page* directive. Code Listing 10-1 enables tracing.

Code Listing 10-1   Trace Hello.aspx
```
<%@ Page Trace="true" language="c#" %>
<form runat="Server">
    <asp:label runat="Server" Text="Hello" />
</form>
```

After our simple *Hello* text is written out, a series of tables with detailed trace information is displayed. Figure 10-1 shows what this output looks like. We'll look at the trace information included in this page output in the section "Reading Trace Output" later in this chapter.

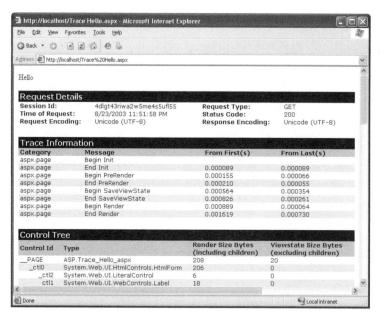

Figure 10-1   Trace output

As you learned in Chapter 9, in addition to turning trace output on and off for a single page, you can turn it on and off for an entire application or even globally for the machine using configuration settings. Code Listing 10-2 demonstrates enabling tracing for an application. We set *pageOutput= "true"* to have the trace information for each page execution included after the page output.

Code Listing 10-2 Trace Enabled Web.config

```
<configuration>
    <system.web>
        <trace enabled="true" pageOutput="true" />
    </system.web>
</configuration>
```

Setting *pageOutput="true"* is equivalent to setting *trace="true"* in the *Page* directive for each page in the application, a convenient option when trouble-shooting an application or looking at performance issues for a site.

Setting Trace Options

Five attributes can be set on the *trace* element to configure tracing. These settings work together to determine how tracing behaves in your application. You can include trace data directly in the page for all to see, or you can limit its visibility so that the data can be viewed only from a separate handler. You can even limit viewing to only when browsing from the server directly.

enabled Attribute

The Boolean *true* and *false* values are the values for the *enabled* attribute. The default value is *false*, meaning that trace information is not available. The trace statements included in the page are short-circuited to minimize the performance impact.

pageOutput Attribute

This Boolean attribute controls whether the output will be included in each page. If *pageOutput* is set to *false* but trace has been turned on explicitly in the *Page* directive, the output will still be included. The default value is *false*.

traceMode Attribute

The default setting for *traceMode* is *SortByTime*. This means that output is arranged chronologically based on when the trace statement occurred. For example, if you include tracing statements in the *Load* event, the output would appear after the *Init* event tracing but before the *PreRender* trace statements.

The other option for the *traceMode* attribute is *SortByCategory*. In this mode, the output is sorted according to category strings passed as part of the *Write* or *Warn* methods.

requestLimit Attribute

When tracing is enabled, data from the most recent requests is cached on the server. You can access this data by requesting the trace.axd handler for the Web application. For example, *http://localhost/trace.axd* would display the list of most recent requests to the default application on the local machine. Figure 10-2, which displays data for three requests, shows how the most recent requests are listed. Because the default *requestLimit* of *10* is in effect, the page also shows that there is room to hold details for seven more requests. When the eleventh request is received, information about the first request is lost. The information retained is for the most recent requests up to the number specified in *request-Limit*. General information about the requests, including the time, the file name, the resulting status code, and the HTTP verb used to retrieve the page, are listed. Clicking the *View Details* link will display the trace output as though it were included in the page, but without the actual page output.

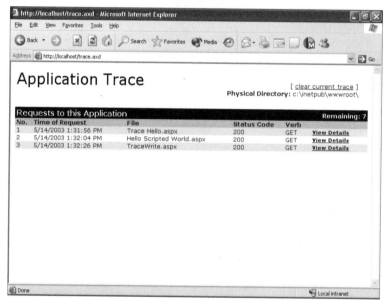

Figure 10-2   Trace.axd listing

localOnly Attribute

Because you might include potentially sensitive debugging information in your trace output, the default behavior for trace is to honor requests to trace.axd only when those requests are made from a browser launched from the server. Requests that are not made to *localhost* will not have access to the data. You can enable remote viewing of trace.axd by setting *localOnly* to *false*.

Reading Trace Output

Now that we've talked about how to configure tracing, let's walk through the information that is automatically gathered during page execution and displayed in the trace output.

Request Details

The request details constitute the top-level information about the request and include which encoding is used for the request and response, what time the request was made, the session ID, as well as which HTTP verb was used and the response status code.

Trace Information

The trace information section has granular information about what is happening during the page life cycle. The *From First* and *From Last* columns reveal how much time has elapsed from the time the request first started and how much time has elapsed from the last trace event.

> **Tip**   Use the trace *From Last* column data to quickly narrow down long-running pieces of code. This is particularly useful in isolating performance issues.

Control Tree

The page itself is the top-level control in the control tree. All other server controls fall somewhere under the page. For example, in Figure 10-1, we see that the page analyzing Trace Hello.aspx contains an *HtmlForm* control and a *LiteralControl*. In this case, the *LiteralControl* has a render size of just 2 bytes, so it's probably just carriage-return/newline white space. The *Label* and more literal elements are contained in the *HtmlForm*.

In addition to tracking the actual size rendered for each control in the tree, the size of the view state data being round-tripped between client and server is also reported. Having an idea of how much view state is being used can help you tailor your application to be more efficient. Databound controls, in particular, can contribute significantly to the size of the view state.

Cookies Collection

The *Cookies* collection shows both the cookies received from the browser for a particular request and any new cookies or updated cookie values returned. Unfortunately, *Cookies* doesn't distinguish between the two types. Code Listing 10-3 simply increments the value of a cookie called *MyCookie* on each request.

In the trace information from Code Listing 10-3, shown in the trace.axd output in Figure 10-3, we see two entries for *MyCookie* with values of *10* and *11*.

Code Listing 10-3   Cookie.aspx

```
<script language="C#" runat="server" trace="true">
protected void Page_Load(object o, EventArgs e) {
HttpCookie outbound = new HttpCookie("MyCookie");

HttpCookie inbound = Request.Cookies["MyCookie"];
if(inbound != null) {
    outbound.Value = (Int32.Parse(inbound.Value) + 1).ToString();
    theLabel.Text = inbound.Value;
}
else {
    outbound.Value = "1";
}
Response.Cookies.Add(outbound);
}
</script>
<asp:label runat="server" id="theLabel"
    Text="no cookie value received" />
```

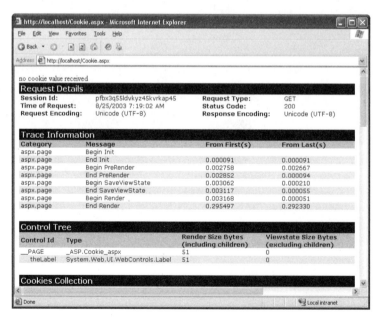

Figure 10-3   Cookie.aspx page output

Headers Collection

The *Headers* collection is an enumeration of all of the HTTP headers sent by the browser. Note that the *ASP.NET_SessionId* cookie is explicitly removed from the *Headers* and *Server Variables* information because it is managed entirely by ASP.NET.

> **Note**   You can distinguish between inbound and outbound cookie values by looking at the *Cookie* row in the *Headers* collection. The value from the *Cookie* header is the value sent by the client.

Server Variables

The server variables are the data that can be retrieved from the Web server about the request and the server environment. This can include information such as the physical path to the application directory unless the application is running at lower trust levels, which would prevent the display of some server variables.

Form Collection

When the HTTP verb used in the request is a *POST* instead of a *GET*, which is the case for postbacks, an additional category of trace information is collected and displayed. The *Form* collection lists the variable names and values for each piece of data posted to the server. This information is particularly useful in tracking exactly what values are coming from the client.

Writing Trace Output

The information provided by ASP.NET when trace is enabled can go a long way toward increasing your understanding of both the page makeup and where the execution and view state costs are. Beyond that, for debugging code, trace provides a replacement for sprinkling *Response.Write* methods throughout your code. Using trace eliminates the need to scour your code to eliminate any lingering debug statements before your code goes into production.

The *Trace* object is actually of type *TraceContext* and is available by accessing the *Trace* property of page. It has two methods for writing trace information: *Warn* and *Write*. Both of these methods have three overrides. The first just takes a string that is the debug data you are recording. The second override adds a category string as the first parameter. When using the *SortByCategory* *traceMode*, the custom category can be very helpful in grouping similar types of output. The third override adds an exception parameter at the end. The exception data is then recorded as part of the trace information.

> **Tip**   Implement an *Application_OnError* handler that traces error information so that if you encounter unusual behavior in an application, you are prepared to gather more information by simply enabling trace.

The difference between messages logged using *Write* and those recorded with *Warn* is the formatting of the output. *Warn* messages are highlighted as providing higher priority information. In Code Listing 10-4, we write messages using both *Warn* and *Write*, including an exception.

Code Listing 10-4   TraceWriteAndWarn.aspx

```
<%@ Page Trace="true" language="c#" %>
<script runat="server">
protected void Page_Load(object o, EventArgs e) {
    Trace.Write("info", "some data goes here");
    try {
        throw new Exception("something exceptional has occurred");
    }
    catch (Exception exception) {
        Trace.Warn("problem", "warn message", exception);
    }
}
</script>
<asp:label runat="Server" Text="Hello" />
```

When the page represented by Code Listing 10-4 executes, information about the exception, including where it was thrown, is included in the trace output. The text in the center of Figure 10-4 ("warn message") is the result of calling the *Warn* method.

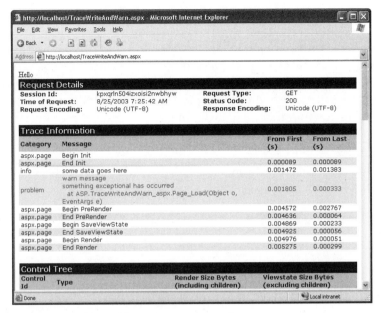

Figure 10-4   Trace *Warn* output

The *Trace* facilities offer an easy way to quickly get good information about the control structure, view state usage, and execution properties of a page. As mentioned earlier, when you need help isolating a problem in your program, *Trace* is the perfect replacement for inserting simple debug info directly into the page code.

How ASP.NET Compilation Works

When ASP.NET receives a request for a page, it first looks to see whether it has a current compiled version of the page. When the sources for a page are modified and saved, ASP.NET invalidates the previous version of the page and creates a new one when it is needed. When the first request for a page in an application is received, ASP.NET will try to generate code for all pages in the directory and compile them into a single assembly for greater efficiency.

Knowing how ASP.NET compilation works is helpful, particularly when troubleshooting a problem with an application. ASP.NET creates a directory under the root Microsoft .NET Framework directory for generating and compiling code. The resulting assemblies (and code, when debugging is enabled) can be found here. The directory used by ASP.NET is called Temporary ASP.NET Files. In a default .NET Framework version 1.1 installation, these assemblies can be found in the \Microsoft.NET\Framework\v1.1.4322 directory under \Windows or \WINNT. Navigate to this directory on your machine, and you'll find a subdirectory corresponding to each application root of your Web server where ASP.NET pages have been requested. For example, *root* corresponds to the default root Web application defined in the Internet Services Manager. Inside that subdirectory is another directory that contains yet another whose name appears to be randomly generated. In that inner subdirectory is a set of files generated by ASP.NET. These files are used to track when pages are updated, when pages need to be recompiled, and dependencies between pages. Figure 10-5 is a view in Microsoft Internet Explorer of the types of files you will find in the temporary directory.

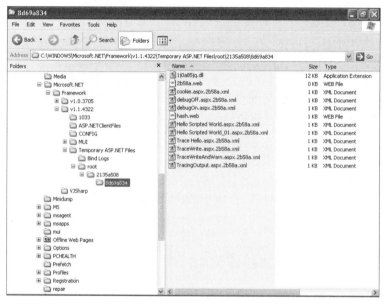

Figure 10-5   Temporary ASP.NET files

The .web files are used by ASP.NET to manage when files are updated. The .xml files correspond to a page in the application directory that has been compiled. In this directory listing, only one .dll is present, although a collection of .xml files exists. If we run ILDASM on that .dll, we can see that the assembly contains page classes for each page in which an .xml dependency file has been created. When a page from the root directory was first requested, a single assembly was generated by creating and compiling code for all the pages present. Figure 10-6 shows the listing as seen in ILDASM.

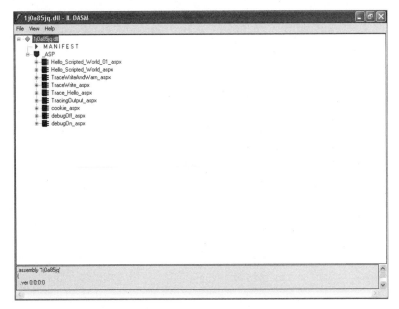

Figure 10-6   Batch compilation

The .xml file contains information about the dependencies used by ASP.NET to track which source files were used in compiling the page class and the name of the resulting .dll. For a simple page, like Cookie.aspx from Code Listing 10-3, the dependencies are simple. Figure 10-7 shows that we've opened the .xml file in Microsoft Notepad and only the .aspx file was used.

The *assem* attribute indicates the name of the assembly into which the page source was compiled; the *filedep* element lists the files that contributed to the final code. If we modify the source file, ASP.NET sees the change and the .xml file is updated when the page is next requested. The *assem* attribute will point to a new DLL that appears in the temporary directory. That assembly will contain just the updated cookie page class, whereas the rest of the page objects will still be executed from the previously created assembly.

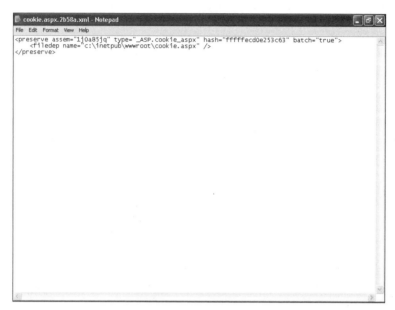

Figure 10-7 Dependency listing

Enabling Debug

Now that you've learned more about how the compilation system works, let's examine the debug options that affect compilation. The *Page* directive supports a *debug* attribute, which is *false* by default. When this attribute is set to *true*, ASP.NET changes the way the file is compiled to provide us with a better debugging experience. The config files also provide a setting that causes all pages in the application to be compiled as though the *debug* directive were set to *true*. Code Listing 10-5 is an example of enabling debugging for all pages in an application.

Code Listing 10-5   Debug Web.config
```
<configuration>
    <system.web>
        <compilation debug="true" />
    </system.web>
</configuration>
```

When debug is enabled for an application, ASP.NET will compile each page separately and generate extra files in the Temporary ASP.NET files directory for the application. A .pdb file is created with symbol information as well as an .err file containing any compilation error output. The flags passed to the compiler are saved in the .cmdline file, and the output from the compiler interactions are saved in the .out file. Interestingly, the source file generated by ASP.NET from the .aspx file is preserved.

> **Tip**   To quickly get to the source code for a page, you do not need to access the Temporary ASP.NET Files directories. Instead, introduce a deliberate syntax error. ASP.NET will flag the error and provide the Show Complete Compilation Source option as well as the compiler output.

Several of the options passed to the compiler are affected by enabling debugging. Usually, the command-line options include */debug-* to disable debug information and */optimize+* to turn on compiler optimizations. When ASP.NET debug is enabled, these settings are reversed to */debug+* and */optimize-* to emit debug information and disable potentially confusing optimizations. Also, */D:DEBUG* is added so that conditionally included debug code will be incorporated.

Sending Data to the Debugger

We've already discussed using the *Trace* object to send *Write* and *Warn* messages to the *Trace* collection facility. You might also want to gather data independently from the page. Much of the debugging that goes on is not directed at the page code but rather at the business objects being used by the page. For example, if you're trying to gather information about code execution in the *Session_OnEnd* event, the .NET Framework provides the objects in the *System.Diagnostics* namespace that allow us to get even deeper into the code and gather more detailed debug information. We can then output debug information without relying on the presence of an executing page to receive the output.

Code Listing 10-6 shows how to use the *WriteLine* method of both the *Trace* and *Debug* objects, which are in the *System.Diagnostics* namespace. (This *Trace* object is not the same as the *Trace* property of page.) Even with the trace and debug *Page* directives set to *true*, we still won't see evidence of the error messages. To view the error data, we must use a process that will listen for the issued debug and trace information. Attaching to the process with Microsoft Visual Studio .NET 2003 and viewing information in the debug pane works.

Another option is to use a system-level debug listener, such as DebugView, available for download at *http://www.sysinternals.com/ntw2k/freeware/debugview.shtml.*

Code Listing 10-6   DiagnosticsDebug.aspx

```
<%@Page debug="true" compileroptions="/d:TRACE" %>
<script language="C#" runat="server">
protected void Page_Load(object o, EventArgs e) {
    System.Diagnostics.Debug.WriteLine("important debug information goes here
");
    System.Diagnostics.Trace.WriteLine("trace information goes here");
}
</script>
<asp:label runat="server" id="theLabel" Text="Debugging info is helpful" />
```

Note that the *Debug* and *Trace* class functionality from the *System.Diagnostics* namespace is available only when the corresponding constants are defined. We get *DEBUG* defined when the debug *Page* directive is *true*, but the trace *Page* directive is unrelated. To define *TRACE*, we must do so explicitly using the *compileroptions Page* directive by setting the exact argument to be passed to the compiler. In this case, the argument is *"/d:TRACE"*. The *compileroptions* directive can be used to pass any arbitrary argument to the compilation of the page.

> **Note**   Do not use ASP.NET debug functionality on a production server. The performance implications are severe. Instead, to gather run time information programmatically, use trace functionality or classes in the *System.Diagnostics.Trace* namespace.

Using Compiler Options

In addition to being able to pass compiler options directly using the *compileroptions Page* directive, we can control another behavior of ASP.NET code generation and compilation that can make investigations easier. By default, ASP.NET generates line-number pragma statements throughout the code. These references indicate the source point of the generated code in the original .aspx page. These pragma statements are not necessary, and can even be distracting, when you look extensively at the generated code. To disable these statements, add the *linepragmas* attribute to the *Page* directive with a value of *false*. Code Listing 10-7 is an example of disabling the source-point line pragmas.

Code Listing 10-7   NoLinePragmas.aspx

```
<%@Page linepragmas="false" %>
<asp:label
    runat="server"
    id="theLabel"
    Text="Disable line pragmas for more readable generated code" />
```

There's really no point in disabling line pragmas generally, but when you find yourself needing to trace through the page class code to pursue some elusive problem, you'll appreciate being able to remove them from view.

Summary

In this chapter, we've looked at the debug and trace functionality of ASP.NET. The trace feature allows us to quickly get some insight into the characteristics of the page. We can see the structure of the control tree and the corresponding view state size, and we can get information about where server resources are spent when executing the page. By using the *TraceContext* object of the *Page* class, we can write output to investigate problems without worrying about removing them for production environments.

We also looked at how ASP.NET code generation and file compilation works and how this behavior can be controlled and leveraged to isolate issues in your code. We also examined how to use objects in the *System.Diagnostics* namespace to trace information that might otherwise be difficult to access in production environments.

11

Moving to ASP.NET

This chapter is not meant to convince you to move to ASP.NET—you should already be convinced! Instead you can think of this chapter as a playbook for how you can move your current application to Microsoft .NET. You'll note that we didn't just say "move to ASP.NET." When you decide to commit to ASP.NET, you're really committing yourself to .NET. To get the most benefit from your investment, you need to think about how all the parts of your system will interact. For example, should you move your existing business logic layer (BLL) or data access layer (DAL) from COM server, written with Microsoft Visual Basic 6 or Enterprise Java Beans, to similar components written in .NET? Or should you use Web services or interop layers?

I firmly believe that before you decide to move to ASP.NET, you should first perform a full review of the technology, including writing up a plan of action for the change. You should fully understand the common language runtime (CLR) as well as the architecture of ASP.NET. Entire books are written about the CLR alone; similarly, we could dedicate an entire book to the architecture of ASP.NET—the point being that, in one chapter, we can't possibly cover every detail you need to know to make the move to ASP.NET. However, we'll provide a basic overview of how ASP.NET works, which will help you get started.

Web Application Architecture

Before Microsoft Active Server Pages (ASP), most dynamic Web applications were hacks; for example, my first Web applications were written on an AIX with Perl scripts. Active Server Pages 1, however, was a complete revolutionary shift in they way dynamic HTML was generated. It was one of the first technologies specifically targeted at simplifying the development of Web applications.

ASP was also one of the first technologies to successfully take advantage of the application programming interfaces, known as ISAPI, of Internet Information Services (IIS). ASP provided a high-level programming paradigm for creating Web applications. So what is ASP exactly?

Active Server Pages is a programming abstraction layer that allows developers to write interactive Web applications without requiring knowledge of low-level IIS programming interfaces such as ISAPI. ASP itself is an ISAPI extension. ASP is automatically registered with IIS.

Within IIS are two main application programming interface entry points known as ISAPI: filters and extensions. *ISAPI filters* participate in each request that comes into and goes out of IIS. Filters are able to filter incoming and outgoing information, adding or removing content when necessary. For example, an ISAPI filter could map incoming URLs to different paths or perform custom authentication routines, such as allowing or denying the request based on an HTTP cookie. (The best resource on ISAPI is the *Microsoft Internet Information Services [IIS] 6 Resource Kit*, published in 2003.)

ISAPI extensions, on the other hand, are the final target of a given request. Whereas information passes through an ISAPI filter, information is mapped to a destination by an ISAPI extension, such as a requested URL into a specific DLL (dynamic link library). For example, ASP is an ISAPI extension. Requests to IIS that end with .ASP are mapped to the asp.dll ISAPI extension.

Applications written directly in ISAPI will outperform any other type of rapid application development abstraction layer. Similarly, hand-coded x86 assembly code can outperform code written in Visual Basic 6. For example, ISAPI code that specifically loops 1000 times and writes "Hello World" would likely outperform an ASP statement that loops 1000 times and writes "Hello World." This performance difference is due to two reasons. First, an ISAPI is composed of C++-compiled x86 instructions that are targeted directly at the processor architecture run by the platform. The ISAPI code is highly task-specific and is responsible only for the single operation of outputting HTML.

Second, an ASP consists of script code, usually Microsoft Visual Basic Script (VBScript), that must be parsed, turned into bytecode, and then executed. The script code is not compiled.

You can get the best possible performance with ISAPI, but the trade-off is the cost of development. Writing ISAPI code is not for the faint of heart. An operation that can be performed in 2–3 lines of ASP or ASP.NET code might take 20–40 lines as an ISAPI extension—and for a task as simple as writing "Hello World." Additionally, since ISAPI is multithreaded, it requires a development language such as C++ and expertise in writing multithreaded code; Visual Basic 6 can produce only code that is apartment-model threaded or single-threaded code.

Active Server Pages Extension Mappings

The mapping of file extensions to the appropriate ISAPI extension is done within IIS. To view the extension mappings on your IIS server, open Internet Information Services. Right-click on a Web site such as Default Web Site and select Properties, which will open the Properties dialog box for your Web site. Select the Home Directory tab, shown in Figure 11-1.

Figure 11-1   Home Directory tab

Next, on the Home Directory tab, click the Configuration button. This will open the Application Configuration dialog box, which displays a table that lists the mappings of file extensions to the corresponding ISAPI .dll. This table is shown in Figure 11-2. The .ASP extension is highlighted.

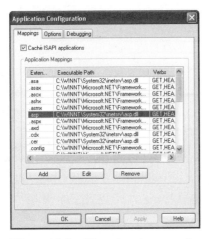

Figure 11-2   File extension mappings

The two extensions, .ASA and .ASP, are mapped to the ASP.dll ISAPI extension, which are handled by ASP. The .ASA extension is a global application file in which global events are defined, such as *Session_OnStart*. Direct access through the browser to this file is not allowed, and this extension is mapped only to prevent unauthorized access. The .ASP extension is the main ASP extension. Files with this extension can be parsed and executed as ASP executables. Figure 11-3 diagrams what happens when IIS receives a request for the .ASP extension.

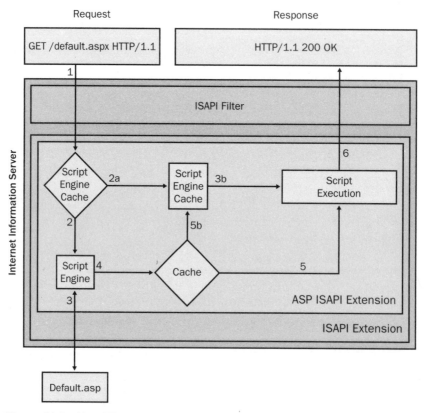

Figure 11-3 How IIS processes a request for a file with the .ASP extension

Here is a description of what Figure 11-3 illustrates:

1. A request is made to an IIS server for default.asp. IIS accepts the request and the request flows through the ISAPI filter layer first and then to the ISAPI extension layer, where it is mapped to the asp.dll extension.

2. Within the asp.dll extension, ASP first determines whether the script responsible for generating the response resides in the *script engine cache*. The script engine cache is a performance technique used by ASP to cache frequently accessed scripts in raw form without reparsing the ASP file. If the script code is found within a script engine cache (2b), the script code is executed (3b), and the response is generated.

3. If a script engine cache is not found for the incoming request, ASP will create a new script parser and parse the .ASP file from disk and generate the script code necessary to create the output.

4. If the requested file is being requested frequently, as we would expect with the home page, the decision to cache the generated script is made (5b).

5. The generated script is handed off to the script execution engine.

6. The generated response page, such as one in HTML, is sent back through IIS to the application that generated the request.

The ASP.NET Difference

Applications built with ASP.NET are still routed through IIS and thus must somehow interact with IIS through ISAPI. Unlike ASP, ASP.NET is written in managed code—nearly 100 percent of the ASP.NET code base is managed code written in C#. However, the interaction point between IIS and ASP.NET is still an ISAPI extension: aspnet_isapi.dll. Table 11-1 shows the extensions that are mapped within IIS to the aspnet_isapi.dll.

Table 11-1   Extensions Mapped within IIS to aspnet_asapi.dll

Entry Point	Description
.ASAX	Global application file for ASP.NET. This type of file serves a similar purpose as ASP .asa files. Global events, such as *Session_OnStart*, and static application variables, are declared within it. As with .ASA, direct requests for .ASAX are not allowed.
.ASCX	Extension used by ASP.NET for user controls. User controls can simply be thought of as ASP.NET pages that can be used within other ASP.NET pages as user interface–generating components.
.ASHX	Specialized extension for creating on-demand compiled ASP.NET handlers. (See Code Listing 11-1.)
.ASMX	Extension used by ASP.NET Web services to allow for SOAP-based interactions.

Table 11-1 Extensions Mapped within IIS to aspnet_asapi.dll

Entry Point	Description
.ASPX	Extension used for ASP.NET pages, similar to .ASP used by ASP. It is within the .ASPX file that all user code resides.
.CONFIG	Extension used by the ASP.NET configuration system, written in XML. Rather than using the IIS metabase ASP.NET application, settings are managed within an XML configuration file.
.CS	Mapping to prevent access to C# source files.
.CSPROJ	Mapping to prevent access to Microsoft Visual Studio .NET C# projects.
.REM	Mapping used by .NET remoting.
.RESX	Mapping to prevent access to .NET resource files. Resource files contain localized strings and other resource information used by projects.
.SOAP	Mapping for .NET remoting use of SOAP.
.VB	Mapping to prevent access to Visual Basic .NET source files.
.VBPROJ	Mapping to prevent access to Visual Studio .NET and Visual Basic .NET projects.
.VSDISCO	Web service discover file. Applications can learn what Web services the server supports by querying the disco file.

Note that extensions related to ASP are not mapped to ASP.NET. This allows ASP and ASP.NET applications to run side by side without conflicting with one another. We'll discuss this in more detail shortly.

Figure 11-4 illustrates what happens when IIS 5 receives and processes a request for the .ASPX extension. After the request is made, IIS routes the request to the ASP.NET ISAPI extension, aspnet_isapi.dll.

Then aspnet_isapi.dll makes a named pipe call from IIS to the ASP.NET worker process: aspnet_wp.exe. This worker process hosts the common language runtime, the executing environment for .NET applications, and additionally hosts the ASP.NET *HttpRuntime* execution environment. The *HttpRuntime* is the request/response processing framework provided by ASP.NET and determines whether the requested page is already compiled. If it is, an instance of the compiled page is created, and the instance is asked to render its contents. If the page is not already compiled, the page parser attempts to load the page.

The page is located on disk and handed back to the page parser. The page parser creates a hierarchy of server control elements found within the page and emits a class file that represents the page.

The class file is given to the appropriate compiler. By default the page is compiled using the Visual Basic .NET compiler, however, you can explicitly select a compiler by specifying the language the page uses within a page directive.

The compiled class (.DLL) emitted by the page parser is stored on the disk again in a special temporary file location dedicated to ASP.NET applications (such as the location C:\WINNT\Microsoft.NET\Framework\v1.1.4322\Temporary ASP.NET Files\MyApp). At this point, an instance of the compiled page is created.

The page is asked to render its contents. *Render* is a special method supported by the page classes and can be thought of as the main method used by a page class. The rendered contents are then sent back through ISAPI. The generated response, such as an HTML page, is sent through IIS again and back to the application that generated the request.

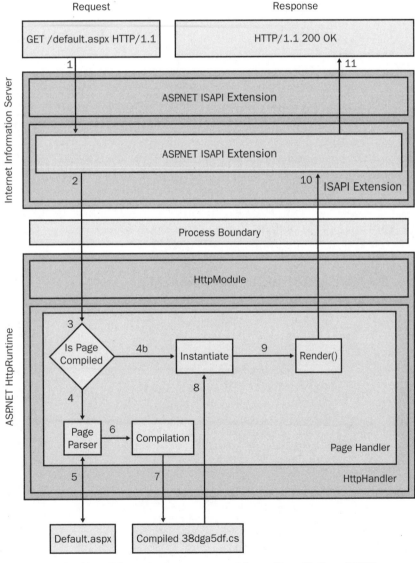

Figure 11-4   How IIS processes a request for a file with the .ASPX extension

In IIS 6, a dedicated IIS worker process hosts ASP.NET. No named pipe calls are made from the ISAPI extension, and the aspnet_wp.exe is not used. Rather, the common language runtime is hosted within the dedicated IIS worker process: w3wp.exe. This process is further divided into subvirtual processes known as *application domains*. An application domain has a 1:1 mapping to either a Web application virtual directory or a Web application root. In the application domain, an instance of the ASP.NET *HttpRuntime* is hosted.

HttpRuntime

The *HttpRuntime* models itself after the IIS ISAPI filter/extension programming model. The ASP.NET *HttpRuntime* is similar to the IIS ISAPI model in that it exposes two main entry points, that is, classes that implement the *IHttpModule* and *IHttpHandler* interfaces. An entry point that implements *IHttpModule* is similar to an ISAPI filter in that it can screen incoming and outgoing requests. A class that implements *IHttpHandler* is similar to an ISAPI extension. It is the target of a given extension of a request, for example, .ASPX.

The major difference between ISAPI and the ASP.NET *HttpRuntime* is that ISAPI filters and extensions can be written only in C++, whereas implementations of *HttpRuntime*'s *IHttpModule* and *IHttpHandler* can be written in any managed language, such as Visual Basic .NET. Code Listing 11-1 is a simple implementation of *IHttpHandler* written in Visual Basic .NET. Note that this code was written within an .ASHX file.

Code Listing 11-1   HelloWorldHttpHandler.ashx

```vb
<%@ WebHandler Language="VB" Class="HelloWorldHandler" %>

imports System
imports System.Web

public Class HelloWorldHandler
    Implements IHttpHandler

    Sub ProcessRequest(context As HttpContext)
        Implements IHttpHandler.ProcessRequest
        Dim Request As HttpRequest = context.Request
        Dim Response As HttpResponse = context.Response

        Response.Write("<html>")
        Response.Write("<body>")
        Response.Write("  <h1> Hello " +
            Request.QueryString("Name") + "</h1>")
        Response.Write("</body>")
```

```
        Response.Write("</html>")
    End Sub

    Public ReadOnly Property IsReusable As boolean
        Implements IHttpHandler.IsReusable
        Get
            return true
        End Get
    End Property
End Class
```

Requests made to this page as *HelloWorldHttpHandler.ashx?name=Rob*:

```
Hello Rob
```

If you're more intimately familiar with ISAPI, you'll be glad to know that ASP.NET replaces the *extension control block* (ECB) with a much easier and friendlier managed class: *HttpContext*. An instance of *HttpContext* is created whenever a request is made to the *HttpRuntime* and contains all necessary information about the request and response.

Now that you've had an overview of how IIS, ASP, and ASP.NET work, let's discuss some specific issues related to moving from ASP to ASP.NET.

Migrating to ASP.NET

ASP.NET has its roots in ASP; however, the technologies are completely separate and do not share a single line of code. In all possible ways, we designed ASP.NET to be backward-compatible with ASP. However, some key areas just aren't, and some language nuances will affect your application.

If you're looking to move an existing project to ASP.NET, you have two options—you can rewrite your existing application, or you can integrate ASP and ASP.NET. If you rewrite your existing application to take full advantage of ASP.NET, you benefit from many of its new capabilities and features, which simplify common tasks such as table rendering and authentication. In ASP, these tasks required lots of custom code. Alternately, if you choose to integrate ASP and ASP.NET—or for that matter, any other application model such as Java Server Pages (JSP) or Hypertext Preprocessor (PHP)—you won't have to worry about ASP.NET colliding with other application extensions. However, in an integration model, you have to define your own methodologies for sharing information between the various application models. ASP.NET does not provide any facilities for sharing any information with ASP.

The good news is that no matter which option you choose, ASP and ASP.NET can coexist within the same directories and IIS applications. Unfortunately, ASP and ASP.NET cannot share any information such as *Session* state data, but you can design around these limitations.

Rewriting for ASP.NET

Rewriting is the recommended option for moving your ASP application to ASP.NET. ASP.NET is a completely different programming model, so even if you do have existing ASP code, for a complex real-world application, you can't simply rename the .ASP file extension to .ASPX.

Why should you rewrite your application? There are many reasons, but five top my list. First, the tool support for ASP.NET through Visual Studio .NET or other tool vendors such as Macromedia is phenomenal. You get features such as statement completion for your source code as well as design-time support for the layout and presentation of your UI.

Second, unlike other Web application programming models that use parsed bytecode or script code (such as ASP), ASP.NET code is compiled when the application is first started.

Third, since ASP.NET code is compiled, you can expect an immediate performance benefit when you rewrite your application. In many cases, you can boost performance by 200 percent simply by typing the variables within your application, that is, specifying that a variable used as an integer is created as an integer type:

```
Dim i As Integer
```

Fourth, ASP.NET introduces a new UI component model called *server controls* that allows for many UI tasks to be encapsulated in reusable components. For example, any table rendering code can be replaced with the ASP.NET Data-Grid server control. Additionally, many specialized server controls are available, such as menuing or charting controls.

Finally, the caching features are my fifth top reason for rewriting your application to take advantage of ASP.NET. These caching features are designed to help you get more performance out of your application by reusing work you've already performed. For example, a dynamic page whose content changes infrequently can be output cached, giving you an additional performance gain of 2–3 times.

You can take advantage of many other great benefits when you rewrite your application for ASP.NET. Let's look at some of the differences between ASP and ASP.NET.

Request Name and Value Pairs

The *Request* API is familiar to all ASP developers—it interacts with request information that is sent to the server. Commonly, we ask this API for any query string or form name value pairs sent along with the request.

For example, if the *ProductID* value is passed in the query string, we would expect to see the following URL: *default.asp?ProductID=10*. In ASP Visual Basic code, we would ask for the value of the *ProductID*, as shown here:

```
' Value on the query string
Dim productID = Request.QueryString("ProductID")


' Value passed as a form name/value pair
Dim productID = Request.Form("ProductID")
```

In ASP, these values were stored in memory as an array. When accessed, the array would be walked to find the corresponding name/value match. The preceding code wouldn't be different in ASP.NET, however, the values would be stored as a *NameValueCollection* rather than as an array. When multiple items such as a list of products are passed in using the same name, the items are programmatically accessed differently. For example, assume that a list of *ProductID* values can be passed in as query string values:

```
Default.asp?ProductID=10&ProductID=5&ProductID=15
```

In ASP, the following code could be used to retrieve and list those values:

```
' Display posted items
For i = 1 to Request.QueryString("ProductID").Count
  Response.Write( Request.QueryString("ProductID")(i) & "<br>" )
Next
```

However, in ASP.NET, the *NameValueCollection* value is 0-based, not 1-based. The preceding code would need to be rewritten as follows:

```
' Display posted items
Dim i As Integer
For i = 0 to (Request.QueryString.GetValues("ProductID").Length - 1)
  Response.Write( Request.QueryString.GetValues("ProductID")(i) & "<br>" )
Next
```

Another option is to use the *String.Split* method if you still desire to work with the items as an array. *Request.QueryString("ProductID")* still returns *10,5,15* in ASP.NET, just as it does in ASP.

```
' Display posted items
Dim arraySize As Integer
arraySize = (Request.QueryString.GetValues("ProductID").Length - 1)
```

```
Dim products As String[arraySize]
products = Request.QueryString("ProductID").Split(',')
```

In-Line Methods

Probably one of the most painful changes for ASP developers is the need to move method declarations from *<% %>* code blocks to *<script runat="server">* code blocks. Functions in ASP could be written as follows:

```
<%
Public Sub DisplayUsername
  Response.Write("<b>Some username</b>")
End Sub
%>
```

When migrating to ASP.NET, the method shown in the next code snippet must be defined in a *<script runat="server">* block.

> **Note**   If you've been working with ASP since version 1, you know that the original version of ASP recommended that methods be defined in *<script runat="server">* blocks. However, most developers—myself included—rarely followed this guideline. Had we followed it, our code would migrate much more easily! If you're still authoring ASP files but anticipate moving them to ASP.NET in the future, define all methods and functions in *<script runat="server">* blocks.

```
<script runat="server" >
Public Sub DisplayUsername
  Response.Write("<b>Some username</b>")
End Sub
</script>
```

Render Functions

A popular ASP trick that many developers took advantage of was partially defining a function in *<% %>* blocks and containing raw HTML output. Such a function was known as a *render function*, which you can see in the following snippet:

```
<%
Public Sub MyRenderFunction
%>
    <font size="5" color="red"><b>Render functions are great!</b></font>
<%
```

```
End Sub
%>
```

```
Q: What do you think about Render functions?
A: <% MyRenderFunction()%>
```

This code would render the following:

```
Q: What do you think about Render functions?
A: <font size="5" color="red"><b>Render functions are great!</b></font>
```

Render functions were handy because functions that rendered HTML could leave the HTML in normal form and avoid performing *Response.Write* for each HTML element added to the output.

You can't use render functions in ASP.NET. Render functions aren't legal in ASP.NET and need to be rewritten using normal *Response.Write* statements. Also, as stated earlier, methods would have to be declared in *<script runat="server">* blocks. The following code still renders the same output as the preceding render function in ASP, and though it is called within *<%* and *%>*, the method is defined within a *<script runat="server">* block and no raw, inline HTML is allowed.

```
<script runat="server">
  Public Sub MyRenderFunction
    Response.Write("<font size=\"5\" color=\"red\">")
    Response.Write("<b>Render functions are great!</b>")
    Response.Write("</font>")
  End Sub
</script>
Q: What do you think about Render functions?
A: <% MyRenderFunction()%>
```

If you desire the benefit of encapsulated rendering, another option is to employ a user control to capture all the HTML output and then use the declarative XML syntax to control where the user control output is rendered on your page.

Parentheses Requirement for Functions and Methods

As you can already see, many of the migration headaches are related to nuances of ASP that developers took advantage of. Another such nuance was that there was no requirement for parentheses when calling functions for ASP code written with VBScript. The most egregious—and unfortunately common—situation in which parentheses were not used was when using the *Response.Write* functionality of ASP to output content.

```
<%
Response.Write "Hello World!"
%>
```

The preceding code is actually more of a VBScript language nuance than an ASP nuance, but we're covering it here rather than in the VBScript section of this chapter. It wouldn't work in ASP.NET. Instead, we would have to rewrite this code to use parentheses:

```
<%
Response.Write( "Hello World!" )
%>
```

If you're still authoring ASP files and plan to eventually convert them to ASP.NET, ensure that you use parentheses for all functions and methods.

Common Tasks Simplified

One of the great benefits of moving to ASP.NET is that many common tasks are simplified. We can't cover all the simplifications offered by ASP.NET, but we can show you one of the most common. The following is standard ASP code for connecting to a database and rendering the contents in an HTML table:

```
<%
' Database connection and table creation
Set objConn = Server.CreateObject("ADODB.Connection")
Set objRS = Server.CreateObject("ADODB.RecordSet")
objConn.ConnectionString = "DRIVER={SQL Server};server=localhost;
    database=pubs; uid=sa; pwd=00password"
objConn.Open()
objRS.Open "SELECT * FROM Authors", objConn

Response.Write "<Table width=""100%"" cellpadding=""3"" border=""1""
    cellspacing=""1"">"
Response.Write "<tr><td>Author Name</td><td>Address</td></tr>"
Do While Not objRS.EOF
  Response.Write "<tr>"
  Response.Write "  <td>"
  Response.Write objRS("au_fname") + ", " + objRS("au_lname")
  Response.Write "  </td>"
  Response.Write "  <td>"
  Response.Write objRS("city") + ", " + objRS("state") + " " + objRS("zip")
  Response.Write "  </td>"
  Response.Write "</tr>"
  objRS.MoveNext
Loop
Response.Write "</Table>"

objConn.Close()
%>
```

This is common code that any experienced ASP developer could author. This type of dynamic table rendering code can be simplified within ASP.NET:

```
<script runat="server">
  Private Sub Page_Load(sender As Object, e As EventArgs)
    Dim sqlString As String
    sqlString = "server=.; database=pubs; uid=sa; pwd=00password"
    Dim sqlConn As New SqlConnection(sqlString)
    Dim sqlCommand As New SqlCommand("SELECT * FROM Authors", sqlConn)

    sqlConn.Open()
    DataGrid1.DataSource = sqlCommand.ExecuteReader()
    DataGrid1.DataBind()
    sqlConn.Close()
  End Sub
</script>
<asp:DataGrid id="DataGrid1" runat="server" />
```

The code uses the ASP.NET *DataGrid* server control and simply binds the results from the executed SQL statement to the data grid. The datagrid then renders its contents as HTML.

> **Note** An additional benefit of server controls is that they can intelligently render the appropriate markup based on the device or browser making the request. For example, *DataGrid's* rendering will be slightly different for Microsoft Internet Explorer than for Netscape. The display is identical, but *DataGrid* can make choices about which display is better for each browser to guarantee correct rendering.

Error Handling

One of the frustrating issues with ASP was the manner in which errors were managed. ASP had no concept of try/catch blocks, unlike ASP.NET. Rather, developers had to aggressively check for errors in ASP pages. The following code demonstrates this:

```
<%
' Database connection and table creation
Set objConn = Server.CreateObject("ADODB.Connection")
Set objRS = Server.CreateObject("ADODB.RecordSet")
objConn.ConnectionString = "DRIVER=(SQL Server);server=localhost;
    database=pubs; uid=sa; pwd=00password"
On Error Resume Next
```

```
objConn.Open()
objRS.Open "SELECT * FROM Authors", objConn

Response.Write "<Table width=""100%"" cellpadding=""3"" border=""1""
    cellspacing=""1"">"
Response.Write "<tr><td>Author Name</td><td>Address</td></tr>"
Do While Not objRS.EOF
  Response.Write "<tr>"
  Response.Write "  <td>"
  Response.Write objRS("au_fname") + ", " + objRS("au_lname")
  Response.Write "  </td>"
  Response.Write "  <td>"
  Response.Write objRS("city") + ", " + objRS("state") + " " +
    objRS("zip")
  Response.Write "  </td>"
  Response.Write "</tr>"
  objRS.MoveNext
Loop
Response.Write "</Table>"

objConn.Close()
%>
```

The preceding code is identical to the ASP dynamic table-generation code shown earlier, with the exception of the addition of *On Error Resume Next*, which instructs the code to continue executing when an error occurs. This instruction assumes that code exists for checking for and handling the error. The result of this code is that when the connection fails, an error will occur, but the code will continue to execute and the end result will be an error message.

> **Note** Error pages in ASP.NET are much more detailed than they were in ASP—another great benefit! Rather than simply stating *ASP Error: 0x8005xxxx*, the system provides a detailed exception message with line number information and other useful details about the error.

The preceding code can be more gracefully rewritten in ASP.NET using the try/catch syntax to catch exceptions, such as the failure to connect to the database server, as shown here:

```
<script runat="server">
  Private Sub Page_Load(sender As Object, e As EventArgs)
    Dim sqlString As String
```

```
sqlString = "server=.; database=pubs; uid=sa; pwd=00password"
Dim sqlConn As New SqlConnection(sqlString)
Dim sqlCommand As New SqlCommand("SELECT * FROM Authors", sqlConn)

Try
  sqlConn.Open()
  DataGrid1.DataSource = sqlCommand.ExecuteReader()
  DataGrid1.DataBind()
  sqlConn.Close()
Catch exp As SqlException
  ' Clean up
  sqlConn.Close()

  Response.Write("Unable to open connection.")
  End Try
End Sub
</script>
<asp:DataGrid id="DataGrid1" runat="server" />
```

Note that all .NET languages support try/catch, which greatly simplifies managing errors within the application.

Visual Basic Language Nuances

You should be aware of some specific Visual Basic language nuances. For example, by default, ASP.NET is configured to require *Option Explicit* for Visual Basic .NET. This simply means that variables must be declared before being used. Whereas with VBScript you could simply declare a variable with first use, in ASP.NET you must explicitly dimension the variable. For example, to dimension a variable *iLoop*, you would simply write *Dim iLoop*.

In VBScript, parameters to methods and functions were passed as by reference (*ByRef*). This essentially meant that a pointer to the memory location of the data was passed to the method. Thus, if a method changed, the value of the parameter was affected. However, with Visual Basic .NET, all values are passed by value (*ByValue*), meaning that a copy of the data is passed as the parameter and changes to the value of the parameter do not affect the memory copied.

The *Let* and *Set* operators are no longer supported in ASP.NET and objects can be assigned directly without needing to explicitly set the value.

Objects in Visual Basic 6 and VBScript supported the concept of default properties. The most common use in ASP is on the ADO *RecordSet* to access a contained item, for example, *adoRS("Title")*. Default properties are no longer supported in Visual Basic .NET, and this code would need to be rewritten as *adoRS("Title").Value*. Do not use default properties if you are still authoring ASP or Visual Basic 6 code that you intend to eventually migrate.

> **Tip**   In addition to dimensioning all your variables, it is also recommended that you type all your variables *Dim iLoop As Integer*. By simply typing your variables, you can increase the performance of your application. You can enforce this by requiring the *Option Strict* Visual Basic .NET compiler option rather than the *Option Explicit* option.

Compiled Code vs. Include Files

One of the tricks that many ASP developers use is to store frequently accessed code libraries in include files that are then included in all the ASP pages that need to use those libraries. Although they appear useful, include files, if misused, adversely affect ASP.

In design reviews and conferences that I've attended, many developers would show ASP pages with very little code but with several includes at the top of the page. These seemingly lightweight ASPs were definitely simplified from an administrative point of view, that is, common code was stored in a single file that was shared. However, these ASPs were anything but lightweight—in fact, they tended to be memory hogs!

When the ASP ISAPI extension loads an .ASP file, it also loads and expands all the include files into one large virtual file in memory. So although developers thought they were getting benefits by moving common logic into include files, they were in fact hurting their programs since many include files would contain routines that were never used by more than 2 percent of the pages. A better strategy would have been to move this common logic into Visual Basic 6 COM servers.

It is recommended that you move code from include files to compiled code in ASP.NET. Take the code from the include file or files and create a single Visual Basic .NET or C# class. Because ASP.NET is compiled, rather than each page having its own copy of all the routines, each compiled ASP.NET page can link to the Visual Basic .NET or C# class instance where this business/rendering logic resides. In addition to compiled classes, you could also use server controls or user controls rather than include files.

Integrating ASP and ASP.NET

In all likelihood, when you begin the move to ASP.NET, you will not be rewriting your existing application but rather slowly migrating it from ASP to ASP.NET. This section focuses on is how to run ASP and ASP.NET together and how to interact with existing investments in COM servers from ASP.NET. I recommend that you also read the "Migrating to ASP.NET" section of this chapter, however, because the points are still applicable for integration.

Configuring Options

The configuration systems used by ASP and ASP.NET are completely separate. Whereas ASP relies on settings found in Internet Information Service's metabase, ASP.NET uses an XML-based configuration architecture. The majority of ASP-related settings can be easily configured by opening up Internet Information Services, right-clicking on a Web site, and selecting Properties. With the Properties dialog box open, select the Home Directory tab and click the Configuration button. This opens the Application Configuration dialog box, which is shown in Figure 11-2, earlier in the chapter.

You can find ASP settings on the Options tab or the Debugging tab of the Application Configuration dialog box. These configuration options include:

- **Enable/Disable Session State**   Indicates whether or not ASP sessions are enabled.

- **Session State Timeout**   Timeout value for *Session*. If the session is not refreshed or used before the timeout expires, the session data is removed from memory.

- **Request Buffering**   By default, request buffering, the ability to buffer the entire request before writing the response back to the calling browser, is enabled.

- **Default Language**   The default script language is VBScript.

- **Script Execution Timeout**   The amount of time a script is allowed to execute before being automatically shut down due to timing out.

- **Client/Server Debugging Options**   Controls debugging ASP applications.

- **Script Error Messages**   Error message displayed when an error occurs within an ASP.

These settings affect only ASP. If ASP.NET was also installed, and ASP.NET pages were present in this Web site or application, these settings would not affect the ASP.NET application whatsoever. ASP.NET uses its own XML-based configuration files.

ASP.NET's XML configuration file is both easier to use and simpler to manage than the one used by ASP. For example, when running in a server farm, rather than having to individually manage each machine by manually configuring IIS through the IIS GUI, the ASP.NET administrator can simply manage the

ASP.NET application by making changes to the XML configuration file and copying that file to the server.

ASP.NET supports two types of configuration files, machine.config and web.config. The machine.config file is the root, or parent, configuration file found in a version-specific directory for the version of ASP.NET you have installed. There can only be one machine.config for each version of ASP.NET you have installed. (ASP.NET is designed to allow different versions to run side by side. ASP.NET 1 and ASP.NET 1.1 can run on the same server without affecting each other another, and in the future ASP.NET 2 will be able to as well.)

Each application can have its own copy of web.config. The web.config file overrides or adds new configuration information to the configuration information originally defined by machine.config.

At the time of writing, two versions of ASP.NET are available: 1.0 and 1.1. These versions correspond to the following directories under either the Windows or WINNT directories: Microsoft.NET\Framework\v1.0.3705\ and Microsoft.NET\Framework\v1.1.4322\. Within each of these directories, you will find a config subdirectory, and within the config subdirectory, you will find the machine.config file.

One of the great benefits of ASP.NET's XML-based configuration files is simplicity. For example, the following markup is the web.config file used to configure settings within ASP.NET that are comparable to the settings we discussed for ASP:

```
<configuration>
    <system.web>
        <httpRuntime executionTimeout="90" />
        <compilation debug="false"
                    explicit="true"
                    defaultLanguage="vb" />
        <pages buffer="true" />
        <customErrors mode="RemoteOnly"/>
        <sessionState mode="InProc"
                    cookieless="false"
                    timeout="20"/>
    </system.web>
</configuration>
```

The preceding web.config file shows a much abbreviated version of what we can expect to find in machine.config. However, it does show how to configure common settings such as session, default language, and page buffering—settings that are similar to those we set for ASP. Another great benefit of the ASP.NET configuration system is that you can write your own configuration section handlers; that is, you can embed your own XML syntax for configuring your application within ASP.NET configuration system. This is done by implementing the *IConfigurationSectionHandler* class. (Chapter 7 reveals more about how the ASP.NET configuration system works and offers a thorough discussion of how to write a configuration section handler.)

Interoperating with COM and *ASPCompat* Mode

In most cases, integration between your existing ASP application and ASP.NET takes place with existing ASP investments with COM. COM is still fully supported within .NET, however, we recommend that if you own the code for the COM objects, you consider rewriting them for .NET. Calling COM from .NET has a performance penalty, namely a marshalling cost incurred where data types must be coerced and converted.

Code written for the common language runtime is commonly referred to as *managed code*; that is, the running code is managed by the CLR. The term *unmanaged code* refers to any code written to run outside of the CLR, such as Visual Basic 6 or C++. (See Figure 11-5.) The CLR has a common type system, and all managed compilers can generate type equivalent code. So you can expect that Visual Basic .NET and C# code are type and functionally equivalent if similar code is written in each language. Unmanaged code relies upon the COM binary standard to dictate a common interface so that objects can interact with one another. For managed and unmanaged code to work together, there must be a coercion of types.

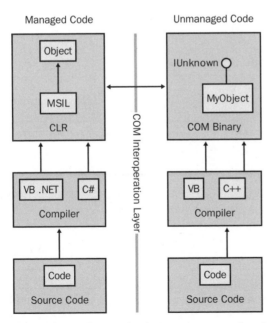

Figure 11-5   Separation between managed and unmanaged code

Some data types can be automatically converted, such as a Visual Basic 6 *Integer* data type, and some types cannot be automatically converted, such as the C++ *BSTR*. Tables 11-2 and 11-3 list the conversions. For types that can't be automatically coerced to a corresponding type on the unmanaged side, you can coerce the type yourself.

Table 11-2 Automatic Conversions

Visual Basic Type	C++ Type	.NET Type
Integer	Short	Short
n/a	unsigned int	UInt32
n/a	__int64	Long
n/a	unsigned __int64	UInt64
Long	Int	Integer
n/a	unsigned short	UInt16
n/a	signed char	SByte
Byte	unsigned char	Byte
Single	Float	Single
Double	Double	Double
Char	__wchar_t	Char
n/a	Void	Void

Table 11-3 Non-Automatic Conversions

Visual Basic Type	C++ Type	.NET Type
Variant	VARIANT	Object
Object	IUnknown	UnmanagedType.IUnknown
Date	DATE	Date
Currency	CURRENCY	Decimal
String	BSTR	String
Boolean	BOOL	Boolean

In the COM world, a type library is used to describe the types used by that COM object. In .NET, all this type information is stored in the manifest of the assembly—simply put, this same type information is stored in the .dll that is generated by a .NET compiler. There is no separate type library. When working with COM objects, you can import a type library. By importing a type library, .NET can create a run-time callable wrapper class for the COM object.

A *run-time callable wrapper* simply provides a wrapper class around the existing COM server and hides the unknown COM types from the .NET developer. A run-time callable wrapper can be generated automatically when using a COM server in a Visual Studio .NET project or by using the command-line tool tlbimp.exe. (Another tool, tlbexp.exe, allows you to create a type library for a .NET class. This then allows the .NET class to be callable and used by COM.)

All code complied for .NET, such as Visual Basic .NET, creates free-threaded objects. One of the major changes for ASP.NET is that it executes in a multithreaded apartment vs. the single-threaded apartment (STA) model used in ASP. Essentially, this means that in ASP.NET, multiple threads can be working together and operating on the same data within the process. Without going into too much detail, from a performance perspective, this is a good thing. ASP.NET uses a different thread for each request and additionally creates new instances of all required pages and classes on each request, so we still get the benefits of a multithreaded environment without having to worry about multithreading issues. The only problem is the interoperation of COM with Visual Basic 6 components or other COM objects that run in a single-threaded apartment.

Visual Basic 6 is capable only of creating code that must be run in an STA. What this means for the ASP.NET developer is that ASP.NET applications that interoperate with a single-threaded apartment COM server, such as Visual Basic 6 components, can behave unpredictably. (The main issue has to do with reference counting of the object and the ability of .NET to properly clean up and dispose of an STA component.) To address this problem, ASP.NET provides an *ASPCompat* page directive that forces the page to run on a special STA thread:

```
<%@ Page ASPCompat="true" %>
```

If you attempt to use a Visual Basic 6 component without marking the page as *ASPCompat="true"*, you might or might not get an exception. You will likely see inconsistent or odd behaviors once you put your application into production.

Another side effect of marking a page as *ASPCompat* is that the ASP intrinsic *ObjectContext* will be available. *ObjectContext* in ASP was used to flow context information about the request from ASP to business objects running within ASP. If your COM code depends on *ObjectContext*, you'll need to use *ASPCompat="true"*. Note that using *ASPCompat* will degrade the performance of the ASP.NET page.

Working Around Session and Application State

Many developers rely upon the *Session* and *Application* objects within ASP to share and store information about users or the application. Although these objects do still exist in ASP.NET, there is no integration point when running ASP and ASP.NET together in the same application. Data stored in *Session* within ASP is not available in the ASP.NET application.

For the *Application* intrinsic object, this lack of integration is usually not too much of a problem. However, if the application relies on *Session*, getting ASP and ASP.NET to work together is more difficult. The usual recommendation is that you replace all ASP and ASP.NET *Session* usage with a common object that is shared by both and stores its data in a database. You'll be writing your own session manager, but you can then take control over where the data is stored and provide a common interop layer for ASP and ASP.NET.

Summary

Migrating to ASP.NET requires thoughtful planning and a good understanding of how ASP.NET works. In this chapter, we discussed in detail the differences between ASP and ASP.NET, including how each of these application models interacts with Internet Information Services. We then discussed the two approaches for migrating an application to ASP.NET: rewriting and integration. You gain the most benefit when you rewrite your application for .NET because you can take advantage of all the great features, such as server controls and caching. However, a more realistic approach is to slowly migrate to ASP.NET, starting with application integration. .NET facilitates integration with existing COM servers through its COM interoperation layer, and ASP.NET provides integration through the *ASPCompat* mode. These compatibility modes have performance costs, but overall performance will still be better with .NET.

Tips and Tricks

In this book, we discussed the concepts underlying ASP.NET and shared the reasons behind some of the design decisions. In each chapter, we offered tips that can help make your development experience more productive, improve the performance of your application, and help you to better understand ASP.NET. This appendix is a compilation of the tips in the book. They are grouped by chapter and appear in the order in which they appear in each chapter.

ASP.NET Page Framework

In Chapter 1, we focused on how ASP.NET interacts with the Web server to receive and handle requests. We examined the application-processing pipeline and looked at how *HttpHandlers* and *HttpModules* are key to the ASP.NET architecture.

- When implementing an *IHttpHandler*, you can get improved performance if ASP.NET is able to reuse a single instance of the handler. The object must be stateless to avoid introducing bugs related to multithreading.

- The final *HttpHandler* or *HttpHandlerFactory* might never be invoked if one of the *HttpModules* ends the request. This can minimize the load on the server when requests are serviced from the cache. When a request fails authentication or authorization checks, there is also no need to execute the handler.

- The order in which *HttpModules* registered for an event is called is not guaranteed. Do not count on one *HttpModule* being called before another.

■ There is a certain amount of overhead related to throwing exceptions in the .NET Framework. Avoid throwing an excessive number of exceptions as part of the regular course of an application.

■ *Server.Transfer* is essentially the equivalent of *Response.End* followed by a call to *Server.Execute*.

■ Add validators to the wizard pages that verify that the set of expected values is in session. If all the required values aren't present, redirect the user to the step where the first missing piece is to be submitted.

■ Add validators at each step of the wizard to enforce the entering of correct input by the user. Let the user proceed only after the values accumulated to that point are satisfactory and errors are corrected, because gathering missing information becomes more complicated after the user reaches the end of the wizard.

Server Controls

The ASP.NET page revolves around server controls that encapsulate user interactions, data, and even business logic. The event-driven architecture of the server controls presents a familiar environment for developers. The automatic management of state allows you to focus on the application instead of overcoming the stateless nature of the HTTP protocol.

■ A certain amount of overhead is associated with all server controls. To preserve application performance when leveraging existing HTML content, do not turn HTML elements into HTML server controls unless you are taking advantage of server events.

■ Remember that updating a user control will cause the compiled pages that reference the user control to become invalidated. When the pages are next requested, they will have to be recompiled.

■ The members of a user control in the output cache can't be accessed from pages that contain the control. The output of the cached control will be included in the page, but the user control object itself will not available. Attempting to access it will result in an error message.

■ If you have to import the *System.Windows.Forms* namespace into your page or Microsoft Visual Studio .NET Web application project, chances are your code is using server-side resources that have no visible desktop on which to be displayed. Thus, they must be disposed of to avoid introducing resource issues under heavy load.

- When the user interface supports multiple simultaneous selections while iterating the list of items, accessing *SelectedItem*, *SelectedIndex*, and *SelectedValue* will return the first item found. To get the complete set of selected items, loop through all items from the list.

- Items added to a list control are carried between client and server in ViewState. If the set of items is a significant size, consider disabling ViewState. That way the control will not bloat the payload by unnecessarily carrying the ViewState in a round trip between client and server. In this case, be aware that the selected items are no longer available, so you must provide code to ascertain when the selected items were changed.

- To create a drop-down list that does not have an initially selected value, add an item to the top of the list that is selected by default and corresponds to no selection.

- Disable client-side validation by using the *Page* directive's *ClientTarget* attribute. Setting this directive to *downlevel* causes ASP.NET to treat the browser as though it does not support JScript.

- When used with sophisticated clients, client-side validation can reduce server load and improve the customer experience by providing immediate feedback about a problem without issuing a request to the server.

- Always verify the data received by the server, even when client-side validation code has been provided. You can't safely assume anything—the client might not have run the code, and the user might have constructed a malicious request with values that would not pass the examination of the client-side code.

- Use the *SaveAs* method of the *PostedFile* member of the HtmlInputFile to specify where the file should be placed on disk. Target a directory that exists on a separate partition, where filling the partition will have minimum impact on the operations of the server.

- If you need to generate random numbers in your application, create a *Random* object and store it in application scope. The object is seeded when it is created and can then be used throughout the application to get differing values easily.

- When deploying in a Web farm without server affinity (meaning that for each request, a client session can be handled by a different server), the validation key must be set explicitly and synchronized between the machines. If the default AutoGenerate setting is used, postbacks handled by a machine other than the one in which the ViewState was generated will not be processed correctly, and the user will get an error.

Data Controls

Applications are fundamentally about gathering, displaying, and manipulating data. The ASP.NET data controls provide the means for easily binding to a data source to create data-driven applications. Data-binding is used to populate lists for user selections as well as for displaying tabular sets of data.

- Use data-binding to declaratively control the display of values combined from the value of other controls.

- Avoid unnecessary data-binding. If the control has ViewState enabled, it needs to be data-bound only for initialization and then again when the underlying data source changes. However, if you disable ViewState for the control or for the page, you must call *Data-Bind* on every page load to repopulate the items.

- Add dynamic items after data-binding. When adding items to a Drop-DownList control from both a data source and code in the page, be aware of the order in which they are added. The data-binding operation clears all the items that exist in the control and replaces them with the set from the data source. After *DataBind* is called, you can safely add items to the list. A good example of where this tip can prove valuable is when you want to add a default value of "Select One" at the top of a list.

- When ViewState is enabled, as it is by default, the data from the data source makes a round trip between the client and server on each request. When the data is significantly large, this round trip can have a negative impact on the user experience. Look at the size of the ViewState for the DataGrid control by using tracing (discussed in Chapter 10) to understand exactly what kind of impact the ViewState is having on page size.

- If ViewState size is problematic for an application, a couple of solutions are available. First, you can completely disable ViewState in configuration for a page or for an individual control. Without View-State, the DataGrid control can no longer automatically store information about the paging state, the item being edited, or the current sort expression. You would need to maintain this data separately. Second, you can simply reduce ViewState by following these steps:

1. Set *AutoGenerateColumns* to *false* and explicitly declare only those columns that are necessary.

2. Set the styles in the code explicitly instead of establishing them declaratively.

3. Do not use the *DataKeyField* member.

■ For frequently accessed but rarely changed data, use the application cache or partial page caching (discussed in Chapter 6) to cut down on trips to the database.

■ Custom paging of the DataGrid can be particularly beneficial when the entire set of data being used is quite large or when retrieving it is expensive. Custom paging can also be used when the data source is a *DataReader* but you still require paging support on the DataGrid. In this scenario, you are responsible for managing the paging in the code, but you might achieve a better result with custom control than by using a *DataSet* with automatic paging.

■ Use two DataGrid controls on a page to allow for a master view and a details view. Synchronize the *SelectedItemIndexChanged* event in the master DataGrid to update the contents of the details view Data-Grid.

■ Consider providing for data filtering and sorting without return trips to the database for throughput. Be aware, however, that storing data in Session has an impact on the amount of memory used on the server. Also, using ViewState to enable the data to make a round trip has an impact on the size of the page and the post data that will be submitted in subsequent requests.

■ Reflecting on the individual items has an impact on performance. For large sets of data with numerous columns to summarize, leveraging the database directly for calculated values might be more efficient.

Developing for Mobile Browsers

More access to the Web is available with browsers in portable devices than ever before. Cell phones and personal digital assistants continue to offer improved screens and compelling features. However, many of these devices do not accept the markup that is usually rendered from Web pages. ASP.NET provides adaptive rendering so that a single Web page can produce WML, cHtml, HTML, and xHtml. In Chapter 4, we looked at how to use the mobile rendering features of ASP.NET to produce a site targeting the mobile user.

■ You might encounter references to the Microsoft Mobile Internet Toolkit on the Web, in magazine articles, and in newsgroups. When version 1 of ASP.NET was released, mobile support was not included. Instead, support was available as part of a separate download called the Microsoft Mobile Internet Toolkit. This mobile support is now included as part of ASP.NET.

■ Mobile pages should limit the amount of input required by the user. Strive for maximum relevant information with the fewest key clicks. Entering data can be tedious on a small form factor, and networks for mobile devices are still relatively slow compared to wired devices, so performing postbacks and following links can be somewhat time consuming.

■ Use a desktop browser as a debugging aid when developing applications for mobile browsers because debug and tracing information is not included in the output from the *MobilePage*.

■ Use cookieless sessions to ensure that your application works correctly on devices that do not support cookies.

■ Device updates installed on ASP.NET 1 using the Mobile Internet Toolkit replace the *browserCaps* section in machine.config with new content. Customizations for the *browserCaps* section will be lost when installing Device Updates 1.

■ When a browser isn't recognized in the *browserCaps* configuration section, the default behavior is to treat it as an HTML 3.2 device without support for client-side scripting.

■ The *AllowCustomAttributes* configuration setting does not cause custom attributes to be passed through to the client. It allows them only to be specified in the server page without causing an error on the server. This setting applies only to the mobile controls where unrecognized attributes on the server controls are treated as an error by default.

■ Be careful when defining and using filters. There is a tendency to want to believe that one capability implies another. Although the capabilities of new devices continue to advance rapidly, it is best to explicitly check for support when customizing.

Managing Client State

Applications need to maintain state for either user- or application-specific data. There are three techniques for managing client state in ASP.NET: Session, View-State, and Cookies. Session state stores user data on the ASP.NET server and relies upon a session ID assigned to the user. The user presents the session ID on subsequent requests, and the user's data is available within Session for the duration of that request. ViewState stores user or application data in the response of the HTML that is sent back to the user in hidden *<form>* variables. Cookies are small chunks of data that can be stored on the user's computer and are sent with each request to the application.

- Use in-process session state (the default) if you have only a single server. In IIS 6, either use out-of-process session state or disable process recycling behavior to avoid data loss.

- Don't use the *Session_End* event; it can be called only for sessions created in the *InProc* mode. The event is not raised for sessions created in one of the out-of-process modes when sessions are abandoned.

- It's important to note that the programming model is transparent. For example, we don't have to change how we access or use session state when we change the storage mode.

- We recommend SQL Server for out-of-process session state because it is just as fast as StateServer, and SQL Server is excellent at managing data.

- Store only basic data types when using out-of-process session state; avoid storing complex types or custom classes. Storing basic data types will decrease the serialization and deserialization costs associated with out-of-process session as well as reduce the complexity of the system.

- If the server running the state service is accessible outside the firewall, the port address of the state service should be changed to a value other than the default. In version 1.1 of ASP.NET, due to security reasons, only local machines can connect to the state server. To allow only non–local host requests in ASP.NET 1.1, open the same registry entry listed earlier for the port setting: *HKLM\SYSTEM\CurrentControlSet\Services\aspnet_state\Parameters*. Change *AllowRemoteConnection* to 1.

■ For ASP.NET 1.0, configure SQL Server for mixed-mode authentication by adding the ASPNET account enabled for the necessary SQL Server permissions (EXECUTE) for ASP.NET session state. (The ASP-NET account is the user that the ASP.NET worker process runs as.) For ASP.NET 1.1 running on IIS 6, configure SQL Server for mixed-mode authentication by adding the NT AUTHORITY\NETWORK SERVICE account.

■ Use integrated authentication rather than store SQL Server credentials within your configuration file. If you decide to use SQL Server user names and passwords, do not use the system administrator (sa) account. Instead use an account that has only the necessary access to the database object required for the operations (for session state, this account is EXECUTE only). If you must use SQL Server credentials, ASP.NET 1.1 supports storing credentials securely.

■ Ensure SQL Server Agent is running before running the Session state installation SQL Scripts. The agent runs a periodic job to purge expired sessions from the database.

■ For out-of-process session, set session state to *enableSession-State="false"* within the configuration file, and set the *EnableSession-State* page directives to either *true* or *ReadOnly* based on what behavior is needed. Note that the length of the session will still be reset (even when set to *false*). This will prevent unnecessary round trips when Session state is not needed.

■ Using the *SessionID* as a key for user data is not recommended. The *SessionID* is randomly generated, and session data—as well as session IDs—do expire. Additionally, although a *SessionID* might be generated on each request, a *SessionID* is set only when a *Session* value is set server-side. This means that if no session values are set server side, new *SessionID*s are issued on each request.

■ If you have to develop an application that supports both cookie and cookieless sessions, your best strategy is to write an HTTP module to redirect the browser to the appropriate application or server for the supported browser feature; for example, configure a dedicated application that is used for cookieless sessions.

■ A Message Authentication Code (MAC) is a key-dependent, one-way hash. A MAC is used to verify *ViewState* data by recomputing the MAC on postback and comparing it to the MAC stored in

VIEWSTATE. If the MACs match, the data in _VIEWSTATE_ is valid. If they do not match, the _ViewState_ data is invalid and an exception is thrown.

■   The view state can be disabled in a page by using <%@ Page Enable-ViewState="false" %>, or in a control by specifying _Page.EnableView-State="false"_ on the server control.

Managing Application and Request State

Application and request state refer to any data that is accessible for the lifetime of either the application or the request. Static variables, the Cache, and Application can all be used to store application state. Per-request state can be stored using _HttpContext.Items_.

■   Unlike session state, data stored within the cache is stored only in the memory of the application in which the data was created. Also, multiple applications on the same server do not share memory and thus cannot share cached data. An application's cache is private to the application that created it.

■   The duration for which a page can be stored in memory is controlled by several dependencies: time, file, and other cache entries. These dependencies are an inherent feature of the Cache API. As they apply to page output caching, these dependencies are controlled by the developer authoring the page.

■   The ASP.NET Cache implements a least recently used (LRU) algorithm. When ASP.NET has need for more memory, the cache can be asked to evict items to reclaim or free memory.

■   When using Microsoft Windows Server 2003 and Microsoft Internet Information Services (IIS) 6, it is recommended to configure the IIS 6 worker process to use 60 percent of the physical memory or to limit the total to 800 MB of physical memory.

■   Use the page directives when possible. There is less risk of introducing bugs in your application because the _OutputCache_ directive is declarative.

■   An _Etag_, or entity tag, specifies an HTTP header sent with the served document to uniquely identify a specific version of the page. Cache servers can query the originating cache server to determine whether a cached document is still valid by comparing the cached documents entity tag to the entity tag returned from the origin server.

■   If *VaryByParam* is not used, why is it required and why is its value set to *none*? The decision was made to force the developer to add *VaryByParam* with a value of *none* to clearly indicate that the page was not varying by any parameters. Requests with parameters sent to an output cached page using *VaryByParam* with *none* will not be resolved by the output cache and are treated as misses.

■   A single parameter can be specified, for example, *VaryByParam="tabindex"*. Multiple parameters to be varied by must be semicolon-separated, for example, *VaryByParam="tabindex;tabId"*.

■   Varying the output cache by various parameters is very useful. However, here is a good rule of thumb to keep in mind: the more specific the request, the less likely it is that the request can be satisfied from the cache. For example, if the page's output is highly user-specific, such as an e-commerce check-out page, the output cached page could be utilized again only by that same user in the same condition (in contrast to output caching the page used to display product information). When items are stored in the cache and cannot be utilized again, the cache is a wasted resource.

■   Do not use *VaryByParam with* * unless absolutely necessary. Any arbitrary data passed in the query string or *POST* body will affect how many versions of the output cached page are created, thus potentially filling memory with many pages that can't be used again.

■   If you have the .NET Framework installed and are using Internet Explorer, a *.NET CLR [version #]* string will be added as part of the *User-Agent* header. This can be useful for users who are downloading .NET applications because you can determine whether they also need to download the .NET Framework.

■   Page output cache directives are additive, and you should plan to use more than just the required *VaryByParam* for pages containing server controls that behave differently for different browser types. Otherwise inconsistencies will occur, as Internet Explorer DHTML could potentially be sent to a Netscape 4 browser (if the output cache is not being varied by browser type).

■   Don't use the *Location* attribute unless you completely understand how it works. In the majority of cases, its use is unnecessary.

- Do not use the page *OutputCache* directive on a page that also uses the output *Cache* APIs. If used together, the more restrictive setting is applied. Thus, if the page *OutputCache* directive has a duration of 60 seconds but the output *Cache* API sets a duration of 30 seconds, the page will be cached for only 30 seconds. (The same is true of the other settings as well.)

- Sliding expiration is usually the recommended approach simply because setting all the pages to expire simultaneously, such as at midnight, would cause the server to re-execute all those pages at midnight, potentially putting an unnecessary load on the server.

- Setting the Boolean value to *true* for *VaryByParams* or *VaryByHeaders* indicates that the output cache is to be varied by the parameter or header. Programmatically, you can decide not to vary by that particular parameter or header later in the processing of the page execution, and *false* could be set to indicate this behavior.

- The *Pragma: no-cache* HTTP header is not officially an HTTP version 1 behavior and is replaced in HTTP 1.1 with the *Cache-Control* header. However, like many characteristics of HTTP, the standard is only loosely followed. Nearly all browsers still use *Pragma: no-cache* and thus ASP.NET must know how to process it.

- When using the page output *Cache* APIs, always set *SetValidUntilExpires* to *true* unless you want clients to be able to remove your output cached pages from memory. The output cache is a performance enhancement, and if clients can arbitrarily remove pages from the cache, performance suffers.

- In the 2.0 version of ASP.NET, we'll add a *AddCacheDependency* method to allow you to add an instance of *CacheDependency* directly.

- No race condition exists when creating a dependency. If the dependent item changes before the item is inserted into the cache, the insert fails and the item is not added to the cache.

- If the page you are output caching relies upon file resources other than those used to execute the page, use the output *Cache* APIs and make the page dependent upon those files. If the files change, the output cached page will be evicted from the output cache.

- Use cache key dependencies where caching is used to enforce behaviors throughout your application. Dependencies do have additional overhead, but for scenarios such as those described thus far, dependencies allow for some powerful behaviors. For example, every page could theoretically be dependent upon a common cache key. When an administrator wanted to flush the cache, she would simply need to invalidate the common key. This would then evict all output cached pages from memory.

■   Don't use *VaryByParam="*"*, which would also resolve to an unknown *HTTP POST* parameter name. Instead, use the *VaryByControl* option.

■   Why doesn't ASP.NET provide a common *Application* or *Cache* out-of-process option similar to *Session?* Unlike *Session*, which is tied to a specific user, *Application* and *Cache* contain application-wide settings that apply, or are available to, all users. Thus, changes to *Application* or *Cache* must be propagated immediately. However, there are two problems with this: managing contentions when two applications simultaneously modify the same data; and decreased efficiency with replication—as the number of servers grows, the data gets exponentially more difficult to replicate between servers.

■   *Cache* supersedes all the functionality provided by *Application* and both simplifies it (because it requires no locking to modify) and provides more advanced functionality (such as expiration, dependencies, and purging of data when necessary).

Configuration

Configuration refers to any settings or data required by an application to run. This data can be as simple as the connection string used to connect to a database, or as complex as the number of threads the running process might require. ASP.NET's configuration system is XML file–based. Many first-time ASP.NET developers expect to configure ASP.NET using the Internet Information Services Manager, much as they would with classic ASP. ASP.NET does not, however, rely upon the IIS metabase. The ASP.NET configuration system requires no proprietary tools to update or manage its configuration system since an XML-based configuration system easily lends itself to manual editing and updating.

- You will find that you might have more than one machine.config on your computer. The .NET Framework is designed to allow multiple versions to run side by side. Each version has its own separate machine.config file. The version of the .NET Framework your Web application is using is determined by the extension mappings, for example, .ASPX, in Internet Information Server. Be sure you edit the correct machine.config if you want to change global settings.

- You can change mappings to allow your application to use a different version of the .NET Framework with the aspnet_regiis.exe tool. This tool is found in the version-specific directory Windows\Microsoft.NET\Framework\[Version]\.

- Don't modify the machine.config file unless you absolutely have to. Changes to machine.config affect the entire server. Instead use web.config in your application to specify desired behavior and configuration options.

- An easy way to tell whether you are working with a root directory for either a Web site or Web application is to look for a \bin subdirectory. The \bin subdirectory is allowed only in the root directory of a Web site or Web application.

- When updating a live site, perform all web.config changes locally and upload the running site with the new copy. This is much more efficient than changing and saving multiple times on the live web.config file.

- Customers often ask us whether they should store data in web.config or global.asax. We recommend you store data within configuration. Storing settings in files such as global.asax implies code. The configuration file allows you to make simple changes without having to recompile your application. Simply add the settings and update the web.config file on your running server.

ASP.NET Security

Application and server security are paramount considerations for the Web developer. Unfortunately, security considerations are often given a low priority in the design process. Application architecture decisions about authentication, authorization, and user impersonation should be considered carefully and reviewed thoroughly as the application is implemented.

- To launch the Computer Management application from the command prompt, enter **start compmgmt.msc**. You can also launch the Internet Information Services Management snap-in directly by entering **start inetmgr**.

- Never use Basic Authentication without requiring Secure Sockets Layer (SSL) so that user credentials are sent in an encrypted form. Using Basic Authentication without encrypting communications is referred to as sending credentials "in the clear" and is a very bad practice.

- A Windows user account is always associated with an executing request. A good way to review the security of a Web application is to walk through what identity is being used by Windows when executing any part of the request.

- Do not run the worker process as an account other than *ASPNET* unless absolutely necessary. Compromising the worker process that is running as *SYSTEM* would give an attacker much higher-level permissions than the *ASPNET* account. Any page will execute as this user unless impersonation is enabled.

- You can force IIS 6 on Windows Server 2003 to use the version 5.0 behavior in the Internet Services Manager by right-clicking the Web Sites folder, selecting Properties, and selecting Run WWW Service In IIS 5.0 Isolation Mode on the Services tab.

- Always use SSL in conjunction with ASP.NET Forms Authentication to secure the transmission of user names, passwords, and authentication tickets from the *FormsAuthenticationTickets* object.

- *RedirectFromLoginPage* relies on the user having been redirected to the login page with a query string to know where to redirect them back to. For example, in the URL *http://www.contoso.com/login.aspx ?ReturnUrl=mypage.aspx*, mypage.aspx is the return URL that the user is redirected to. If the user requests the login page directly, he will be sent to the page configured as the default for the Web application in the Internet Services Manager, usually default.aspx.

- Never store user passwords in clear text.

- File Authorization works only against file types that are mapped in the Internet Services Manager to ASP.NET. File types that are not handled by ASP.NET will be subject to the IIS authorization checks.

- *Allow* and *deny* tags are processed sequentially by ASP.NET. The first match found is used, so if you allow a user with one statement and deny them with another, the order of elements will determine whether the user gains access.

- Do not set *validateRequest="false"* in the page's *configuration* element unless absolutely necessary. The better option is to set *validate_Request= "false"* in the page directive for those pages where validation will be handled in your custom code. Such a page directive is shown on the first line of Code Listing 8-11.

- Call the *Server.HTMLEncode* method on all user input before displaying it.

- Disable services on the Web server that aren't being used. For example, if you type **net start** at the command prompt, you will probably be surprised at the number of services running on the server. You might not need Simple Mail Transfer Protocol (SMTP), Infrared Monitor, or DHCP client running on the server. Look at the demands of the Web application, and be sure that the running services are needed to make the server and the application run correctly.

Tuning ASP.NET Performance

Performance work is often neglected until it dramatically surfaces as a major blocking issue. Do not wait until deployment to discover the performance characteristics of an application. Performance tuning is best handled as an iterative process where the biggest gains can often be had easily at first. You should understand the reasons behind the time-to-first-byte and time-to-last-byte numbers for the most frequently accessed pages of an application. Output caching and data caching can enhance the speed and efficiency of your application more than code changes alone.

- When simulating real-world load, use various pseudo-random user-agent strings and completely random requests with large query strings and quantities of posted data. Live servers must endure this type of load, so accurate analysis should include malformed requests along with the valid ones.

- The time-to-first-byte throughput metric translates directly into how the user perceives the performance of the Web application. Even when throughput numbers look adequate, the user might feel that the response time is inadequate. The user is not concerned with how many requests the server can manage; she just notices how fast her request is handled.

■   Become proficient at using the load generating tool you choose. This might seem like obvious advice, but we can't emphasize it enough. Almost all test packages include various parameters that can be customized to vary the mix of client connection speeds, SSL connections, user-agents, and security credentials. To effectively utilize the tool and thus measure Web application performance accurately, you must understand how to vary the settings in accordance with your application requirements.

■   Keep batch compilation enabled, but make requests to each Web application while bringing a site online so that the first user to issue a request to the site does not see the delay of batch compilation, and the whole directory can be batch compiled.

■   Store application-wide data in the *cache* object instead of the *application* object. The *cache* object does not have the same locking semantics and provides more flexibility.

■   Do not create COM objects in a page constructor, either explicitly or by declaring the object as a page-scoped variable. If you must use legacy COM objects, create them when they are needed and release them as soon as you are done with them.

ASP.NET Debug and Trace

ASP.NET tracing facilities provide a simple method for seeing the structure and performance characteristics of a page. Additionally, it can be leveraged easily to output custom debug information. Understanding the generated code for a page can be key to tracking down unexpected behavior in custom code.

■   Use the trace *From Last* column data to quickly narrow down long-running pieces of code. This is particularly useful in isolating performance issues.

■   You can distinguish between inbound and outbound cookie values by looking at the *Cookie* row in the *Headers* collection. The value from the *Cookie* header is the value sent by the client.

■   Implement an *Application_OnError* handler that traces error information so that if you encounter unusual behavior in an application, you are prepared to gather more information by simply enabling trace.

- To quickly get to the source code for a page, you do not need to access the Temporary ASP.NET Files directories. Instead, introduce a deliberate syntax error. ASP.NET will flag the error and provide the Show Complete Compilation Source option as well as the compiler output.

- Do not use ASP.NET debug functionality on a production server. The performance implications are severe. Instead, to gather run time information programmatically, use trace functionality or classes in the *System.Diagnostics.Trace* namespace.

Moving to ASP.NET

Moving to ASP.NET from ASP or another Web application technology not only requires changes to code but also might require some changes to the way your applications are designed. You need to be aware of some nuances so that you can plan ahead for them.

- If you've been working with ASP since version 1, you know that the original version of ASP recommended that methods be defined in *<script runat="server">* blocks. However, most developers—myself included—rarely followed this guideline. Had we followed it, our code would migrate much more easily! If you're still authoring ASP files but anticipate moving them to ASP.NET in the future, define all methods and functions in *<script runat="server">* blocks.

- If you're still authoring ASP files, don't use render functions.

- If you're still authoring ASP files and plan to eventually convert them to ASP.NET, use parentheses for all functions and methods.

- An additional benefit of server controls is that they can intelligently render the appropriate markup based on the device or browser making the request. For example, the *DataGrid*'s rendering will be slightly different for Internet Explorer than for NetScape. The display is identical, but the *DataGrid* can intelligently make choices about which display is better for each browser to guarantee correct rendering.

- In addition to dimensioning all your variables, it is also recommended that you type all of your variables: *Dim iLoop As Integer*. By simply typing your variables you can increase the performance of your application. You can enforce this by requiring the *Option Strict* Microsoft Visual Basic .NET compiler option rather than the *Option Explicit* option.

- Do not use default properties if you are still authoring ASP or Visual Basic 6 code that you intend to migrate. Default properties are no longer supported in Visual Basic .NET.

- You shouldn't have any reason to use include files in ASP.NET. Instead use server controls or user controls, or move your code into compiled classes.

- ASP.NET is designed to allow different versions to run side by side. That is, ASP.NET 1.0 and ASP.NET 1.1 (and in the future ASP.NET 2.0) can all run on the same server without affecting one another.

- ASP.NET uses a different thread for each request and additionally creates new instances of all required pages and classes on each request. This prevents you from having to worry about multithreading issues, but you still gain the benefits of a multithreaded environment.

- Using *ASPCompat* will degrade the performance of the ASP.NET page.

The Cassini Sample Web Server

Cassini is a sample Web server, written entirely in managed code. The source code is freely available, which allows us to see exactly how it hosts ASP.NET in conjunction with its own HTTP listener. You can modify the sources and recompile the code to create your own enhanced version of a Web server. Note that because Cassini is a sample, it lacks many of the features you are accustomed to seeing in Microsoft Internet Information Services (IIS). It does not support Secure Socket Layers (SSL) or perform user authentication. It supports only one ASP.NET application per port, and it will process only those requests issued from the local machine.

With all these limitations, why would you be interested in using Cassini? As we mentioned, Cassini is a great example of how the hosting APIs are used to run ASP.NET pages. Cassini will run side by side with IIS or another Web server, so ASP.NET support can be easily added to an existing Web server. The functionality can be embedded into another application, allowing you to run ASP.NET pages without an Internet connection. And of course, you could modify the sources to make a more robust server, using Cassini as the starting point.

System Requirements

Cassini requires one of the following operating systems: Microsoft Windows 2000 Professional or Microsoft Windows 2000 Server, Microsoft Windows XP Professional or Windows XP Home, or Microsoft Windows Server 2003. Because Cassini is written entirely in managed code, it requires the .NET Framework version 1.0 or version 1.1.

Downloading the Cassini Web Server

You can download the Cassini Web Server and its sources from the ASP.NET Web site's project download page (*http://www.asp.net/Projects/Cassini/download*). When you click the download link, you will be prompted to save or run the installation program, Cassini.exe, which at the time of this writing is just 211 KB. When the installation program is launched, you will be prompted to accept the License Agreement. After you read and agree to the terms, the source files are installed to the location of your choice. The default installation location is C:\Cassini. Notice that no .DLL or .EXE is installed—only the sources and some support files.

Files Installed with Cassini

Just nine .CS files make up the Cassini source code. The first eight files compile into the Cassini .DLL library that constitutes the Web server functionality. The final .CS source file compiles into a Windows executable, named CassiniWeb-Server, that is used for controlling the sample Web server. An .SNK file is used for strong name signing of the assembly so that the assembly can be placed into the Global Assembly Cache (GAC); the .CS file also provides an icon for the CassiniWebServer executable. There is, of course, a README file and a batch file for compiling the library and executable.

Building Cassini

The Cassini download is all source files. You must compile these files on your own machine to use the code. Run the build.bat file from the installation location to build both the Cassini .DLL and the CassiniWebServer executable. Figure B-1 shows the command prompt output after you build Cassini.

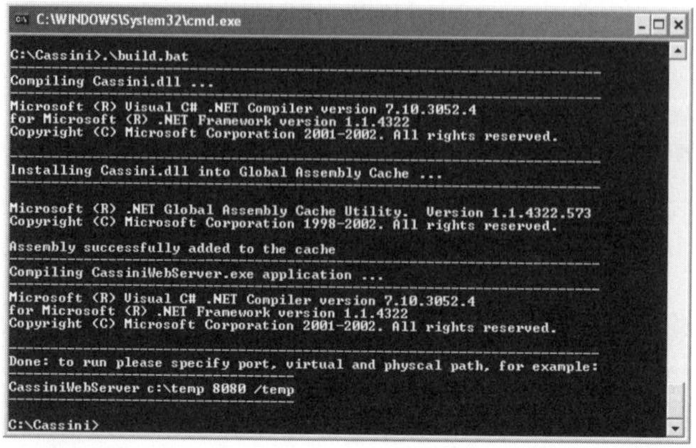

Figure B-1   Command prompt output from building Cassini

Notice that after the library is built, it is installed into the GAC as part of the build process. Because the hosting requires the ability to perform cross–application domain remoting, the library is placed into the GAC. After the Cassini .DLL is built and installed, the CassiniWebServer executable is compiled.

Running Cassini

Launch the CassiniWebServer controller executable from the command prompt by typing **CassiniWebServer.exe** or by double-clicking on the file in Windows Explorer. Next you see the dialog box shown in Figure B-2, which you use to configure and start the Web server.

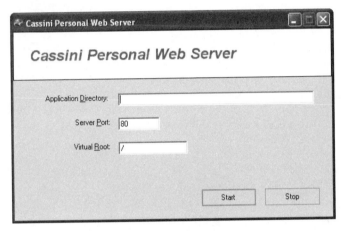

Figure B-2   Cassini controller program

In the first text box, enter the physical directory in which the .ASPX pages exist. The directory must exist before you click the Start button. In the second text box, enter the port that should be used to listen for requests. By default, this is port 80, as it is for IIS, so if you are running side by side with another Web server, you will need to pick a different unused port. Note that the port number, when not the default of port 80, must be specified after the machine name in the address bar of your browser. For example, if you chose port 8080, the address for a request to SomePage.aspx on the local machine would be *http://localhost:8080/SomePage.aspx.*

The third text box accepts a virtual path for the application. The default is a single slash, corresponding to the top level. You can add nesting levels that mimic the structure of nested virtual directories, but be aware that Cassini supports just a single application, and no configuration data from root paths is applied. Remember that only a single directory was given, and Cassini does not know about any other virtual directories.

When you click the Start button, the Web server begins listening on the specified port. Also, in the CassiniWebServer dialog box, a link appears for browsing the application. When you click the link, your browser will launch and take you to the application root. When no page is specified, as in this case, the sample Web server generates a listing of links corresponding to the pages contained in the application directory. Figure B-3 is an example of the directory listing produced by Cassini.

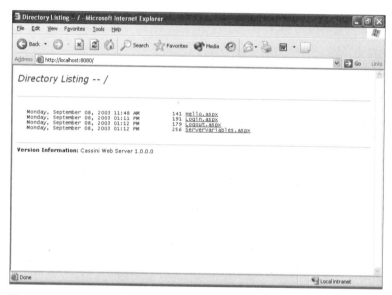

Figure B-3   Directory Listing produced by Cassini

Getting Help With Cassini

Peer support and community discussions are available on the ASP.NET Web site (*http://www.asp.net*) in a forum dedicated to the Cassini Sample Web Server. The forum can be accessed directly at *http://www.asp.net/Forums/Show-Forum.aspx?tabindex=1&ForumID=67*.

Index

Symbols
Of Exceps Thrown counter, 228

A
Accept-Language headers, 146–147
accessKey with mobile browsers, 102–103
Active Server Pages. *See* ASP
adapters for mobile browsers, 89–90, 102–104
advantages of ASP.NET, 2, 268
Alert.aspx, 33–34
allow tags, 297
analyzing performance, 223–224. *See also* performance
anonymous access
  denying, 217
  file upload problems from, 46
  purpose of, 204
apartment model–threaded components, 111, 237
Application API, 133, 171. *See also* application state
Application Center Test program, 226
Application Restarts counter, 229
application settings, 194–195
application state
  API preferred for. *See* Cache API
  Application API, 133, 171
  Application vs. Cache API, 171
  ASP vs. ASP.NET, 282
  browser history method, 163
  cache key dependencies, 162, 293
  cache privacy, 291
  cascading removal of entries, 162
  controls, partial page caching of, 164–169
  defined, 110, 133
  dependencies, inserting, 173–176
  dependencies, removing, 160–162
  deterministic page serving, 158–163
  HTTP cache headers, 138–140
  invalidation headers, 155–157
  location of cache, selecting, 151–152
  nonremovable cache items, 177
  out-of-process option, 294
  OutputCache. *See* OutputCache directives
  partial page caching, 163–169
  programmatic removal of pages, 163
  removing cached items, 163, 177
  setting cache items, 172–177
  shared user control entries, 169

  static variables for, 177–179
  techniques for, table of, 133
  varying by control state, 167–169
  what to cache, 172
Application_OnError handlers, 250, 298
appSettings section of web.config, 194–195
.asax files, 263
.ascx files, 263
.ashx files, 263
.aspx files, 264–265
.asmx files, 263
ASP (Active Server Pages)
  advantages over prior technologies, 259–260
  ASPCompat directive, 281
  backward-compatibility with, 267
  error handling, 273–275
  include files, 276
  integrating with ASP.NET, 276–282
  ISAPI, compared to, 260
  mapping to ISAPI, 261–263
  migrating to .NET. *See* moving to ASP.NET
  name value pairs, 269–270
  render functions, 270–271
  session state for, 110–112
  settings for, 277
  upgrading to .NET. *See* moving to ASP.NET
ASPCompat, 300
ASPNET account, 206, 296
ASP.NET Authentication, 205–206
aspnet_setreg.exe, 200
assemblies
  directory for, 251
  performance overhead of, 234
authentication
  anonymous access, 46, 204, 217
  ASP.NET options, 205–206
  Basic Authentication, 204, 296
  client certificates, 204
  configuration section, 188
  cookies for, 210
  defined, 201
  Digest Authentication, 205
  Forms Authentication, 206, 208–211, 213–215, 296
  IIS authentication, 203–205
  impersonation with, 206–208
  Integrated Authentication, 119, 205, 290

rendering
  configuration section, 188
  mobile browser, 89, 93–94
  render functions, 270–271, 299
  Render method, 265
  scriptless, 93–94
Repeater control, 56–59
request state
  defined, 133
  HttpContext.Items, 291
requests
  .aspx files, processing for, 264–265
  counter for, 228
  ending, benefits of, 283
  HttpContext creation, 7
  IHttpHandler interface, operation of, 4–6
  IHttpHandlerFactory interface, operation of, 4–6
  IHttpModule interface, 7–9
  measuring, 225, 228
  name value pairs, 269–270
  processing overview, 3–9
  requests per second metric, 225, 228
  SimpleHandler.cs sample, 5–6
  SimpleModule.cs sample, 7–8
  web.config files for adding handlers, 6
RequiredFieldValidator control, 41
response buffers, 137
response time, 225
Response.Redirect method, 11–13
restarts, counter for, 229
.resx files, ISAPI mapping of, 264
reverse proxies, 111
rewriting ASP for .NET. See moving to ASP.NET
roles
  checking, avoiding, 216
  Forms Authentication with, 213–215
  Global.asax for, 214–215
  IsInRole method, 212
  purpose of, 212
  URL authorization with, 216
  Windows Authentication with, 212–213
rows
  filtering, 78
  selection in DataGrids, 72–74
run time, ASP.NET, 4
runat="server" blocks, 25, 270, 299
run-time callable wrappers, 281

S

security
  anonymous access, 46, 204, 217
  ASP.NET Authentication, 205–206
  ASPNET account, 296
  authentication for. See authentication
  authorization for. See authorization
  client certificates, 204

config file security, 199–200
configuration section, 189
cross-site scripting, 218–219
detecting running services, 221
Digest Authentication, 205
Forms authentication, 206, 208–211, 213–215, 296
hardening servers, 221
hashing passwords, 211
IIS for, 202
impersonation, 202, 206–208
importance of, 201
Integrated Authentication, 205
loginUrl pages, 209–211
Passport authentication, 206
passwords, 209, 211, 296
patches, 221
role-based, 212–215
tickets, Forms authentication, 209
user accounts, 296
user names, 211
validating input, 218–220
Windows Authentication, 204–205, 212–213
Windows mode authentication, 205
Windows user accounts, 296
worker process, 296
server controls
  base class for, 26
  binding data to. See data-binding
  Calendar.aspx, 27–28
  capabilities of, 27
  CheckBoxList, 35–36
  CompareValidator, 42
  CustomValidator, 44–45
  defined, 23
  disabling client-side validation, 285
  DropDownList, 37–38, 54–55, 285, 286
  event handlers, adding, 25
  event-driven model, 25
  HTML element equivalents, 26
  HTML type. See HTML controls
  HtmlHelloWorld.htm, 23
  iterating items, 285
  list controls. See list controls
  ListBox, 36–37
  message box, client-side, 33–34
  MessageBox object, 33
  mobile controls. See mobile browsers
  overhead from, 284
  partial page caching of, 164–167
  performance issues, 25
  place in page structure, 23
  RadioButtonList, 39–40
  RangeValidator, 42–43
  RegularExpressionValidator, 43–44
  RequiredFieldValidator, 41
  runat="server" blocks, 25, 270, 299

About the Authors

Matt Gibbs is a lead Software Design Engineer on the Microsoft ASP.NET team. Previously he was part of the product teams for Active Server Pages 3.0, Internet Information Services (IIS) versions 4.0 and 5.0, Mobile Internet Toolkit version 1.0, and Microsoft .NET Framework version 1.1.

Matt has a master's degree in computer science from the University of Washington and a bachelor's degree in computer science from the University of Utah. He enjoys traveling as well as playing golf and squash. You can reach Matt at mattgi@microsoft.com.

Rob Howard is a Program Manager on the Microsoft ASP.NET team. He has contributed to ASP.NET features such as session state, Web services, and caching as well as to many of the new features coming in ASP.NET 2.0. He also is actively involved in the ASP.NET community, working closely with groups such as ASPInsiders, Microsoft MVPs, and community user groups. You can contact Rob at rhoward@microsoft.com.

Get a **Free**
e-mail newsletter, updates,
special offers, links to related books,
and more when you

register online!

Register your Microsoft Press® title on our Web site and you'll get
a FREE subscription to our e-mail newsletter, *Microsoft Press
Book Connections.* You'll find out about newly released and upcoming
books and learning tools, online events, software downloads, special
offers and coupons for Microsoft Press customers, and information
about major Microsoft® product releases. You can also read useful
additional information about all the titles we publish, such as detailed book descriptions, tables of contents and indexes, sample
chapters, links to related books and book series, author biographies,
and reviews by other customers.

Registration is easy. Just visit this Web page and fill in your information:

http://www.microsoft.com/mspress/register

Microsoft®

- -

Proof of Purchase

Use this page as proof of purchase if participating in a promotion or rebate offer on
this title. Proof of purchase must be used in conjunction with other proof(s) of
payment such as your dated sales receipt—see offer details.

Microsoft® ASP.NET Coding Strategies with the Microsoft ASP.NET Team

0-7356-1900-X

CUSTOMER NAME

Microsoft Press, PO Box 97017, Redmond, WA 98073-9830